THE LIMPING HERO

GROTESQUES
IN LITERATURE

Peter L. Hays

New York
NEW YORK UNIVERSITY PRESS
1971

Contents

Introduction 3

1   Myth and Ritual Backgrounds 11

2   Fertility Figures 33

3   Sterility Figures 63
     Part 1 Victims 63
     Part 2 Victimizers 106

4   Limited Man 125

5   Conclusion 187

Appendices
1   Continental Literature 195
2   The Hospital 219

Index 233

Acknowledgments

I wish to thank the publishers of the following authors for permission to reprint lengthy extracts from their works:

Edward Albee—from *The American Dream*, copyright © 1960, 1961 by Edward Albee. Reprinted by permission of Coward-McCann, Inc.

Saul Bellow—from *Herzog*, copyright © 1961, 1963, 1964 by Saul Bellow. Reprinted by permission of The Viking Press, Inc., U.S., and George Weidenfeld & Nicolson, Ltd for British Commonwealth and Empire.

E. E. Cummings—from "in Just—", from *Poems 1923–1954*, copyright © 1954 by E. E. Cummings. Reprinted by permission of Harcourt Brace Jovanovich, Inc. and by MacGibbon & Kee, Mr. Cummings' British publishers.

T. S. Eliot—from *The Waste Land* and *Murder in the Cathedral*, the latter copyright © 1935 by Harcourt. Brace & World, Inc.; renewed, 1963 by T. S. Eliot.

The illustration that appears in Chapter Three is reprinted through permission of Philosophical Library.

Three sections of this book appeared in altered form in the following journals, whose editors were kind enough to allow republication:

Critique
The University Review
Educational Theatre Journal
The CENTENNIAL REVIEW

I also wish to thank those who have helped me with this book, its conception, gestation, and delivery: Eric Solomon, Julian Markels, and Charles W. Hoffmann for their ideas; Ginnie Johnson Overton, Norna Wilkin Ferrara, Judy Kalivas, and Betty Kimura for their nimble typing fingers; the editors of NYU Press for their skillful midwifery; and, especially, my wife Myrna, for her love and tolerance for me and this "lame, foolish, crooked, swart, prodigious" project.

THE LIMPING HERO

Fig. 1. Symbol of the fecundity of sacrifice: the cross bears fruit
(after an engraving dated 1512).

Not only are the archetypal patterns the basis of literature, . . . but at least for our own time literature is one of the great disseminators of the archetypal patterns.
—*Stanley Edgar Hyman*
The Armed Vision *(p. 165)*

Introduction

This book began in graduate school when, in the course of my reading, I was struck by the number of lame characters I encountered. In addition to Faulkner's Ab Snopes and Cash Bundren, Tennessee Williams' Laura Wingfield, Melville's Ahab, and other modern literary figures, it seemed to me a disproportionate number of figures in Greek mythology were either lame, like Hephaestus and Oedipus, or met death through a leg wound, as did Achilles, Paris, Cheiron, and Eurydice. I wondered whether there were many more limpers and whether anything united all of them beyond the obvious similarity of a wounded leg or foot. I have now spent the greater part of several years reading books which contained lame characters. The list of limpers, if nothing else, is rather impressive, and the reader may consult it at the end of this text in Appendix Two, appropriately named The Hospital. As for a thematic bond, one did emerge, and its explication and application comprise the body of this book.

My investigation was inductive; the pattern I saw was one that emerged as the reading progressed. I knew of approximately one hundred limpers before I attempted any synthesis. Since then, I have applied my thesis where it has seemed appropriate and have refrained from forcing it on works that have appeared inhospitable to it. Unlike Procrustes, I have been content to record limpers without creating any of my own.

By "limpers," I mean literary characters who are actually lame or symbolically so—that is, actually or figuratively castrated, for, as I shall show in the first chapter, lameness as a literary device is usually either symbolic of or a euphemism for a genital wound; the wound, in turn, symbolizes a social disability. To stress the point for clarity's sake: castrated or sexually impotent man's disability, whether physical or psychological, is only the first in a series of injuries. He cannot enjoy the full satisfactions of normal sexual intercourse, cannot beget children, and undoubtedly suffers—as Hemingway graphically depicts Jake Barnes suffering—from feelings of inferiority as a result of his loss of virility. Sometimes this is all the author intends; more often the maimed individual's inability to assert himself as fully as he feels he should is meant to suggest every man's inability to order his destiny. Thus, baldly stated, sexual impotence represents other disabilities in dealing with the world.

In a literary study of this kind—one that proposes to trace the history, development, and significance of a symbol in certain works of art—it is helpful to cite evidence from other disciplines: mythology, anthropology, and etymology, for example. But I do not consider myself a disciple nor this work an argument in behalf of C. G. Jung, Maude Bodkin, Sir James G. Frazer, Lord Raglan, Joseph Campbell, Robert Graves, Northrop Frye, or anyone else. I mean to demonstrate only the thesis that most limpers in literature can be seen to fit into several related categories, and that seeing them in this way either reinforces or augments our understanding of the works in which they appear. Where it has seemed appropriate, I have sought to trace the course of the archetype's transmission, or its use by one author because of the influence of another author, but I have not considered the symbol's provenance as important as its function in any given work.

Admittedly, I use archetype and symbol interchangeably. Even so, I mean more by archetype than simply "a typical or recurring image"; [1] cattle are typical and recurring images in westerns but are usually just conventional scenery or plot devices and do not carry any deeper significance. I use the term as Jung defined it:

. . . forms or images of collective nature which occur practically all over the earth as constituents of myths, and at the same time as autochthonous, individual products of unconscious origin.[2]

The primordial image or archetype is a figure . . . that repeats itself in the course of history. . . .[3]

Or as Stanley Edgar Hyman describes archetypes:

basic age-old patterns of central human experience . . . [which] lie at the root of any poetry (or any other art) possessing special emotional significance.[4]

Because of its "special emotional significance," the lame figure has suggested itself to literary artists for centuries, and thus, quite clearly, it can be regarded as such an archetype, although Jung does not mention it in his *Archetypes and the Collective Unconscious.* Jung believed that archetypes arise from the collective unconscious, inherited memories of mankind's collective past, and as such remain latent until actualized in dream vision or artistic creation.[5] This study deals only with literary actualizations of one archetype—the maimed figure. When I speak of such characters from myth as Hephaestus, Achilles, or Uranos, therefore, it must be remembered that I am dealing with them only as they appear in the works of Homer, Hesiod, and other mythographers. Since I am not especially concerned with provenance, there is no attempt to make a case here for or against the collective unconscious.

Because I believe that the maimed figures to be discussed are archetypal, are related to ancient rituals (Hyman's "age-old patterns of central human experience"), and are especially significant emotionally, I have chosen these characters with care. Not everyone in literature who limps is a limping hero. An author who writes about war invariably deals with wounded individuals, just as an author of westerns deals with cattle. But to take two examples from the same author, Sergeant Quirt's leg wound in *What Price Glory?* by Laurence Stallings and Maxwell Anderson is, so far as I can determine, merely a plot device of no symbolic value: Quirt's wound has no role in the authors' commentary on war and little special meaning in their portrait of professional soldiers. But Richard's injuries in Stallings' novel *Plumes* are paralleled by his mental condition: he must readjust to a changed, postwar world although he, too, is altered in mind and body. His physical wounds are "objective correlatives" for the limitations of his body and of his world. Again, in Bertolt Brecht's short story "Socrates Wounded," [6] the thorn that pierces Socrates' foot and lames him, in this tract on the stupidity of war and accidental heroism, is simply a convenience, a stratagem, like the thorn in the paw of Androcles' lion. The sprained ankles, real and false, in the same volume of stories are equally devoid of typological or emotional significance.[7] Brecht does use castration, though, for its figurative value (see Appendix One), and it is with such use that I am concerned, that is, with those maimed characters, important in their respective works, whose crippled state seems to me symbolically significant and relevant to an interpretation of the works in which they appear.

What I say of crippled figures in this study may appear equally relevant to others who are not lame or castrated: the blind or deaf, those missing hands or arms. But I have limited my work to lame or emasculated characters for several reasons. First, the number of characters in literature who are in some way maimed must be enormous; it would be next to impossible to organize them except perhaps in an encyclopedia of literary characters, alphabetically arranged by name, with cross references to types of physical disability. If this list were then expanded to include all characters with lame or bruised psyches, whom could it exclude?

One last remark about the plan of this book. Following presentation of the ritual origins of castration in Chapter One, which identifies such limping heroes as Adonis, Osiris, Dionysus, and Jacob as sacred kings or ancient fertility gods, I discuss the literary uses that have been made of this archetype. Chapter Two, then, is devoted to fertility figures as they appear in works by D. H.

Lawrence, Tennessee Williams, and Bernard Malamud, among others. The first part of Chapter Three deals with the archetype accepted literally, that is, with sterility figures, for whom the Fisher King (who, in spite of his wound, has begot many literary children) is the obvious paradigm. The second part of that chapter deals with another lame prototype, the Devil, who usually causes blight and destruction. The final chapter deals with limpers whose wounds mark them as limited, restricted men —real men in a reasonably realistic world, as opposed to the obviously fictitious characters of the chivalric world of romance who surrounded the Fisher King. These crippled characters express their authors' views of life and its possibilities as finite and restricting. To some extent the discussion of *la condition humaine* in Chapter Four may seem to overlap the previous one on sterility. If an author views life as futile and joyless, he can write about a limited protagonist in a sterile, moribund environment. One can, however, for the sake of discussion, make distinctions between the two. I do not consider my categories iron-bound, nor my placement of a work in one or another as essential to my argument; on the contrary, the categories are primarily heuristic, intended simply to give some order to a mass of material. Hence I have had no compunction in placing the same character in two different chapters and discussing him from a different point of view in each.

To reiterate briefly then, all the limpers discussed in this study are to some degree impotent. Although the converse is frequently true—e.g., the Fisher King—it is not necessarily so: all who are emasculated do not limp. For the sake of this study, however, I have labeled all such maimed figures *limpers,* using the term metaphorically to include not only the lame and impotent, but the impotent though not lame. Moreover, in literary works the wound itself is frequently less emphasized than the associated rituals of fertility/sterility.

No doubt I have omitted characters—from some obscure works, or, more to my shame, from well-known and important works—who, had I known of them, would have provided better examples than those I did use. For such omissions, I have no excuse. This book could undoubtedly be more inclusive in ten or twenty years, but just as certainly it would still be incomplete. However, if my analyses of the included works are enlightening, then my remarks and my method should have relevance to similar but omitted works. Consequently this book defines a new symbolic image for literary criticism, that of the limping hero, a concept which I hope will compare in usefulness with such others as "quest" and "rebirth."

Notes

1. Northrop Frye, *The Anatomy of Criticism* (Princeton, 1957), p. 99.
2. C. G. Jung, *Psychology and Religion* (New Haven, 1938), p. 63.
3. Jung, "On the Relationship of Analytical Psychology to the Poetic Art," *Contributions to Analytical Psychology*, trans. H. G. and Cary Baynes (London, 1928), p. 246.
4. Stanley Edgar Hyman, *The Armed Vision* (New York, 1948), p. 143.
5. See *Complex/Archetype/Symbol in the Psychology of C. G. Jung* by Jolande Jacobi, trans. Ralph Mannheim (New York, 1959), p. 33.
6. Bertolt Brecht, *Tales from the Calendar*, prose trans. by Yvonne Kapp (London, 1961), pp. 83–99.
7. *Ibid.*, "The Augsburg Chalk Circle," p. 18, and "The Experiment," p. 43.

All the children of Jacob's thighs. . . .

The knees of a human being also possess a sort of religious sanctity in the usage of nations.

The foot . . . often has a generative or phallic significance.

1.

Myth and
Ritual Backgrounds

These epigraphs are but a fraction of the testimony in literature to the sacred or procreative quality of thighs, knees, and feet.[1] In the Bible, children come from the thighs—the word is usually translated as "loins," but *yarekh,* in the Hebrew texts of Genesis 46:26 and Exodus 1:5, does mean "thigh." The thigh is a sacred object for swearing oaths in Genesis 24:2 and 47:29; and a special curse is reserved for it in Numbers 5:21. Also, thighbones are one part of the sacrificial animal especially reserved as an offering to God: Exodus 29:22, 27; Leviticus 10:21, etc.; the same is true of Greek sacrifices: *Iliad* I, 460 ff.; II, 423 ff.; VII, 240; *Odyssey* III, 455—among other examples that might be cited. The *Rig-Veda* (III, 21, 5) describes sacrifice of thighbones; they were also used in ancient Egyptian rituals for the dead.[2] Greek legends also mention marrow—presumably from the thighbones—as a special diet for royal children: *Iliad* XXII, 501, and Fulgentius, *Mitologiarum libri tres,* III, 7.

The Hebrew word for knee, *barekh,* is cognate with the word for bless, *barukh.* Its etymological relations in other languages show the knee's, like the thigh's, connections with procreation: Greek gonu (γονυ), Latin *genu,* English *gonad, genital, genus, generate, generation, genius,* and *genuine.* There are similar cognates—*knee* and *generation*—in Assyrian-Babylonian *birku,* Russian *koleno,* and Finnish *polvi;* and the Latin *femur, femora,* the thighbone, is cognate with *feminine, fecund,* and *foetus.* Homer refers to the knees as if they were the source of a man's strength and vitality (*Iliad* IV, 313; XIX, 354; XXII, 388; *Odyssey* XVIII, 133. Cf. Job 4:4 and Isaiah 35:3), and also speaks of killing as a "loosing of the knees" (*Iliad* V, 176; XV, 291). Elsewhere (*Iliad* I, 550 ff.; XI, 608; XVIII, 457; and *Natural History,* XI, CIII, 250) Homer says and Pliny echoes, "Suppliants touch the knees and stretch out their hands toward them and pray at them as at altars. . . ." The act of adopting or recognizing a child as one's own consisted of placing him on the new parent's knees (Genesis 30:3, 48:9–12, 50:23); children are born from a man's knee in African folklore, and cloud-maidens from a god's knee in the *Kalevala,* just as Dionysus was reborn from Zeus's thigh.[3] Birth can be prevented, in folklore, by crossing the knees or lacing one's fingers around them.[4]

The foot, similarly, is a "source of procreative substance" and a "seat of procreative life-soul."[5] Among the examples that might be cited to attest to this strange-sounding notion is the Chinese legend about the formation of the Chou dynasty, which occurred when Chiang-yuan conceived through her feet when "she stepped on the print of the Sovereign's great toe," and the Siamese fertility rites which Frazer cites: "By keeping up his foot, the temporary king of Siam gained a victory over the evil spirits, whereas by letting it down he imperilled the existence of the state." Frazer also mentions many tribal rulers who were never allowed to set even one foot on the earth: "The divine personage may not touch the ground with his foot"—presumably so that his royal *mana* may not be drained off. Similarly, Frazer mentions the many instances of girls at puberty who may not touch the ground, presumably so as to preserve their fertility.[6] Perhaps the same tabu governed the behavior of the Welsh king—"Math son of Mathonwy was lord over Gwynedd. . . . At that time Math . . . might not live save while his two feet were in the fold of a maiden's lap . . . ,"—and the Irish hero Oisin, who succumbs to old age when his foot touches the ground.[7] Unlike Oisin, whose foot causes him personal debility, Cuchulainn, hero of one of the great Irish epic cycles, has special power in his foot: "Thus it was that Cuchulainn let fly the white *gae bulga* [barbed spear] from the fork of his irresistible right foot. . . . 'Ah, that blow suffices,' sighed Ferdiad. 'I am fallen of that! But, yet one thing more: mightily didst thou drive with thy right foot.' "[8] In Greek myth, Antaeus could renew his strength only by touching the earth. And many ancient coronation rites included shoeing the king in an attempt, perhaps, to guard his sacred foot.[9] Furthermore, in a discussion of the phallic significance of feet, Jung cites a Coptic belief that the Nile flows from the feet of God, comparing it to the Indian belief about Gitche Manito which Longfellow put in *Hiawatha* (I, 9): "from his footprints flowed a river." Jung also mentions the fertility dances of Pueblo Indians, which feature a kicking of the earth with the heel, and says "Feet . . . have a fertility significance. . . . The foot and the treading movement are invested with a phallic significance." [10] And we ourselves define *tread* as meaning both "to step" and, of birds, "to copulate."

The obvious question, of course, is what—if anything coherent—do all of these tidbits of lore and gossip mean? Is there any one, basic explanation for them?

A most cogent and compelling argument is provided by Richard Broxton Onians in his *Origins of European Thought* (1954), a work to which I am deeply indebted in this chapter. Onians' thesis, based on the evidence not only of ancient narratives and drama, but also of the writings of such naturalists as Aristotle and Pliny, is that the ancients believed the source of life to be the head— the brain—and that the stuff of life was carried in cerebrospinal fluid, as Aristotle says: "The semen passes from the brain through the spine." [11] One ancient definition of marrow still records its identification with the spine and the brain: ". . . the marrow pass[es] down from the brain through the orifices in the vertebrae. It is inferred that the spinal cord is of the same substance as the brain for the reason that, if its extremely slender membrane is merely cut into, death follows immediately" (N.H., XI, LXVII, 178).[12] Hence, when the Hebrews and Greeks offered thighbones in sacrifice, they were not benefiting from the trick that, as Hesiod describes, Prometheus played on Zeus (*Theogony* 521–564), but were in fact offering to the gods the very containers of the stuff of life. This would also explain, better than the legend that Jacob wrestled with an angel and had his thigh dislocated, why the thigh was sacred to the Hebrews, why they swore oaths by placing their hands under it, and why they believed that children could be born from the thighs.

The same marrow was to be found in those capacious receptacles, the knees. In fact, the *Oxford English Dictionary* lists the knees specifically under the heading "marrowbone," and equates marrow, as Pliny did, with the spine and with life, strength, and vitality, which explains why Homer associates strength with the knees, and killing with "loosing" the knees. In addition, the respect paid them, the "religious sanctity" to which Pliny refers, helps us to understand the ritual way in which they were clasped in pleading: one begged to be spared at another's knees (e.g., *Od.*, XXII, 310, 337) because he appealed for his life at a source of life. Montaigne cites this practice, and his particular reference confirms the ancient life-giving chain: "In petitioning or saluting any great man they touched his knees. Pasicles the Philosopher, brother of Crates, instead of laying his hand upon the knee, laid it upon the private parts [*genitoires*], and being roughly repulsed by the man whom he thus approached, he asked: 'Is not this yours as well as the knees?' " [13]

The feet were physiologically connected to the sources of vitality in two ways. Fulgentius, in his discussion of Achilles' life (*Mitologiarum*, III, 7), mentions a belief among doctors which he says goes back to the time of Orpheus: that veins ran from the kidneys and genitals, through the thigh, to the heel. Aristotle quotes the similar belief of Polybus: "There are four pairs of veins. The first extends from the back of the head, . . . until it reaches the loins and passes on to the legs, . . . to the outer side of the ankles and on to the feet. Another pair . . . goes on inside along the backbone, past the muscles of the loins, on to the testicles, and onwards to the thighs, . . . to the inside of the ankles and to the feet.[14]

This concept of anatomy helps to explain why foot wounds are so quickly fatal in mythology—not only to Achilles, but to Pholus, Diarmuid, Paris—who dies not from his head wound but a heel wound, and Talos— whose vein structure resembles that described by the early physiologists: "He had a single vein extending from his neck to his ankles" (Apollodorus, I, ix, 26, Frazer's translation). It also explains why the myths contain so many leg wounds. They are the rationalized remains, in sophisticated stories, of more primitive rituals, of live sacrifices that involved the genital organs or legs, as I shall explain further on in this chapter.

The path of the life-stuff, semen, into the lower limbs was through the marrow. In classical times the testes were not regarded as the sources of semen, but simply as reservoirs between the places of generation and emission. As Aristotle says, "The testes are no [essential] part of the ducts but are only attached to them" (*De Generation Animalium*, 717a, 34–35). Moreover, it was known empirically that castration did not kill, which would certainly happen if the source of life were destroyed, and so castration was regarded as an act which, by preventing the emission of semen, preserved it within the body. Thus Aristotle records that the legs of eunuchs swell because of the trapped fluid.[15]

Despite the boar's status as a symbol of fertility and virility, *chlounes* (χλούνης), a Greek word for boar, is also a word for eunuch. *Chlounes* literally meant "greenish" (it is cognate with *chlor-*, as in *chlorophyll*), thus growing. Latin provides similar etymologies. "Boar" is *verres,* cognate with *ver,* which means "the spring season," but no doubt originally signified "green" (vernal), sappy (*virus*—slimy liquid); other related terms are *man* (*vir*), *vireo* (to be green), and *vigor* (*vis*), as well as *virile, virility*. In Greek again, the same word *ear* ('ἔαρ) means "spring" and "sap" or "juice." Spring was full of sap, green, vital, and that paradigm of ancient procreators, the boar, earned the epithet of green for his vitality—which, along with the toughness of a boar's hide, helps explain why the image of a boar crowned so many shields and helmets from the Aegean to the Baltic (see Apollodorus III, 6, 1 and *Beowulf*, lines 304, 1111, 2152).[16]

Aristotle's testimony indicates that the ancients believed castratos were equally full of vitality, though unable to vent it, and this belief helps explain many preclassical sacrificial rites, especially the frequency with which heroes of mythology—Tammuz, Adonis, Odysseus, Osiris, and Diarmuid—fight with and are at least wounded by boars.

J. G. Frazer and other anthropologists record that many primitive peoples regarded their kings as the embodiment of the spirit of fertility. While the king was healthy and sexually potent the land was fertile and herds increased, but if the king were to grow old or sicken, and his virility diminish, the land would suffer. Therefore the sacred king was not allowed to die a natural death "lest with his diminishing vigour the cattle should sicken and fail to bear their increase, the crops should rot in the fields, and man, stricken with disease, should die in ever-increasing numbers." [17] Instead, at the first sign of aging—or after a fixed time—the king was killed, and his undiminished powers, it was believed, were inherited by his successor—often the man who had killed him. Frazer goes on to say that "the king is slain in his character of a god or demigod, his death and resurrection, as the only means of perpetuating the divine life unimpaired, being deemed necessary for the salvation of his people and the world." Again:

> The killing of the god, that is, of his human incarnation, is therefore merely a necessary step to his revival or resurrection in a better form. Far from being an extinction of the divine spirit, it is only the beginning of a purer and stronger manifestation of it. . . . Thus the killing of the representative of the tree-spirit in spring is regarded as a means to promote and quicken the growth of vegetation. For the killing of the tree-spirit is associated always . . . with a revival or resurrection of him in a more youthful and vigorous form.[18]

Readers of Frazer, the myth interpretations of Robert Graves, Lord Raglan's *The Hero,* or Joseph Campbell's *The Hero with a Thousand Faces* can supply hundreds of examples of deaths of sacred kings as fertility sacrifices. Frequently this death explicitly involved castration. Thus Cronus castrated his father Uranus and ruled in his place. Set killed his brother Osiris and rent the body to pieces; all were recovered except the genitals. This loss undoubtedly represents an act of ritual emasculation, for models of the phallus of Osiris played an important part in worship of ancient Egypt. A similar incident of mutilation occurs to Bata, younger of the famous Egyptian Two Brothers. That these mutilations are connected with fertility can be seen in the parallel instance of the Egyptian sun-god Ra, from the blood of whose self-mutilation sprang the gods Hu and Sa.[19] Similarly, Aphrodite is supposed to have been born from the blood that spilt into the sea from Uranus' severed genitals. Still another fer-

tility figure who suffered castration was Attis, better
known by the name of his Cyprian and Greek counterpart, Adonis. Agdistis, an androgynous Phrygian god, was
emasculated by other gods (or in some versions, self-muti-
lated), and from his severed male parts an almond tree
sprang. From its fruit Nana conceived Attis, with whom
Agdistis (a doublet of the Phrygian earth mother Cybele)
fell in love. In order to prevent Attis from marrying anyone else, Agdistis caused the beautiful lad to castrate
himself and to bleed to death under a tree.[20] In later
versions of the tale, Attis was gored to death by a boar,
but the symbolic involvement of his death with fertility
is suggested by Frazer in his description of the rites of
Attis, performed alike in Rome and Phrygia, and closely
resembling Syrian rites of Tammuz.

[On March 24, the Day of Blood, the] high priest
drew blood from his arms and presented it as an
offering. . . . The inferior clergy whirled about in
the dance with waggling heads and streaming hair,
until, rapt into a frenzy of excitement and insensible
to pain, they gashed their bodies . . . in order to
bespatter the altar and the sacred tree with their
flowing blood. . . . The novices sacrificed their virility. Wrought up to the highest pitch of religious
excitement they dashed the severed portions of themselves against the image of the cruel goddess. These
broken instruments of fertility were afterwards rev-
erently wrapt up and buried in the earth or in subterranean chambers sacred to Cybele, where, like the
offering of blood, they may have been deemed in-
strumental in recalling Attis to life and hastening
the general resurrection of nature, which was then
bursting into leaf and blossom in the vernal
sunshine.[21]

What Frazer did not know, but what now seems evident, is that the significance of the sacrifice lay not in the "broken instruments of fertility," but in the emasculated priests' inability to vent semen—becoming vessels, better instruments of fertility, as the castrated gods Osiris, Tammuz (or Thammuz), Attis, and Adonis had been before them.[22]

These gods all died following their castration, which in turn followed their mating to a fertility goddess, Isis, Ishtar, Cybele, and Aphrodite, respectively. Undoubtedly, theirs was a sacred marriage, described by Frazer and the other anthropologists, a ritual union of male and female fertility figures to insure continued increase of crops, herds, and children. After the marriage, whether immediately at the change of the seasons or at the end of a longer period of time, the male was castrated to preserve the life-stuff within him, and then killed. His successor, the new representative or spirit of fertility and inheritor of the vitality of his predecessor, mated with the then-current representative of the fruitful great mother, the female fertility principle. He was slain in turn and replaced to insure good crops, and so the cycle went on. Mary Renault provides us with her reconstructions of these rituals in her novel *The King Must Die* (New York, 1958), especially the deaths of Kerkyon at Eleusis and the surrogate of Dionysus at Naxos.

In time, whether because of increasing civilization and a concurrent aversion to live sacrifice or because the sacred king refused to terminate his reign and allow himself to be sacrificed—or both—various substitute practices were effected, as Frazer and Graves explain. Sometimes a temporary king was substituted and killed, or kings alternated, each feigning death at the end of his allotted reign but returning to rule after the supposed death of his tanist, e.g., Acrisius and Proetus, Pelias and Neleus, Eteocles and Polyneices, Atreus and Thyestes, Castor and Pollux, and Romulus and Remus. "Originally the king died violently as soon as he had coupled with the queen. . . . Later, emasculation and laming were substituted for death; later still, circumcision was substituted for emasculation and the wearing of buskins for laming." Thus does Graves summarize the process, and Bruno Bettelheim, in his discussion of the relation of circumcision to castration, confirms parts of it when he remarks that "Loeb is convinced that circumcision was originally performed as a sacrifice to a female goddess. . . . He follows Barton, who holds that originally all Semitic circumcision was a sacrifice to the goddess of fertility." [23]

This process, which included hamstringing and dislocating the thigh as methods of laming, helps us to understand a great deal about characters of early mythology. First, generation after generation of sacred kings were killed by an arrow wound in the ankle: Talos, the bronze guardian of Crete was killed when Poeas shot him in his only vulnerable spot, his ankle; Poeas' son was wounded in the foot, some say by a serpent's bite (Homer, *Iliad*, II, 121–25; Sophocles, *Philoctetes*, 1, 266; Apollodorus, *Epitome*, III, 27), another says by one of Heracles' poisoned arrows (Servius on Virgil, *Aeneid* III, 402), but Philoctetes recovered and fought at Troy, where he killed Paris with an arrow in the ankle, the same spot where Paris himself had slain Achilles; and Achilles' tutor Cheiron, and the latter's friend Pholus, also died from leg wounds by the poisoned arrows of Heracles.[24] Many characters of mythology died of poison directly administered to the foot by its manufacturer, a serpent. Besides Philoctetes (if we believe the account of the majority that he was snake-bitten) there were Acrisius, Munitus, Mopsus, and Eurydice.[25]

Presumably, Acrisius, Munitus, and Mopsus lost their lives to successors who took the form—in ritual—of serpents to slay them; others—Tammuz, Adonis, Osiris, Idmon, Carmanor of Lydia, Ancaeus of Arcadia, Ancaeus of the Calydonian boar-hunt, Cretan Zeus, and Diarmuid—were slain by their tanists in boar form. Thus Set slew Osiris, Apollo slew Adonis, and Finn mac Cool slew Diarmuid.[26] Originally both serpent and boar were probably tribal totems, but both continue to figure in mythology. The role of boars as fertility symbols I have already discussed. It needs to be added though that the boars' tusks were likened to the crescent moon and also to the sickle—like that which Cronus used to castrate Uranus—with which the first ear of grain was ritually reaped each year. Serpents, their fellow murderers in these ritual deaths, also had a reputation for sexual vitality long before Freud or even Genesis. According to a Pelasgian creation myth, Eurynome, goddess of all things, was impregnated by the North Wind in the form of the serpent Ophion. Eurynome, in the form of a dove, laid the Universal Egg. Ophion then coiled about the egg and caused it to split, hatching "all things that exist." Eurynome and Ophion then made their home on Mt. Olympus, where the Greek gods later lived. There Ophion vexed Eurynome by claiming to be the creator of the Universe. "Forthwith she bruised his head with her heel . . . and banished him. . . ." (*G.M.*, I, p. 27). Although there is no mention of Eurynome's injuring her heel, one is tempted to equate her with Eurydice, and with Eve, for Yahweh or Jehovah is etymologically related to "dove," and man will bruise the serpent's head and the serpent, man's heel (Gen. 3:15). Since that time, of course, snakes have been associated in homiletics and artistic imagery with sex. But as Onians points out, in antiquity serpents were believed to be the living form assumed by those who had died or to be spontaneously generated from the spinal marrow of the dead. Jung proposes that analogy might have suggested such a belief: "The snake, because it casts its skin, is a symbol of renewal. . . ." Jane Harrison refers to similar notions among Africans and cites the same belief among the Greeks:

> The form taken by the traditional hero and also the king is unquestionably that of a snake, and the snake is also used in phallic ceremonies for the promotion of fertility.
>
> The snake we are constantly told is the vehicle of the dead man, the form in which he is apt to appear.
>
> The snake then is the symbol and the vehicle not of mortality but *im*mortality. . . .[27]

Thus in the murders of heroes by snakes and boars the significant fact was not the death of the individual, but the preservation of his vitality, his *mana,* which was inherited intact by his successor. The man (in the form of a boar or serpent) [28] who killed the sacred king did so to ensure the undiminished fertility of land, flocks, and people.

This ritual conflict—often represented as the clash of seasons, the young summer king against the old king of winter—evidently did not always end in death. In some myths, and for unclear reasons, the hero survives the attempt on his life by his tanist in animal form. Philoctetes survives the serpent's bite to fight at Troy, and Odysseus survives the boar's slashing of his sacred thigh. Or perhaps their myths recount in garbled form an enactment only of ritual murder, a period of royal inactivity while tanists ruled in place of the king, and then ritual rebirth: Philoctetes from his tomb on Lemnos, Odysseus from war, wandering, and a visit to the Underworld—and return to slay the substitutes.

Sometimes the conflict and survival of the hero does not involve a ritual animal, but human or at least anthropomorphic antagonists; the outcome in each case, though, bodes a certain enrichment for posterity. Thus Jacob—whose name means to seize by the heel, presumably the sacred heel that denotes kingship—usurps his brother's patrimony. In a wrestling match with an angel Jacob's thigh is dislocated, causing him to limp, or to be unable to touch his heel to the ground. And so Jacob receives God's blessing and becomes Israel, the eponymous founder of a nation (Gen. 32:24–31). Similarly, Aeneas was lamed in the battle for Troy when Diomedes threw a rock which "struck Aeneas on the groin where the hip turns in the joint that is called the 'cup-bone.' The stone crushed this joint, and broke both the sinews. . . ." (*Iliad*, V, 303 ff.). (In Gen. 32:25, the angel touched "the hollow" of Jacob's thigh, that is, where it meets the hip, and the Jews are forbidden to eat "the sinew of the hip which is upon the hollow of the thigh" [vs. 32].) But Aeneas was rescued by his mother Aphrodite, healed by other goddesses, and went on to become the father of Rome, as Jacob was of Israel. Anchises, the father of Aeneas, was also lamed, by Zeus, as punishment for boasting of having slept with Aphrodite (as Adonis had also done).[29]

Still another lover of Aphrodite, her husband Hephaestus, was lame. According to the *Iliad* (XVIII, 394 ff.), he was born so and thrown from Olympus by his mother Hera, who was ashamed of him. Yet Hesiod, in his *Theogony*, speaks of the birth not of a sickly child but of "glorious" Hephaestus.[30] Admittedly, "glorious" might refer to Hephaestus' artistic ability and not to his physique. But it is noteworthy in these descriptions of the births of the gods that Hesiod does not mention the smith god's lameness. At the end of Book I of the *Iliad,* however, Homer mentions another tradition concerning Hephaestus, that when Zeus hung Hera up by a golden chain from heaven for rebelling against him, Hephaestus tried to interfere and release his mother. For challenging his father Zeus, Hephaestus was hurled again from Olympus, this time falling on Lemnos and having his legs broken.[31] Is it not possible that we have here the mythic device of doubling, where a significant feature of a tale, after differentiation from the original by variant tellings of the story, is reincorporated to stand beside the original feature as similar but not identical, as for example with the unlikelihood of two Isolts in the story of Tristan? Is it not equally implausible that the same god should be thrown twice from Olympus, once by each parent, and that originally lame, he has his twisted legs broken as a result of his second fall? It seems more likely that Hephaestus was born well-formed as any of the gods and that his lameness is the result of his unsuccessful rebellion against his father, as Zeus had rebelled against Cronus, and Cronus against Uranus. In any case, Hephaestus, master craftsman, mechanic, and consort to the fertility queen Aphrodite, was lame, as was the Norse smith Weyland.[32]

Another Greek hero who challenged his father's authority and was, presumably, lame from having his feet pierced just after birth was Oedipus.[33] The actor who represented Oedipus in the tragedies concerning The House of Atreus in the Greek dramatic festivals would have worn buskins, as would the player who took the part of Dionysus in Aristophanes' *The Frogs.* That Dionysus is identified by buskins [34] is significant, for Greek drama originated in rites celebrating Dionysus, as Cornford and Murray among others have established. There is only a meager explanation of why tragic roles alone, with the one exception in *The Frogs* just mentioned, were associated with buskins: that buskins gave the wearer added height. But this does not explain why buskins are a regular part of many coronation ceremonies, for most monarchs would be crowned in any event on an elevated platform for visibility's sake; nor would it explain the presence of a carried buskin in either the Eleusinian or Orphic mysteries.[35] If a buskin had a built-up heel, it would cause the wearer to stand on tip-toe (to keep his sacred heel from touching the ground) and, possibly, to walk unsteadily. An actor's stance in buskins, then, would attest to the sacred nature of the wearer, his lameness presumably due to hamstringing, as with Zeus, to dislocation, as with Jacob, to fractures or other wounds, as with Hephaestus, Oedipus, and Odysseus, or to castration, as with Attis. Hence buskins undoubtedly represent the last stage in the evolution or displacement of the ritual sacrifice and identify their wearers as sacred kings, which helps explain why Aegeus left his son Theseus sandals as a means of identification, and why Jason frightened his usurping uncle Pelias by limping into Iolcus on one sandal. It may be for the same reason that Hermes (Mercury) is invariably pictured on tiptoe, with wings guarding his heels, and that winged sandals are also an important identifying feature of Perseus' scanty costume (as in the statue of him by Cellini).[36]

In sum, the ritual practices of castration and live sacrifice changed to castration alone or ritual laming, and finally to the wearing of buskins to imitate laming. Regardless of form, all of these signs manifested sacred kingship: the lame figure was a fertility deity whose disfiguration or wound portended greater goods—more crops, flocks, children—and, thereby, greater happiness for his people. This, I am convinced, is the origin of the archetype. And, as we trace the limping hero through literary history, we shall see that the original significance has been preserved by several modern authors.

Notes

1. Genesis 46:26; Pliny, *Natural History*, The Loeb Classical Library (Cambridge, Mass., 1940) vol. III, trans. H. Rackham, XI, CIII, 250; C. G. Jung, *Symbols of Transformation* from The Collected Works, vol. 5, trans. R. F. C. Hull (New York, 1956), p. 239. All subsequent references to Pliny or Jung, unless otherwise specified, will refer to these books.

2. E. A. Wallis Budge, *Osiris* (New Hyde Park, 1961), I, 345.

3. John A. Macculloch, gen. ed., *The Mythology of All Races* (Boston, 1925), VII, Alice Werner, ed., 156; *Kalevala*, poem or runo IX, 34–36; Ovid, *Metamorphoses*, III, 3, 310–312.

4. Sir James George Frazer, *The Golden Bough*, one-volume abridgement (New York, 1922), pp. 239–240 (unless otherwise indicated, subsequent references to Frazer will refer to this edition of *The Golden Bough*); Pliny, XXVIII, 17, 59; and Ovid, *op. cit.*, IX, 298–311.

5. Richard B. Onians, *Origins of European Thought* (Cambridge, 1954), p. 524. Cf. Jung, pp. 126, 239, 315; and Paul Diehl, *Le Symbolisme dans la Mythologie Grecque* (Paris, 1966), pp. 150–153.

6. L. Wieger, *A History of the Religious Beliefs and Philosophical Opinions in China*, trans. E. C. Werner (1927), p. 41; Frazer, pp. 284–288, 593, 169–170. Cf. Robert Graves, *The White Goddess* (London, 1952), pp. 323–331.

7. Math: *The Mabinogion*, trans. Gwynn Jones and Thomas Jones (London, 1949), p. 55; Oisin: *The Mythology of All Races*, ed. Louis Gray, vol. III, ed. John A. Macculloch (Boston, 1918), p. 181.

8. Tom Peete Cross and Clark Harris Stover, *Ancient Irish Tales* (New York, 1936), pp. 319, 320.

9. A. M. Hocart, *Kingship* (Oxford, 1927), pp. 71 *et seq.*, esp. pp. 163–164, and Tor Istram, *The King of Ganda* (Stockholm, 1944), p. 26; both cited by Herbert Weisinger, *The Tragedy and the Paradox of the Fortunate Fall* (London, 1953), pp. 33, 35.

10. Jung, pp. 314–315. The Coptic reference is from E. A. W. Budge, *Coptic Apocrypha in the Dialect of Upper Egypt* (London, 1913), p. 243. Jung also cites Dr. Aigremont (pseud. Siegmar Baron von Schultze-Gallera), *Fuss- und Schuhsymbolik und-Erotik* (Leipzig, 1909).

11. *Problemata*, 897b, 25–26. The passage is from *The Works of Aristotle*, ed. W. D. Ross, as are all my quotations from Aristotle; this passage is from vol. VII (Oxford, 1927), trans. E. S. Forster. Cf. *Historia Animalium*, trans. D'Arcy Wentworth Thompson (Oxford, 1910), 512b, 1–6: "There is also another pair [of veins] running on each side through the spinal marrow to the testicles. . . . These veins are termed the spermatic veins," Aristotle quoting Diogenes of Apollonia; or Plato in *Timaeus*, 73, ". . . [God] made the marrow . . . to be a universal seed of the whole race of mankind. . . . That which, like a field, was to receive the divine seed, he made round every way, and called that portion of the marrow, brain . . . ; but that which was intended to contain the remaining and mortal part of the soul he distributed into figures at once round and elongated, and he called them all by the name 'marrow' " (*The Dialogues of Plato*, trans. Benjamin Jowett [Oxford, 1892], III, 495). See also *Timaeus*, 91.

12. Onians, *op. cit.*, pp. 109, 149. The translation cited is Rackham's but is substantially the same as Onians'; there seems to be some discrepancy in the numbering of the *Natural History*.

13. *The Essays of Michel de Montaigne*, trans. Jacob Zeitlin (New York, 1934), I, xlix, 262. In his notes to this passage, Professor Zeitlin cites Montaigne's source as Diogenes Laertius, VI, lxxxix, and remarks that both the Greek original and the Latin translation used by Montaigne speak of hip joints, not *genitoires* (p. 410).

14. Onians, p. 528; Aristotle, *Historia Animalium*, 512b, 13–24.

15. *Problemata*, 876b, 31; of course, this work is only apocryphally Aristotle's, but whether or not genuinely his, it does establish the presence of this physiological concept in ancient Greece. The same volume, 877a, 5 ff., says that bare feet are "preju-

dicial to the performance of the sexual act." Though Forster translates *hypodesis* (μποδεσις) simply as "covering," Onians translates it as "binding" of the feet to facilitate sexual intercourse, and suggests an analogy to the Chinese practice of binding the feet of their women (pp. 246, 524 ff.). Since sandals were the normal covering of feet in classical times, and were bound on, Onians' reading is not necessarily farfetched.

16. Sir James G. Frazer's note to this passage in his two-volume translation of and commentary on Apollodorus (London, 1921), I, 353, n. 4, says that vase-paintings indicate that boars were a common shield device.

17. Frazer, *The Golden Bough*, pp. 267, 265–266, 274. See also Robert Graves, *The Greek Myths* (Baltimore, 1955), I, pp. 12–13, 16–20. Subsequent references to Graves' *Greek Myths* will be distinguished by the initials *GM* from references to his *The White Goddess*. The initials of only the former will be cited in the text, as it is referred to frequently. Citations to the latter will be footnoted.

18. *Ibid.*, pp. 282, 300.

19. Budge, I, pp. 7, 65, 373, 386–387; II, pp. 222, 295. Cf. Frazer, p. 365.

20. *The Oxford Classical Dictionary*, ed. Cary *et al.* (Oxford, 1949), pp. 119–120. Cf. Pausanias, VII, 17, 10–12.

21. Frazer, p. 349. Cf. Graves, *GM*, I, pp. 71, 263.

22. "Adonis" is not a name but a title meaning "lord" and was probably conferred on the vegetation deity Tammuz as worship of him moved west from Mesopotamia. These castrated and resurrected fertility gods have much in common with Dionysus, whose worship in Greece Herodotus (II, 42, 49, 144) compared to that of the similarly rent-to-pieces and resurrected fertility god of Egypt, Osiris. (Cf. Diodorus Siculus, I, 11, 3; I, 13, 5, etc.; and Plutarch, *Isis et Osiris*, pp. 28, 34, 35.) On the identification of Thammuz, Attis, and Adonis, see *Oxford Classical Dictionary*, p. 7; Graves, *GM*, I, p. 72; and Jessie Weston, *From Ritual to Romance* (New York, 1957), pp. 8, 38.

23. Graves, *GM*, I, pp. 223, 225; and his *The White Goddess*, p. 331. Graves' theory is reinforced by the work of other scholars. On emasculation, Frazer, pp. 347–350, 365, 579–580; Weston, pp. 42–44, 48; Bruno Bettelheim, *Symbolic Wounds* (New York, 1962), pp. 91–92. On circumcision, Bettelheim, pp. 93–95; B. M. Loeb, "The Blood Sacrifice Complex," *Memoirs of the American Anthropological Association*, No. 30 (1933), p. 18; George A. Barton, "Semitic Circumcision," *Encyclopedia of Religion*

and Ethics (New York, 1911), p. 680. On the wearing of buskins, Frazer, pp. 592–594; Graves also cites other examples of
buskin-wearing on pages 323–331 of *The White Goddess.*

24. "Poisoned arrows dropped upon, or shot into, a knee or foot,
caused the death not only of Pholus and Cheiron, but also of
Achilles, Cheiron's pupil: all of them Magnesian sacred kings"
(Graves, *GM*, II, 115–116). Cf. I, 318: "The Thessalian sacred
king was, it seems, killed by an arrow smeared with viper
venom, which the tanist drove between his heel and ankle."

25. Graves suggests that the myth of Orpheus and Eurydice is a
misinterpretation of early pictures, and that actually "Eurydice's victims died of snake bite, not herself"; "male human
sacrifices were offered to . . . Eurydice, their death being apparently caused by viper's venom" (*GM*, I, pp. 115, 128).

26. *Ibid.,* I, pp. 13, 72; II, pp. 115, 235; I, 41. Cf. on Osiris and Set,
Budge, I, pp. 42, 62–63; on Apollo and Adonis, Ptolemy Hephaestionos, I, pp. 306; on Diarmuid and Finn, *The Mythology
of All Races,* ed. Louis Gray, III, "Celtic," ed. John A. Macculloch (Boston, 1918), 177.

27. Onians, pp. 206–207; Jung, 269; and Jane Harrison, *Epilego-
mena and Themis* (New Hyde Park, 1962), pp. 268–270. Cf.
Pliny, *N.H.,* X, LXXXVI, 188; and Plutarch, *Vit. Cleomenes,*
39.

28. Interestingly, boar and serpent myths combine. Set, as he was
known by the Egyptians, is associated with a boar; but his
Greek name, Typhon, is identified with a monstrous serpent-
cum-dragon.

29. *Aeneid,* II, 649. Robert Graves provides the following commentary on that myth:

> Aphrodite . . . was the nymph-goddess of mid-sum-
> mer. She destroyed the sacred king, who mated with her
> on a mountain top, as a queen bee destroys a drone: by
> tearing out his sexual organs. Hence the heather-loving
> bees . . . in her mountain-top affair with Anchises [Servius
> on Virgil's *Aeneid,* ii, 649]; hence also the worship of
> Cybele, the Phrygian Aphrodite of Mount Ida, as a queen
> bee, and the ecstatic self-castration of her priests in mem-
> ory of her lover Attis. Anchises was one of the many sacred
> kings who were struck with a ritual thunderbolt after
> consorting with the Death-in-Life Goddess. In the earliest
> version of the myth he was killed, but in later ones he
> escaped. . . . His name identifies Aphrodite with Isis,
> whose husband Osiris was castrated . . . ; 'Anchises' is,
> in fact, a synonym of Adonis. (*GM*, I, 71–72)

30. *Hesiod,* trans. Richard Lattimore (Ann Arbor, 1959), *Theogony,* 1, 930. Subsequent references to Hesiod's works will refer to this edition and will be cited in the text.

31. Hesiod, *loc. cit.,* declares that Hephaestus was the parthenogenous son of Hera, but in *The Iliad* (I, 578–579), Hephaestus refers to Zeus as father.

32. Cf. Graves: "It is not generally recognized that every Bronze Age tool, weapon, or utensil had magical properties, and that the smith was something of a sorcerer. . . . That the Smith-god hobbles is a tradition found in regions as far apart as West Africa and Scandinavia" (*GM,* I, 87–88).

33. Gilbert Murray, in his chapter "Ritual Forms in Greek Tragedy" which appeared in Jane Harrison's *Themis* (see n. 27 above), recounts much of what I have said in this chapter about the ritual murder of the fertility hero or *daimon*—as, of course, have many others. What is of particular interest at this point is his statement that "Oedipus-Jocasta are a vegetation pair, like Adonis-Aphrodite, Hippolytus-Artemis, etc." (p. 353).

34. *A Greek-English Lexicon,* ed. Henry George Liddell and Robert Scott, rev. ed. Henry Stuart Jones and Robert McKenzie (Oxford, 1961), under κόθορνος, meaning 2, "emblem of Tragedy in the person of Dionysus."

35. Robert Graves, *The White Goddess,* p. 325: "[in] the Eleusinian Mysteries, . . . the initiate said: 'I have fitted what was in the drum to what was in the *liknos.'* We know what was in the *liknos*—a phallus—and on the analogy of the buskins ceremonially presented to the sacred king at his marriage, it may be concluded that the drum contained a buskin into which the phallus was inserted as a symbol of the sexual act."

Graves does not cite his source of information about the contents of the *liknos.* There is a bas-relief on the so-called Lovatelli funeral urn which purports to show scenes from the Eleusinian Mysteries: someone fondling a serpent which enfolds Demeter, another figure holding a *liknon* or winnowing fan, still another figure holding a basket carrying images of phalli and pouring a libation over a sacrificial pig. The urn, however, dates from the first century A.D., when the Eleusinian Mysteries were some fifteen centuries old and, seemingly, had been conflated with Orphic rites. Jung (pp. 342–343) offers the same interpretation as does Graves but gives his source as Albrecht Dieterich's *Eine Mithrasliturgie* (Leipzig, 1903; 2nd ed. 1910), pp. 123 ff. and Jung's text (*Symbols of Transformation*) shows the relief of the Lovatelli urn as plate IVb.

George E. Mylonas, in *Eleusis and the Eleusinian Mysteries* (Princeton, 1961), pp. 296–305, summarizes the opinions of Dieterich and those who follow, more or less, his sexual explanation of the rites, and also the opinions of others who, like himself, believe in a different interpretation. Mylonas concludes that interpretations such as Dieterich's, Jung's, and Graves' apply either to "the mysteries of Rhea-Kybele-Attis, or to those celebrated [not in Greece but] in Alexandria," that the information seems mainly Orphic in origin and has nothing to do with the Mysteries of Eleusis, of which we may never know the exact details.

Whether Mylonas or Graves and his predecessors are right does not greatly affect what I have been trying to establish, for it does not change things if buskins were involved in the Orphic but not the Eleusinian rites; we do know that they were an essential part of Greek tragedy, which evolved from religious festivals for Dionysus, and the fact that they figure in both the myth and art of ancient Greece is evidence of their special nature.

36. At a still further remove, we have the strange fact that Passover, the Jewish holiday celebrated every spring to commemorate the Exodus from Egypt (or as Christian apologists would have it, redemption of the Israelites from bondage, prefiguring Christ's redemption of mankind), is called *Pesach* in Hebrew, and *pesach* is cognate with the root verb that means lame or limping. Undoubtedly a spring fertility rite was subsumed into the present festival, lending an unusual name to the occasion. (Cf. Theodor Herzl Gaster, *Passover* [New York, 1949], pp. 23–25.)

IN JUST-

in Just-
spring   when   the   world   is   mud-
luscious   the   little
lame   balloonman

whistles   far   and   wee

. . . .

it's
spring
and
*   the*
*   goat-footed*

baloonMan   whistles
far
and
wee

—*e. e. cummings*

2.

Fertility Figures

Barbara Seward has said that "the eras most favorable to symbolism have been the Catholic Middle Ages and the romantic nineteenth and twentieth centuries," [1] and for the most part this is true. The myths referred to in the previous chapter have been interpreted symbolically, especially by depth psychologists such as Jung; but such interpretations have often been rejected by iconographers, anthropologists, and those literary critics willing to tread the sword bridge of authorial intention. Presumably any collocation of events by an individual consciousness possesses some significance for psychoanalysts, but since I wish to limit this study to aesthetic considerations, it seems advisable to use ancient myths—of doubtful origin and moot purpose—only as background material and to concentrate on what are more generally agreed to be aesthetic works, the plays of Sophocles, for example, or Apuleius' *The Golden Ass.* In the latter, Lucius is punished for his unnatural lust for diabolical knowledge when, in his transformed shape as an ass, he is lamed by excessive labor, twice threatened with hamstringing, and twice threatened with gelding. However, he is reformed and saved by the fertility goddess Isis, initiated into her mysteries, and then initiated into the mysteries of her husband Osiris, god of the dead and victim of Set to whom the ass was sacred, by a lame high priest of Osiris named, significantly, Asinius.[2] Lucius' transformation from a beast, literal and figurative, occurs in the rich springtime of the year and is presided over by a goddess of fertility (described as such by Lucius in chapter seventeen) and a lame priest of an emasculated god of fertility. Lucius' life thereafter is enriched both spiritually and materially.

Lame figures upon whose health the welfare of the land depends appear next, directly after the Classical Age, in the Middle Ages. These characters, most of them variants of the Fisher King, symbolize sterility and will be discussed in the next chapter. The Renaissance, with such obvious exceptions as the work of Shakespeare, is an age that preferred allegory to symbolism, and there appear few limping heroes until the Romantics revived an interest in symbolic technique at the opening of the nineteenth century.

Today we no longer believe in the direct relation of a ruler's health to that of his land. In fact, with few exceptions, gods, kings, and even presidents rarely appear as protagonists in works of deliberate fiction. Our literary "heroes" are such only because of the frames of reference in which they appear; they are usually men whose problems have meaning for us but whose successes or failures do not affect our lives directly—as opposed to our aesthetic senses and, possibly, our emotions—except perhaps by way of example. However, although the surface concerns of our literature may seem to have altered, the pattern of the dying and reviving hero remains.

Such a death and rebirth for the sake of fertility occurs very explicitly in D. H. Lawrence's short novel *The Man Who Died* (1928).[3] Lawrence tells the story of Christ after the crucifixion and earthly resurrection.[4] The protagonist, never named but called by Lawrence "the man who had died" (p. 7), is identified in the first half of the novelette with a gamecock, an obvious fertility symbol: "He is good for twenty hens" (p. 3); or as the protagonist says of him, "I believe the bird is full of life and virtue" (p.21). Besides symbolic identification between the fertilizing bird of morning and the newly risen source of spiritual life, Lawrence puns obviously on "cock" as the male sexual organ, for the story, which Lawrence intended to title "The Escaped Cock," [5] records Christ's escape from ascetic denial to a richer, fuller life that includes sexual experience. As Lawrence himself expressed it: "As he heals up, he begins to find what an astonishing place the phenomenal world is, far more marvellous than any salvation or heaven—and thanks his stars he needn't have a 'mission' any more." [6]

The Man Who Died is still literally and figuratively distant as the story opens—"Don't touch me. . . . Not yet!

I am not yet healed and in touch with men" (p. 12). But he knows that he has died to be reborn, not as a symbol for other men, as he is usually taken to be, but that he might live more truly, more fully, than before.

"My mission is over, and my teaching is finished, and death has saved me from my own salvation. . . . I want to take my single way in life. . . . My public life is over . . ." (p. 13).
    Risen from the dead, he had realised at last that the body, too, has its little life, and beyond that, the greater life. He was virgin, in recoil from the little, greedy life of the body. But now he knew that virginity is a form of greed; and that the body rises again to give and to take, to take and to give, ungreedily. Now he knew that he had risen for the woman, or women, who knew the greater life of the body, not greedy to give, not greedy to take, and with whom he could mingle his body (pp. 16–17).

In the spring of the year, the time of Pesach and Easter, the Man Who Had Died goes forth "across the green wheat among the olive trees. He felt the cool silkiness of the young wheat under his feet that had been dead" (p. 8). He takes with him the bantam rooster, the escaped cock, and at an inn matches the bird against the inn's rooster, which it defeats. The protagonist says, "Thou at least has found thy kingdom, and the females to thy body" (p. 22), that is, the defeated rooster's hens. Thus the first part of the novelette ends, leaving the Man Who Died to find his earthly kingdom and a female for his body.
    The problem for the Man, as for Lawrence, was to find life and love that was based on free give and take,

sharing, with no compulsion. "It was the mania of cities and societies . . . to lay a compulsion upon a man. . . . He thought of his own mission, how he had tried to lay the compulsion of love on all men. And the old nausea came back on him." And so he searches for experience of the world and human contact, paradoxically, as "he looked again on the world with repulsion, dreading its mean contacts" (p. 22). Like Lucius, he succeeds in his quest, however temporarily, through a priestess of Isis. Like the Man, the woman is never named. She is just the priestess of Isis, "but not Isis, Mother of Horus. It was Isis Bereaved, Isis in Search. . . . She was looking for the fragments of the dead Osiris. . . . She must gather him together and fold her arms round the re-assembled body till it became warm again, and roused to life, and could embrace her, and could fecundate her womb" (p. 25). At winter time, and into her need "for the re-born man" (p. 27), Lawrence deliberately introduces the Man Who Had Died, and his need. She calls him Osiris (pp. 32, 34, 39), and he prays to Isis, "Ah, Goddess, . . . I would be so glad to live, if you would give me my clue again" (p. 40). For Lawrence, the clue is obvious: "There dawned on him the reality of the soft, warm love which is in touch, and which is full of delight" (p. 41).

Lawrence goes on to use scripture extremely idiosyncratically to describe the Man's experiences: "He knew only the crouching fullness of woman there, the soft white rock of life. . . . 'On this rock I built my life' "; of his subsequent erection, "I am risen!" (pp. 42–43). The season passes into spring, then summer, and the woman conceives: "Thou art like a tree whose green leaves follow the blossom, full of sap." And so both have received new life themselves and created more. At this point, Lawrence describes the thought of the Man Who Died: "So he knew the time was come again for him to depart. He would go alone, with his destiny. Yet not alone, for the touch would be upon him, even as he left his touch on her. And invisible suns would go with him" (p. 45).

This story by Lawrence, written late in his career, is a lucid and at times unesthetically blunt enunciation of his philosophy. At the same time it is a perfect example of the use of the limping hero of ancient myths, Egyptian and Christian combined, to express in modern literature the theme of fertility.

Lame gods, Christ in particular, figure once again in a character's conversion from self-pity to a life of true possibility. Robert Penn Warren's novel *Wilderness* (New York, 1961) concerns a clubfooted Bavarian Jew named Adam Rosenzweig, who comes to America in search of freedom. Christ, the second Adam, wandered forty days in the wilderness; Adam Rosenzweig, in Warren's novel of strained parallels, wanders through the Civil War's Wilderness campaign. Rosenzweig finds that laws alone do not inhibit freedom; to be free he must know himself. One of the epigraphs to the novel is from Pascal's *Pensées,* number 397: "The greatness of man is great in that he knows himself to be miserable. A tree does not know itself to be miserable. It is then being miserable to know oneself to be miserable; but it is also being great to know that one is miserable." [7]

Fleeing rebels overpower Adam and steal his boots, including the surgical one that enables him to walk with a minimum of difficulty. The novel ends, in Warren's trite and blatant metaphor, as Adam manages to stand on his own bare two feet. He is alone in a strange country on a field of war; he is a Jew among Gentiles, a cripple without friends or special talent. We might well expect him to be miserable, but he accepts his lot, and Warren

would have us think Adam great. Of course, to the extent
that a man's self-knowledge and self-confidence open new
possibilities for him, Adam's self-discovery is one of
fertility.

Tennessee Williams used allusions from Greek mythology to express the sexual philosophy he derived from
Lawrence.[8] Nor are these classical allusions accidental.
Writing of his childhood, Williams has said, "I would
rather read books in my grandfather's large and classical
library than play marbles and baseball and other normal
kid games." [9] Moreover, he studied Greek at Washington
University, St. Louis.[10] Examples of this classical influence
may be seen in the title and general outline of *Orpheus
Descending,* the sacred grove of "royal palm trees" that
forms the background for *Sweet Bird of Youth,* and the
setting of *Streetcar Named Desire* as Williams describes
it in his notes before the play and has Blanche repeat
them: "They told me to take a streetcar named Desire,
and then transfer to the one called Cemeteries and ride six
blocks and get off—at Elysian Fields! . . ." (Act I, sc. 1).
Blanche, like Val Xavier of *Orpheus,* has come to a hellish
other world.

In *Cat on a Hot Tin Roof* elements of Greek mythology are set in a tale of sexual and spiritual regeneration.
The night before the action of the play takes place, Brick
Pollitt, in a vain drunken effort to recapture the glory
and sense of accomplishment he had as a high school and
college athlete, breaks an ankle trying to jump hurdles
on a high school track. Throughout the play Brick hobbles with cast and crutch, which symbolize his moral
crippledness; he tries, too, to withdraw from the men-
dacious world (as he calls it) into himself and into an
existence anesthetized by alcohol.

Brick had had a latently homosexual friendship with

another football player, Skipper, and Brick's wife Maggie obviously disliked the resultant triangle. In jealousy, she had told Skipper either to admit his homosexual feelings toward Brick or to leave Brick to her. Skipper tried to do the former, but Brick, disgusted by the idea of homosexuality and the suggestion that he might have any such tendencies, had rejected their relationship on those terms —and rejected Skipper. Skipper turned instead to drugs and alcohol and died shortly thereafter. Brick blames himself for his friend's death, but projects his guilt onto Maggie for precipitating the crisis, disgustedly tinging with abnormality her sexual desire for him. During the months since Skipper's death, Brick has not slept with Maggie, and on that fact the play turns.

Brick's father, Big Daddy, is dying of cancer. His other son, Gooper, and Gooper's again-pregnant wife, Mae, want to be sure to inherit Big Daddy's wealth and his plantation for themselves and their five "no-neck monsters" [11] (another mythological allusion?). Maggie wants the inheritance for herself and Brick, but Brick wants only to escape, by means of alcohol, from the world of "mendacity"—including his own. He is, as he says to his father, "almost *not* alive" (p. 94). Big Daddy would prefer to leave the plantation to Maggie and Brick, if they have children who can inherit it in turn and thus perpetuate him. So Maggie lies to Big Daddy and the rest of the family, saying that she does carry Brick's child; and in the last moments of the play, having taken away Brick's crutches—the wooden one he walks on, and the alcohol he lives on—she literally forces Brick into bed with her to turn the lie into truth. She forces him back into an active life and into an attempt to have children, this dialogue accompanying the scene:

BRICK: I admire you, Maggie.

MAGGIE: Oh, you weak, beautiful people who give up with such grace. What you need is someone to take hold of you—gently, with love, and hand your life back to you. . . . (p. 158).[12]

Maggie seems to do just that: she gives Brick his life back, and from him, Williams implies, she will conceive more. For in spite of Maggie's childlessness during the play, which contrasts her with her teeming sister-in-law Mae, Williams identifies Maggie-the-cat as the fertility goddess, Diana, in her earlier Greek identity as Artemis, bow-carrying mother-deity and birth-goddess.[13] When Mae comes on stage with a bow she has found, asking Brick if it is his, Maggie replies:

Why, Sister Woman—that's my Diana Trophy. Won it at the intercollegiate archery contest on the Ole Miss campus. . . . Brick and I still have our special archers' license. We're goin' deer huntin' on Moon Lake as soon as the season starts. I love to run with dogs through chilly woods, run, run, leap over obstructions— (pp. 28–29).

Moreover the cat is a sacred animal of Artemis and is itself regarded as a fertility spirit.[14] Thus Williams carries on, here at least, Lawrence's distinction between mindless, spiritless sexuality, as between Mae and Gooper, and a bodily union between Brick and Maggie which represents a union of souls as well.

The continuation of life, the fertility of land and

people, is a major theme of the play: childless Maggie is taunted by her prolific sister-in-law Mae; Big Mama is a literal translation of Magna Mater; and Big Daddy wants Brick to have a son who can inherit the plantation, repeatedly described (pp. 65, 93, 154) as rich and fertile; even Big Daddy's dirty joke about an elephant in heat echoes the theme in his allusion to the "excitin' odor of female fertility!" (p. 151)

In *Cat on a Hot Tin Roof*, then, Brick has watched Big Daddy face impending death from cancer, he has seen Maggie endure him in spite of his antipathy toward her, and he has seen her defend her marriage to him before his family. At the end of the play, Williams makes us feel that Brick has, if not solved, then at least learned to live with his problems. We feel that Brick will give up his excessive self-pity and the liquor that nourishes it, and that he will "stand on his own two feet" as much as his newly broken ankle will permit. He has not only received his life back from Maggie, as the contest-scarred victor received the crown of sacred kingship from the fertility goddess' representative or priestess, but Williams intimates that Brick will propagate more life, father children who will follow him in ruling over Big Daddy's plantation, 28,000 acres "of the richest land this side of the valley Nile."

Similarly, Truman Capote's short story, "Among the Paths to Eden" [15] treats the theme of death and spiritual rebirth suggested by the title and graveyard setting. The heroine, Mary O'Meaghan, is a spinster of nearly forty, whose life had been devoted to her father. But he is now dead and she, on the advice of a "practical" friend, is seeking a husband among the widowers she meets in a nearby cemetery, men who she hopes miss the comforts of a well-kept, well-cooked-for home. The man she con-

fronts in this story is Ivor Belli, who has finally paid a
grudging visit to his not terribly lamented wife's grave.
It is a Saturday in March, "a hard winter had just passed,"
and the day is adorned with "handsome, spring-prophesy-
ing weather" (p. 238). As a token of the season, Mr. Belli
brings jonquils to his wife's grave. Here, as in all the
works discussed in this chapter, early spring flowers suggest rebirth, renewal; jonquils are especially appropriate
since they are a variety of narcissus, named for the beautiful Greek youth who took his own life but was reborn as
the flower.

Mary and Ivor talk, share her peanuts, and sit on the
gravestone, though the very invitation to do so causes
Mary to blush "as though he'd asked her to transform
Mrs. Belli's bier into a love bed" (p. 242). One of her
difficulties in finding a husband, besides her age and plain
looks, is that she is crippled: her left leg will not bend.
"An accident. You know. When I was a kid. I fell off a
roller coaster at Coney. . . . Nobody knows why I'm alive"
(p. 242). Like the Man Who Died, she has returned from
death, entombed not for three days but for most of her
life. And though she fails to interest Belli enough for him
to wish to marry her, she does, like the Man Who Died,
cause a renewal of life.

Her pleasant conversation, her reminiscences of times
past, her very person make Belli feel younger and more
alive:

". . . I'm fifty-one," he said, subtracting four years.
"Can't say I feel it." And he didn't; perhaps it was
because the wind had subsided, the warmth of the
sun grown more authentic. Whatever the reason, his
expectations had re-ignited, he was again immortal,
a man planning ahead (p. 245).

He begins to think with more nostalgia of his past marriage, remembering the pleasant aspects of it, and wishes he had brought his wife, instead of jonquils, orchids like those she had saved after their daughters' dates and "stored in the icebox until they shriveled" (p. 244). With an increasing sense of vigor and rejuvenation—"clouds were fewer, the sun exceedingly visible" (p. 249)—he decides to take his secretary to dinner, to buy her an orchid, a flower named in Greek "testicle," appropriate to his resurging sense of masculinity. "And where, he wondered, do couples honeymoon in April? At latest May" (pp. 249–250).

Lame Miss O'Meaghan has played the part of Pan: she has ushered in the spring, Ivor Belli's second. She brings no new life to herself, no renewed fertility, but Mr. Belli she brings to a "hopeful, zestful, live-forever mood" (p. 250).

In Bernard Malamud's novels there is often a similar blend of success and failure, as well as a quest for self-knowledge, self-fulfilment, and an end to the wasting away of the lives involved. Besides imagery from nature, Malamud uses mythic patterns constantly: the Grail Quest in *The Natural*,[16] a pattern of rebirth in both *The Assistant* and *A New Life*,[17] and the dark journey of the soul in *The Fixer*. Of these, *The Assistant* and *A New Life* are most obviously concerned with fertility. *A New Life* concerns Seymour Levin, who is teaching in college for the first time, attempting to make something of his life. As he tells Pauline Gilley, the wife of his supervisor, when first they sleep together:

> My father was continuously a thief. Always thieving, always caught, he finally died in prison. My mother went crazy and killed herself. One night I came home

and found her sitting on the kitchen floor looking at
a bloody bread knife.

. . . I mourned them but it was a lie. I was in love
with an unhappy, embittered woman who had just
got rid of me . . . I was mourning myself. I became
a drunk, it was the only fate that satisfied me.

. . . For two years I lived in self-hatred, willing to
part with life. . . .[18]

That period is over: Levin has left the land of the
dead for that of the living, but is only a novice and has
not yet learned to live fully. The hierophant who initiates
him into the "mysteries" is Pauline Gilley. Through her,
Levin learns to love, and through love he learns to bear
responsibility. At the end of the novel, Gerald Gilley asks
Levin why, why take on "an older woman than yourself
and not dependable, plus two adopted kids, no choice of
yours, no job or promise of one, and other assorted head-
aches." To which Levin replies, "Because I can, you son
of a bitch" (p. 360).

Pauline's love has made Levin "patient and kind. . . .
Love bears all things, believes all things, hopes all things,
endures all things." Many of Malamud's characters, including Levin, "rejoice in . . . sufferings, knowing [Mala-
mud at least, if not they] that suffering produces endurance, and endurance produces character, and character
produces hope. . . ." The quotations are from the works
of St. Paul (1 Corinthians 13:4 and Romans 5:3–4, respectively), making one wonder whether Malamud meant to
suggest Pauline doctrine through Pauline Gilley. Certainly
Malamud agrees with Paul's "Make love your aim" (1
Corinthians 14:1), although the latter means only *caritas*

and love of God, while Malamud means a fusion of *eros* and *caritas*.

St. Paul says, "We were buried therefore with him [Christ] by baptism into Death. . . . We know that our old self was crucified with him so that the sinful body might be destroyed . . ." [Romans 6:4 ff.]. Levin undergoes a bodily death. He dwells in a tomb-like cellar (p. 201) and is partially resurrected by his own desire to live, then more fully by Pauline's love. He is a teacher of English, but as Paul notes, "If I speak in the tongues of men and of angels, but have not love, I am a noisy gong or a clanging cymbal" (1 Corinthians 13:1). And while Levin makes love to Pauline Gilley without committing his life to her, fending off his conscience (p. 210), he suffers:

> The next time after making love, Levin experienced a fiery pain in the butt. . . . It moved up the side, then to the scrotum, then back to the butt, a harrowing embarrassment after sex and shameful way to be vulnerable.
>
> After another such spasm he began to dread going to bed with her. At the same time he was disgusted with himself— . . . for every pleasure, pain. . . . Levin paid the price of emission, a fiery pain in the ass (p. 213).

Says Paul, "But I see in my members another law at war with the law of my mind. . . . Wretched man that I am! . . ." (Rom. 7:23–24). Levin confronts the problem of his enforced impotence, tries to analyze it, and winds up psychoanalyzing himself.

> What was the painful egg the rooster was trying to lay? . . . He was asking himself what he was

hiding from: That he too clearly saw her [Pauline's] shortcomings and other disadvantages, and was urgently urging himself to drop her before it was too late? That he was tired of the uneasy life, fed up with assignations with the boss's wife, sick up to here with awareness of danger and fear of consequences? . . . After mulling these and related thoughts, Levin . . . fell over one regarding himself: the dissatisfaction he had lately been hiding from, or feeling for an inadmissibly long time, was with him for withholding what he had to give. He then gave birth. Love ungiven had caused Levin's pain. To be unpained he must give what he unwillingly withheld.

. . . Through fields of stars he fell in love (pp. 215–216).

To quote St. Paul once more: "Let love be genuine" (Rom. 12:9).

The controlling image of the long paragraph from egg to "He then gave birth" is that of the novel's title, *A New Life*. "The new life" appears in Romans 7:6; it is also, of course, the title of Dante's paean to Beatrice that celebrates the transmutation of earthly love into love of God, a theme parallel to St. Paul's. By accepting the responsibility of his love for Pauline, Levin undergoes an initiation, a ritual rebirth that commences after he realizes the cause of his psychosomatic genital wound.

The primary message of St. Paul was that one should follow God and His commandments willingly, not because of law, secular or religious, but because one loved God and had faith. Thus willingness to serve and freedom from compulsion are tenets that unite three extremely disparate authors, all of whom concern themselves with fertility—St. Paul, D. H. Lawrence, and Bernard Malamud.

There are other elements of fertility and sterility in the novel. There is the cycle of seasons and directions: Levin arrives in the far West at the end of summer, the begining of fall; he begins a return to the East at the beginning of summer one year later; the dramatic turning point of the novel occurs when Levin and Pauline enjoy their first romantic idyll in the forest in late March, when neophyte naturalist Levin discovers trees, birds, and love (pp. 194–199).

Gerald Gilley is sterile and red-headed (pp. 192–193; 1), the latter characteristic being, as Sidney Richman says, a diabolical sign as employed by Malamud. Similarly, characteristics of the breasts signify fertility or sterility in his female characters.[19] Pauline is at first quite deficient: "Her chest had the topography of an ironing board" (p. 193); "her chest was barren" (p. 207), "bereft of female flowers. He [Levin] mourned that motherless breast, the lost softness over the heart to pillow a man's head" (p. 216). But like Levin, she too undergoes rebirth. The first sign of fertility that Malamud associates with her is fruit—oranges and lemons—as with Iris Lemon in *The Natural*. The confirming sign of Pauline's fecundity, of more new life in the novel, is her pregnancy by Levin, marked by her growing breasts; moreover, "Her body smelled like fresh-baked bread, the bread of flowers" (p. 366).

Malamud had used the words "a new life" and a similar pattern of ritual rebirth and redemption in an earlier novel, *The Assistant*.[20] The protagonist in *The Assistant* is Frank Alpine, a wanderer without home and without values, except for some basic human compassion tempered by prejudice. Desperately poor and hungry and without direction to his life, he helps Ward Minogue, an acquaintance, rob Jewish grocer Morris Bober one November day. Frank is more willing to participate in the robbery because his victim is a Jew, someone for whom he need not feel sympathy. Yet when Ward impatiently pistol whips the old man, Frank gives Bober a cup of water. Alpine is twenty-five and looks much older. Of Italian extraction, he was raised in an orphanage as a Catholic, but he no longer believes in that religion or much of anything. He has never known love, success, or satisfaction; he is a born loser, a *schlemiel*. As he says:

> "I've been close to some wonderful things—jobs, for instance, education, women, but close is as far as I go. . . . Sooner or later everything I think is worth having gets away from me in some way or other. I work like a mule for what I want, and just when it looks like I am going to get it I make some kind of stupid move, and everything that is nailed down tight blows up in my face.
> . . . With me one wrong thing leads to another and it ends in a trap" (p. 36).

In this case, the trap is Morris' grocery. Frank, ashamed of his part in the robbery and sorry for Bober, returns to help the old man—to become Bober's assistant in work as he was Ward Minogue's in theft. As Fitzgerald had about the rich, Alpine has conflicting feelings about goodness. In the orphanage where he was raised, Alpine has been taught about St. Francis, of whom he says:

> "He said poverty was a queen and he loved her like she was a beautiful woman. . . . Every time I read about somebody like him I get a feeling inside of me I have to fight to keep from crying. He was born good, which is a talent if you have it" (p. 31).

But Alpine lacks this talent and comprehends neither St. Francis nor his own feelings about the saint. Yet he sees that Bober's life, like St. Francis', is one of both poverty and goodness; in his longing for a code to live by, an end to his own aimlessness, he is attracted by Bober's endurance in the face of calamity, by his acceptance of life with all its hardships, by his compassion, and by his religion. At the same time, Alpine is repelled by the pain and suffering that Morris' code brings the grocer. He asks Morris what it is to be a Jew. The grocer replies:

> ". . . The important thing is the Torah. This is the Law—a Jew must believe in the Law. . . . This means to do what is right, to be honest, to be good. This means to other people. Our life is hard enough. Why should we hurt somebody else? . . . We ain't animals. . . . This is what a Jew believes" (p. 124).

Frank is also attracted to Bober's daughter Helen and gradually wins the friendship of father and daughter —only to lose both. Unable to do right even when he wants to, Frank continuously steals meager sums from the grocery store cash register, causing Morris, when the grocer can finally prove theft, to fire him. The same night Frank goes to the park to meet Helen who is falling in love with him and has been meeting him in spite of her mother's objections. He arrives at their rendezvous and finds Ward Minogue attempting to rape Helen. But after he drives off Ward, Frank takes her by force himself. Later when Bober becomes ill, Frank sneaks back into the store, operating it while Morris recuperates. When the grocer is better, he forces Frank to leave. At the end of March, however, Morris catches pneumonia while shoveling snow and dies three days later. At his

funeral, a warm spring-like April day, Frank slips and
falls into Morris' grave, landing on the grocer's coffin.
Afterwards he goes back to the store that had been Bober's
tomb-in-life for twenty-two years, assuming the support
of Mrs. Bober and Helen and working at an additional
night job as well so that Helen can attend night school.
He also assumes Morris' values, his honesty and compassion: his descent into Bober's grave marks Frank's
death as an uncommitted wanderer and his rebirth as
Bober's spiritual son—one who lives by the Law. The
last paragraph in the novel relates the events of the spring
a year after Bober's death:

> One day in April Frank went to the hospital
> and had himself circumcised. For a couple of days he
> dragged himself around with a pain between his legs.
> The pain enraged and inspired him. After Passover
> he became a Jew (p. 246).

That Frank should have himself circumcised and
formally convert to Judaism at Passover-Easter time is
highly significant: it is the season of Nature's renewal of
life and it coincides with the resurrections of Christ, Attis,
and Adonis. It is also the time of the redemption (resurrection) of the Jewish nation from Egyptian bondage.[21]
That Frank should drag himself around during these holy
days is also significant, for *pesach,* the Hebrew word for
Passover, is etymologically related not only to *pasahu,* an
Assyrian word meaning to propitiate, but also to several
Hebrew words meaning lame or hobbling.[22] Thus Malamud has used, consciously or not, religious and mythic
allusions as well as obviously purposeful seasonal changes
—the novel moves twice from wintry fall to warm spring

—to mark the pattern of death and rebirth. Frank undergoes a rite of initiation, begun at Morris' side in the living death of the grocery store, marked by his descent to the grocer's grave and by his circumcision, and expressed by his conversion from a spiritually empty life; he experiences resurrection, which prepares him for his new life, based on the role of the grocer and endowed with Bober's responsibilities, beliefs, and values. Frank's material gains are negligible but he does grow in heroic stature and in our admiration. We can measure Frank's conversion from his sterile, self-centered life in terms of his relationship with Helen, who is also endowed with mythic characteristics.

Although critics disagree about their relationship at the novel's conclusion,[23] I feel that they probably will marry. At the end of the novel Helen confesses to herself her feelings for Frank.

> Although she detested the memory of her experience in the park, lately it had come back to her how she had desired that night to give herself to Frank. . . . She had wanted him. . . . If he had made his starved leap in bed she would have returned passion. She had hated him, she thought, to divert hatred from herself (p. 239).

She learns how hard Frank is working and thinks:

> He had kept them alive. Because of him she had enough to go to school at night. . . . It came to her that he had changed. It's true, he's not the same man, she said to herself. I should have known by now. She had despised him for the evil he had

done, without understanding the why or aftermath, or admitting there could be an end to the bad and a beginning of good. . . . He had been one thing, low, dirty, but because of something in himself— something she couldn't define, a memory perhaps, an ideal he might have forgotten and then remembered—he had changed into somebody else, no longer what he had been. She should have recognized it before. What he did to me he did wrong, she thought, but since he has changed in his heart he owes me nothing (p. 243).

The next week she enters the store and speaks to Frank— only the second time in almost a year since her father's death, and for the first time of her own volition—to thank him for all of his trouble. She tells him, blushing as she does so, that she will consider his offer to take more money from him so that she can go to college during the day, and also tells him that she is still using a volume of Shakespeare he had given her as a present long before. That night Frank hears her fight with and leave—perhaps permanently—her one boy friend.

Frank and she may never become completely reconciled, but most of the barriers that had existed between them have been removed. After Frank's assault on Helen, the one comment from her that Malamud gives us, the one that closes the chapter, is "Dog—uncircumcised dog!" (p. 168). The adjective, at least, is no longer valid.

As Baumbach has noted, "Frank's attraction to Helen is an uneasy fusion of the sensual and the spiritual. . . ." (p. 117); also, his "redemption is made possible by his uncompromising love for Helen, which provides the impetus of his commitment to the store" (p. 120). It is undoubtedly part of the impetus for his commitment to Judaism as well. Frank was strongly attracted to Judaism and to Helen, and wished to "belong" to both; and he has taken what steps he can, accomplishing the first goal and doing as much as he could to achieve the second. The first brings him a form of rebirth and spiritual peace; the second would bring him sexual fulfillment, a satisfaction of his social needs, and probably children. " 'Helen' was the name of the Spartan Moon-goddess, marriage to whom . . . made Menelaus king," and her name is etymologically related to Helle, bright goddess of death and resurrection.[24] To the extent to which Helen has redeemed Frank, she is a fertility goddess.

To emphasize her role, Malamud frequently describes her in terms of obvious symbols of fertility: flowers (harbingers of spring's renewal) and birds (roosters; the doves of Noah, Aphrodite, and Christian symbolism; the Thanksgiving turkey). Morris thinks Helen "looks like a little bird" (p. 20); when Frank spies on her in the bathroom he thinks of her "breasts like small birds in flight, her ass like a flower" (p. 75). And like Aphrodite, Helen leaves a floral fragrance about her in the air (p. 184).

There is still another sign that attests to the special nature of Helen's role. In *Symbolic Wounds,* Dr. Bruno Bettelheim discusses the relationship of circumcision to ritual forms of emasculation. Speaking of the self-mutilation of the priests of Cybele, he says, "This example of ritual castration, and many others not mentioned here, indicates that it was exacted by maternal figures as a sign of devotion and submission on the part of their male followers. . . ." [25] If Mrs. Bober objects to Helen's consorting with a non-Jew, if Helen herself loathes Frank because he is "an uncircumcised dog," then Frank is willing to have himself circumcised as a sign of "devotion and submission"—to the Law of Judaism as Morris Bober spoke of it, and to Helen. Bettelheim also says, as I quoted before, "Loeb is convinced that circumcision was originally performed as a sacrifice to a female goddess. . . . He follows Barton, who holds that originally all Semitic circumcision was a sacrifice to the goddess of fertility." [26] Frank's circumcision for love and religion during the Paschal season, the time of propitiation, coincides not only with the death and resurrection of Christ at the time of hobbling, but also with the castration of Attis and Adonis (and their priests) on behalf of their respective loves and fertility goddesses, Cybele and Aphrodite. To call Helen a fertility figure, however, to compare her to Cybele and Aphrodite, is not to say that Malamud has written modern Greek myth, as John Updike has in *The Centaur*. The source of the power that Helen may dispense, the nature of her *mana*, is the same as that with which the priestess of Isis heals Lawrence's Man Who Died. As Baumbach and Richman have noted, redemption comes to Malamud's protagonists through their ability to give of themselves unselfishly, to love.[27]

Saul Bellow, Malamud's great contemporary, has had fun in using fertility myth material, and in using it more obviously than any other recent American writer. As many authors may use "Christ" as half curse, half prayer, so Bellow uses the stuff of myth half in joke and half in earnest. In "A Sermon by Doctor Pep" (1949), Dr. Pep is a soap-box prophet of a fuller, healthier life. He begins his harangue in "Bughouse" Square, Chicago, with a reference to approaching Easter and the resurrection of life that spring will effect on the sidewalks of Chicago. Soon

Bellow, who was a student of anthropology as well as literature, has Dr. Pep infusing his speech with repeated fertility references:

> Spring and Easter make me think of these things, dear listeners. The slaughtered Osiris gets himself together again and his scattered body comes to life; the grave-cold Redeemer rises up; . . . We little dream of the love-raging cults that preceded when we see those sprays of cloth flowers worn in the parade or of the legs that trembled for the touch of panting Attis in the hobbled march of tight skirts. And pretty soon there'll be little cake and fudge lambs in the windows that the children croon at and eat. Yes, eat the lamb made to eat; . . . Learn biting love with the little pure divinity lamb; . . . Or turn your thoughts to eucharistic wine and wafers. "You shall eat my body and drink my blood"—terrible to the blood-avoiding law of Moses. But consider it as an order to feel no blame and have an innocent appetite. In things like this the secret of health and eating is to be found. A Paschal lamb. To the ancient Greek islanders, a fish. And if Christ's blood ran for us, why shouldn't the blood of steers run . . . ? [28]

Dr. Pep preaches the theme of resurrection through the dependence of life upon death, and the necessity of acknowledging the closeness and ever-presence of death, facing up to it, and then ignoring it to concentrate on life: "We can keep death too near us by secret care. It inhibits the bite, it poisons the mouthful, closes the digestion and sends us to an early grave" (p. 462; 75). Dr. Pep, who has paid for his present life by the loss of a limb—· "I ransomed my body with my leg" (p. 455; 68)—urges not to deny death, but recognize its inevitability and then stop worrying about it.

In *Henderson the Rain King* (1959), Bellow has written a quasi parody of all fertility myths ("quasi" because while the occasions for humor are evident, it is not clear how much Bellow meant them to detract from the seriousness of the book). Eugene Henderson is a fifty-five-year-old, twice-married Connecticut millionaire who asserts both his contempt for society and something of his own personality by being a pig farmer. Like his first totemic beasts (there are several), Henderson is beset by an inner voice demanding, *"I want, I want!"* One gets the impression while rereading this motto the many times it appears in the novel that the stress is ambiguous and may be applied to either the first or second word of this chant.

To satisfy his craving, Henderson sets out on a quest —with critically noted parallels to Odysseus, Don Quixote, Faust, Conrad's Marlowe and Jim, Coleridge's Ancient Mariner, and another African big game hunter whose initials were also E. H., Ernest Hemingway. At the first village he visits, that of the matriarchal Arnewi, Henderson finds the tribe and its cattle dying for lack of water in the dry season, their cistern of collected water polluted by a plague of frogs. Taking upon himself the hero's task of freeing the waters, Henderson makes a bomb and succeeds only too literally: his bomb cracks the cistern, frees the water—with its burden of dead frogs—and allows it to run off.

In shame and despair, he goes deeper into the dark continent and soon meets the Wariri, a tribe whose sacred king is strangled when he cannot satisfy his many wives, and whose vice-regent is Sungo (Sun-go), a rain king. Henderson arrives to find the former Sungo strangled for inability to perform his requisite tasks, and unwittingly becomes the new Sungo himself. He participates in a phallic ceremony which consists of his moving the statue of a fertility goddess Mummah (all puns obviously intended by Bellow) by embracing, erecting, and carrying it in his arms. This ritual brings clouds out of the hot, clear sky. Subsequently Henderson is stripped naked by a troop of Amazons, plunged into a pond of the only remaining (stagnant) water (an act of homeopathic magic), and then lashed in a scapegoat ceremony—all of which one can find dutifully recorded in Frazer. And rain does come to the Wariri.

Their king Dahfu befriends Henderson and attempts to increase his self-respect and enjoyment of life by making him switch to the king's own totemic animal, the lion. Henderson undergoes a period of Reichian therapy which includes his imitating Dahfu's pet lioness, crawling around on all fours and roaring. Finally Henderson escapes and returns to America, taking with him a symbolic lion cub (as a pet for his daughter), and caring for a small orphan, one of his first truly altruistic acts in the novel.

Henderson is obviously a fertility figure: he brings rain to the Wariri. And he is a limping hero: on the third page of the novel Henderson recounts how he "fell off a tractor while drunk, and ran myself over and broke my leg. For months I was on crutches, hitting everyone who crossed my path, man or beast. . . ." [29]; and he was wounded in the leg by a land mine in the Second World War (p. 303). But the extent of fertility with which Bellow endows him is moot. The New-found-land he dances over with the child at the novel's end is described as "frozen ground of almost eternal winter" (p. 340). His altruistic desire to serve humanity by becoming a doctor is commendable, but the idea of ex-pig-farmer, ex-rain-god Henderson entering medical school in his late fifties is more than a bit ludicrous. Bellow always has difficulty reconciling the romanticism of his visions (what he wants to happen) with his naturalism (their likelihood).

Like "Dr. Pep," *Henderson* teaches the necessity of facing and accepting death in order to enjoy life. In addition it encourages selflessness and altruism—limits to one's individualism—as necessary prerequisites to love and fulfillment. Perhaps the reader will make more lasting use of these lessons than (as he has good cause to believe) will Henderson.

In "good" English and American literature today, accounts of victims, sufferers, and antiheroes are far more prevalent than stories that end optimistically. In *The Man Who Died, The Assistant, Cat on a Hot Tin Roof,* and *Henderson the Rain King,* the better long works mentioned in this chapter, the authors imply only that the protagonists have achieved lives that are healthier than and morally superior to what they had been before; in no case is there more than an implication, for strongly affirmed positive endings would probably have been regarded by critics and public alike as false, sentimental, and "Hollywoodish." Despite their use of symbols, Bellow, Lawrence, Malamud and Williams are all regarded as realists. Nevertheless Lawrence explicitly continues the story of a dying and reviving god; Malamud and Williams incorporate the same theme in their works. They, Bellow, and Robert Penn Warren express the belief that man can undergo degradation, a spiritual death, as a *rite de passage* to a life that is better, fuller, and more meaningful. All of these authors, and Truman Capote also, have kept alive the ancient ritual of fertility out of sacrifice, a sacrifice marked by a leg wound.

Notes

1. Barbara Seward, *The Symbolic Rose* (New York, 1960), p. 4.
2. *The Golden Ass of Apuleius,* trans. Robert Graves (New York, 1954), pp. 70, 71, 131, 135, 151, 154, 174. Interestingly, Apuleius' allegory contains the story of a rival's killing one whose wife he desired, at a boar hunt by a spear-thrust in the thigh, and letting it be known that the dead man had indeed been killed by a boar: a clear example of ritual killing of a king by a supplanter in boar form (p. 157).
3. *The Short Novels* (London: The Phoenix Edition of D. H. Lawrence, 1956), II. Quotations from *The Man Who Died* cited in the text will refer to this edition.
4. The resurrected Christ of the Gospels shows his nail-pierced hands and feet, but he is not described as limping; Lawrence's Man Who Died did limp as "he saw his hurt feet touching the earth again . . . his dead feet . . . naked scarred feet" (p. 6). Similarly, in Robert Graves' euhemeristic account of Christ's life, *King Jesus* (New York, 1946), Jesus undergoes a tribal rite of royal initiation prior to His appearance in Jerusalem. The rite includes a ritual combat that ends, as Jacob's did, in a dislocation of a thigh (pp. 263–264). As proof of his assumption that Jesus was lamed, Graves cites this passage (the editorial insertions are Graves'): ". . . Balaam the Lame [i.e., Jesus] was 33 years old when Pintias the Robber [i.e., Pontius Pilate] killed him. . . . They say that his mother was descended from princes and rulers, but consorted with carpenters" (p. 6; from the *Lexicon Talmudicum,* sub "Abanarbel," and the *Talmud Babli Sanhedrin,* 106b, 43a, 51a).
5. Harry T. Moore, *The Collected Letters of D. H. Lawrence* (London, 1962), II, 975.
6. *Ibid.*
7. Blaise Pascal, *Pensées,* trans. W. F. Trotter (London, 1931).
8. Besides the various biographies and general studies of Williams —Benjamin Nelson's (London, 1961), Nancy Tischler's (New York, 1961), and Signi Falk's (New York, 1961)—which include mention of his pilgrimage to Taos and the Lawrence ranch, specific discussions of influence are "Jesus and the Osiris-Isis Myth: Lawrence's *The Man Who Died* and Williams' *The Night of the Iguana*" by George Hendrick, *Anglia,* 84 (1966),

398–406; and Norman J. Fedder's brief but valuable book, *Influence of D. H. Lawrence on Tennessee Williams* (The Hague, 1966).

9. From an article in *The New York Times*, March 8, 1959, which appears as a foreword to Williams' *Sweet Bird of Youth* (New York, 1962).

10. Francis Donahue, *The Dramatic World of Tennessee Williams* (New York, 1964), p. 10.

11. Tennessee Williams, *Cat on a Hot Tin Roof* (New York, 1955), pp. 15, 16 et passim. Subsequent quotations from this play will be noted by page number in the text and will refer to this edition.

12. It should be noted that the play ending described is that of the Broadway or acting version, written by Williams at Elia Kazan's request, and that it differs from Williams' original ending. However, the dialogue is Williams', it appears in most published versions of the play, and Williams has never seen fit to repudiate it as inappropriate.

13. Frazer, *Golden Bough*, pp. 139 ff:; Graves, *The Greek Myths*, I, 83–85; *Oxford Dictionary*, p. 104; Jane Harrison, *Themis* (Cambridge, 1912), pp. 503–504.

14. Frazer, p. 453; Graves, *GM*, I, 134–135; and *The White Goddess*, pp. 234–235.

15. Truman Capote, *Selected Writings* (New York, 1963), pp. 238–252. All quotations are from this source and are noted by page number in the text.

16. Leslie Fiedler seems to have been the first to recognize the presence of myth in *The Natural (No! in Thunder* [Boston, 1960], p. 105); among others who refer to or discuss its presence are Jonathan Baumbach, *The Landscape of Nightmare* (New York, 1965), pp. 107–111; Charles Alvah Hoyt, "Bernard Malamud and the New Romanticism," *Contemporary American Novelists*, ed. Harry T. Moore (Carbondale, 1964), p. 78; Sidney Richman, *Bernard Malamud* (New York, 1966), pp. 28–49; and Robert Shulman, "Myth, Mr. Eliot, and the Comic Novel," *Modern Fiction Studies*, XII (Winter, 1966–1967), 400–403.

17. Baumbach, pp. 103, 106, 111–121; Hoyt, pp. 68, 69; Richman, pp. 71, 85, 89.

18. Bernard Malamud, *A New Life* (New York, 1961), pp. 200–201.

19. Richman, p. 34. Richman is wrong, however, in saying that (in *The Natural*) Memo Paris is unlike Harriet Bird because only the former has a fibroma of the breast; Harriet also denies her breast to Roy when they are riding on the train *(The Natural* [New York, 1952], p. 35) and it is this denial that marks lack

of warm femininity. The fibroma is only an additional sign, an objective correlative of the disease that denial of love is, like the crippled state of Zinaida Nikolaevna Lebedev in Malamud's *The Fixer.*

20. Bernard Malamud, *The Assistant* (New York, 1957). "A new life" occurs on p. 60. All subsequent quotations from this novel will be taken from this edition, page numbers only being given in the text.

21. J. G. Frazer, *The Golden Bough,* pp. 336, 248–351; and Joseph Campbell, *The Masks of God* (New York, 1964) III, 138. Cf. God's renewal of His covenant with the children of Israel, His removal of their guilt, through their circumcision at Passovertime, Joshua 5:2–8.

22. See *Webster's New World Dictionary* under *Pasch,* and *A Hebrew and English Lexicon of the Old Testament,* ed. Brown, Driver, and Briggs (Oxford, 1953), p. 820. Cf. Ch. 1, n. 36.

23. Granville Hicks feels that Frank and Helen may marry ("Portraits of the Authors as Men," *Saturday Review,* July 10, 1965, p. 29), but Baumbach (p. 119) and Theodore Solotaroff ("Bernard Malamud's Fiction," *Commentary,* March 1962, p. 198) do not—Baumbach explicitly, Solotaroff implicitly. Nor does Ihab Hassan hold out hope for them *(Radical Innocence* [Princeton, 1961], p. 166).

24. Robert Graves, *GM,* II, 276; and *The White Goddess* (New York, 1948), p. 277. See also *Webster's New World Dictionary* under *hell* and *Hel.*

25. Bruno Bettelheim, *Symbolic Wounds* (New York, 1962), p. 92. Cf. C. G. Jung, *Symbols of Transformation,* trans. R. F. C. Hull (New York, 1956), p. 430.

26. *Ibid.,* p. 95; B. M. Loeb, "The Blood Sacrifice Complex," *Memoirs of the American Anthropological Association,* No. 30 (1933), p. 18. George A. Barton, "Semitic Circumcision," *Encyclopedia of Religion and Ethics* (New York, 1911), III, 680. Cf. Ihab Hassan: "The act is one of self-purification, of initiation too, . . . if not of symbolic castration" *(op. cit.,* p. 168).

27. Baumbach, pp. 101–122, Richman, pp. 43–44, 60, 87–90, 136.

28. Saul Bellow, "A Sermon by Dr. Pep," *Partisan Review,* XVI (May, 1949), 457–458. This story is reprinted in Herbert Gold's *Fiction of the Fifties* (New York, 1959), and the section quoted appears on p. 70. For subsequent quotations in the text, the first numbers are page references from the *Partisan Review* printing, the second from the Gold anthology.

29. Saul Bellow, *Henderson the Rain King* (New York, 1959), p. 5.

I, that am curtailed of this fair proportion,
Cheated of feature by dissembling Nature,
Deformed, unfinished, sent before my time
Into this breathing world, scarce half made up,
And that so lamely and unfashionable
The dogs bark at me as I halt by them;
Why, I, in this weak piping time of peace,
Have no delight to pass away the time,
Unless to spy my shadow in the sun
And descant on mine own deformity:
And therefore, since I cannot prove a lover,
To entertain these fair well-spoken days,
I am determined to prove a villain . . .
                    —*Shakespeare,* Richard the Third
                    Act I, scene I, 18–30

3.

Sterility Figures

Part 1. Victims

In the Middle Ages the emblematic or iconographic nature of the particular fertility sacrifice characterized by leg wounds was preserved, but the significance of the rites was altered. Most likely it was the Catholic Church in Western Europe that sought to repress the most pagan-seeming elements commonly practiced at the time, although obvious elements of ancient fertility rites were retained in the Morris dances and maypole festivities, as

63

Miss Weston tells us, and in planting and harvesting, as Frazer records.[1] Priests still bless fields and sprinkle them with holy water for richer harvests and do the same to fishing fleets for greater catches, acting in a manner similar to the blood-sprinkling priests of ancient history and like Moses in Exodus 24: 6,8. However, Christ's immediate relation to fertility, material as well as spiritual, in the late medieval period can be seen in the engraving (fig. 1) of Christ, crucified upon a rich and fertile tree bearing an abundant crop of various fruits.

Thus we see again the relationship between the health of the king and that of his land: when the king's vitality is destroyed the land suffers. This tradition existed in the classical period symbolizing sterility as well as fertility. Thus Oedipus is crippled, having pierced feet, but sexually capable; yet his impotence, his inability to appease the gods for his unwitting patricide and regicide causes Thebes intense suffering:

> . . . Thebes is tossed on a murdering sea
> And cannot lift her head from the surge of death.
> A rust consumes the buds and fruits of the earth;
> The herds are sick; children die unborn,
> And labor is vain. The god of plague and pyre
> Raids like detestable lightning through the city,
> And all the house of Kadmos is laid waste,
> All emptied, and all darkened: Death alone
> Battens upon the misery of Thebes.[2]

Medieval Canterbury suffers similarly in T. S. Eliot's *Murder in the Cathedral* (1935), involved as it is in the fate of Thomas à Becket:

God is leaving us, God is leaving us, more pang,
    more pain, than birth or death.
Sweet and cloying through the dark air
Falls the stifling scent of despair;
The forms take shape in the dark air:
Puss-purr of leopard, footfall of padding bear,
Palm-pat of nodding ape, square hyena waiting
For laughter, laughter, laughter. The Lords of
    Hell are here.
They curl round you, lie at your feet, swing and
    wing through the dark air.
O Thomas Archbishop, save us, save us, save your-
self that we may be saved;
Destroy yourself and we are destroyed.[3]

In the literature of the Middle Ages there is a lame
king, like Oedipus, whose land "is laid waste, all emptied
and all darkened." He was known as *le Roi Mehaigne,*
the maimed king, or *le Roi Pescheur,* the Fisher King,
and he appears in hundreds of Medieval manuscripts in
Old French, Middle High German, Welsh, and Middle
English, in both prose and poetry.[4] The cause of the
king's wound varies with his name and the story in which
he appears, but the wound itself and the sterility it causes
his domain are sometimes seen—as the Black Death often
was—as God's punishment for the king's sins.[5]

The Fisher King's wound in Wolfram von Eschenbach's *Parzival* is a lance point through the testicles as
divine punishment for the king's neglect of his sacred
trust, the Holy Grail, in order to gain renown through
jousting for the sake of a lady. For this sin the land of
Grail is laid waste and barren, the people made desolate.
Among the King's predecessors is Bendigeidfran, more

popularly known as the Blessed Bran, a Welsh king who ruled all of England, and whose status as a fertility deity is confirmed by his ownership of a cauldron in which slain warriors are brought back to life.[6] Bran is wounded in the foot with a poisoned spear in a battle with the king of Ireland over Branwen, Bran's sister, who exclaims, "Woe is me that ever I was born: two islands have been laid waste because of me!" [7] Among the Fisher King's literary successors is Sir Percivale in Thomas Malory's *Le Morte D'Arthur* (Book 14, Ch. 10). When almost tempted to break his vow of chastity, Percivale does penance by running himself through the thigh with his sword.[8] Thus for some four centuries of literary creation in England and on the continent, authors depicted a maimed king (or doublets of him) who presided over lands whose vitality was linked with his, and whose ruin is concomitant with his.

As he, preeminently among literary characters of the period, reigned over blighted lands, so he and the Waste Land have become common symbols in modern literature for a stultifying, limited existence in a desolate, crippling environment. T. S. Eliot acknowledges his debt to Jessie Weston's *From Ritual to Romance* and Sir James George Frazer's *The Golden Bough* in his introductory note to *The Waste Land* (1922), the initial obscurity of which prompted many readers of the poem to seek at least the Weston book for elucidation, and an introduction to the Fisher King and his suitability as symbol par excellence for lost and dispirited generations.

The Waste Land expresses Eliot's concept of the spiritual aridity of life in the 1920s and the lack of real love, faith, and values among the inhabitants of the great urban deserts. Edmund Wilson summarized the poem well:

The terrible dreariness of the great modern cities is the atmosphere in which "The Waste Land" takes place . . . ; all about us we are aware of nameless millions performing barren office routines, wearing down their souls in interminable labors of which the products never bring them profit—people whose pleasures are so sordid and so feeble that they seem almost sadder than their pains. And this Waste Land has another aspect: it is a place not merely of desolation, but of anarchy and doubt. In our post-War [I] world of shattered institutions, strained nerves and bankrupt ideals, life no longer seems serious or coherent. . . .[9]

Eliot echoes the incoherence by the seeming formlessness of his poem, its rapid shifts and abrupt juxtapositions. He achieves a sense of utter sterility by describing the landscape as a "dead land" (1. 2), "A heap of broken images, where the sun beats,/ And the dead tree gives no shelter, the cricket no relief,/ And the dry stone no sound of water" (1. 22–24). In this landscape, the Grail Quest has been debased into the quests for wealth of the one-eyed seller of currants and of Phlebas the Phoenician. The prophecy of the Sibyl or of Ezekial becomes the commercial charlatanism of Mme. Sosostris. Love does not exist. Instead there is Philomela, "so rudely forced: (1. 100); toothless Lil, who aborts her pregnancies; and the typist, who lets the carbuncular clerk

. . . engage her in caresses
Which still are unreproved, if undesired.
Flushed and decided, he assaults at once;
Exploring hands encounter no defence;

His vanity requires no response,
And makes a welcome of indifference.
. . . Bestows one final patronising kiss,
And gropes his way, finding the stairs unlit. . . .

She turns and looks a moment in the glass,
Hardly aware of her departed lover;
Her brain allows one half-formed thought to pass:
"Well now that's done: and I'm glad it's over
          (11. 237–252).

All takes place in an unreal city under brown fog (11.
60–61, 207–208), in a land where there "is no water but
only rock/Rock and no water and the sandy road" (11.
331–332), and "dry sterile thunder without rain" (1. 343).
Eliot depicts a barren landscape—in Jonathan Baumbach's
phrase, a landscape of nightmare—devoid of love and pity,
devoid of all human emotions except lust, greed, fear, and
apathy. Dominating the poem by his presence, as he has
the subsequent literature of the twentieth century, is the
maimed Fisher King.[10]

Offspring of the maimed king follow in quick succession. Although the Fisher King himself is not mentioned, his presence is felt in F. Scott Fitzgerald's *The
Great Gatsby* (1925) with its valley of ashes; Gatsby quest-
ing after a Grail of sorts, Daisy paraphrasing Eliot's neu-
rasthenic woman by asking, "What'll we do with ourselves . . . ?" and Tom also paraphrasing Eliot when he
says, "Civilization's going to pieces." [11]

Fitzgerald's friend and rival Ernest Hemingway pictured another civilization going to pieces in *The Sun Also
Rises* (1926), the biography of the lost generation. The
characters in this, Hemingway's first and probably best
novel, search nervously and desperately for the only satis-

factions left them after the deracination and disillusionment—indeed, the very derangement—of war. All that
seems left them are sensual pleasures: warm sunshine and
cold, clear water, fine wine, the excitement of bullfight-
ing, or of fishing, or of lover after lover—in short, the
peripatetic and self-defeating search for fun. Jake Barnes
and Brett Ashley love one another, but Jake, emasculated
in the war, cannot satisfy her sexually. So Brett, a nym-
phomaniac, goes from one unsatisfying affair to another,
while Jake tries to exist solely in a world of work, sport,
and drink. Jake, as maimed fisherman, is the Fisher King
in this novel of misfits.[12] Most of the characters are chased
across Europe by their own ennui. Jake's wound is echoed
in those of Count Mippipopolous and other veterans of
public wars and private battles; his sexual impotence, his
failure to achieve a normal relationship with Brett, represents the separateness of all the characters—the prostitute
Georgette and the homosexuals who accompany Brett at
the beginning of the novel, Cohn and Frances, Mike, the
Count, even Romero the bullfighter, who, although sexually capable, must limit his sexual activities and even his
love for Brett because it interferes with his dangerous
profession.

The pessimism, the cynicism, the general malaise that
infect the waste land these characters inhabit are suggested repeatedly by Hemingway. Georgette complains
that she's sick, that everybody is.[13] A waiter, commenting
on a young married man and father of two children, who
has been killed during the running of the bulls, says:
"Badly cogido through the back. . . . A big horn wound.
All for fun. Just for fun. What do you think of that? . . .
Right through the back. A cornada right through the
back. For fun—you understand" (pp. 197–198). Brett tells
Jake that she has ended her affair with Romero and is

going back to Mike because Mike is "so damned nice and he's so awful. He's my sort of thing" (p. 243). "You know," she continues, "it makes one feel rather good not to be a bitch. . . . It's sort of what we have instead of God." Their theological discussion ends with Brett's saying of God, "He never worked very well with me," and Jake's replying, "Should we have another Martini?" (p. 245), as if a cocktail were a suitable surrogate for God. A final instance of bitter irony concludes the novel. Brett says, "Oh, Jake, we could have had such a damned good time together," and Jake replies, "Yes . . . Isn't it pretty to think so?" (p. 247). The novel ends on a note that tells us that Jake's wound is deeply symbolic. The people of this lost generation cannot relate, cannot form abiding spiritual unions. Emasculated or not, they cannot love: almost all are impotent.

Hemingway shows especial sensitivity to lame characters as figures representing impotence. He was himself severely wounded in the leg during World War I, and most of his characters who have been to war (and several who have not) are similarly scarred. The wound, "the unreasonable wound" [14] as Frederick J. Hoffman calls it, is more than just an item of personal history for Hemingway: it figures symbolically in many of his works.

In "Indian Camp" (1924), one of Hemingway's first published short stories,[15] such symbolism is evident. The story takes place in a poverty-stricken Ojibway Indian camp in Michigan where Dr. Henry Adams goes with his son Nick to aid an Indian woman who has been two days in labor. Dr. Adams performs a Caesarian section with a jack-knife, then sews the woman up with "nine foot, tapered gut leaders," all without an anaesthetic for the woman, whom four men hold down in the lower bunk. In the upper bunk lies the husband, unable to help or even to stand and watch because he had cut his foot badly with an ax three days before. After having finished working on the mother, Doctor Adams says "Ought to have a look at the proud father. They're usually the worst sufferers in these affairs. . . . I must say he took it all pretty quietly." [16] He has taken much quietly, but not without suffering: unable to bear his wife's pain without being able to do anything, unable to listen to her screams any longer, the man slit his throat and bled to death while the doctor was at work in the bunk below bringing the infant into the world.[17]

A recent interpretation [18] suggests that the baby Dr. Adams delivers is not the son of the wounded Indian, but of George, the Doctor's brother. George passes out cigars to the Indians who have brought the Adamses to the camp. He is bitten by the mother in the pain of delivery, but the suggestion is present that he had been bitten before under more pleasant circumstances. And he stays behind after the doctor and his son depart. If George is the boy's father, then the Indian's wound represents still more impotence. The Indians at the camp grub out an existence, and the husband cannot do anything to ease his wife's pain, prevent his own, or prevent the abuse of himself or his people (symbolized through his cuckoldry by George) except by violence.

In this classic initiation story Nick learns about the pain of birth and death, the two great events of life, which Hemingway presents cyclically. As combats between mythical heroes are often represented as conflicts between seasons, contests that did not achieve any final resolution but were in fact merely opposite points on a cycle, so here Hemingway succinctly represents life and death as just such a cycle, presenting it both literally and symbolically. Nick and his father enter the camp at dusk and leave at dawn, when a bass jumping from the lake makes "a circle in the water" which Nick thinks feels "warm in the sharp chill of the morning" (p. 95): life and death, day and night, light and dark, warm and cold, and the eternal circle sum up the situation here. Just as fish have been a symbol of vitality and fertility, so maiming has foreshadowed death.

In a later story, "God Rest You Merry, Gentlemen" (1933), Hemingway again uses the symbol of the Fisher King to denote waste and futility, but he has split the maimed king's role between two characters: an unnamed, sensitive boy who mutilates himself and a Jewish physician, Doc Fischer. This morbid tale, which takes place in Kansas City on Christmas Day, is narrated by a persona called Horace, a newspaper reporter, and concerns a boy of about sixteen who considers his erections sins against purity. The boy pleads with two doctors, Fischer and Wilcox, asking that they castrate him. They refuse, and the boy, not actually knowing what castration is, amputates his penis with a razor. He is brought to the hospital, but bungling Dr. Wilcox cannot stanch his loss of blood, and the boy bleeds to death on Christmas.

Several points, especially a full comprehension of the nature of each character, are essential to an understanding of the story's meaning. Wilcox insists on his full title (possibly reflecting his lack of confidence in his own ability): Horace never refers to him except as Doctor Wilcox, whereas Fischer is always the more familiar "Doc." Not only is Wilcox incompetent, he is also harsh and insensitive. When the boy makes his request, Wilcox replies crudely:

> "You're just a goddamned fool. . . . Oh, go and
> ———[*sic*]."

"When you talk like that I don't hear you," the boy said with dignity to Doctor Wilcox. . . .

"Get him out of here," Doctor Wilcox said (pp. 394–395).

When Fischer mentions that it is "the day, the very anniversary, of our Saviour's birth," Wilcox's prejudiced reply is "*Our* Saviour? Ain't you a Jew?" (p. 396). Besides his inability to save the boy's life, Wilcox drinks on duty (p. 393) and relies entirely on *The Young Doctor's Friend and Guide.* As Horace says,

Doctor Wilcox was sensitive about this book but could not get along without it. . . . He had bought it at the advice of one of his professors who had said, "Wilcox, you have no business being a physician and I have done everything in my power to prevent you from being certified as one. Since you are now a member of this learned profession I advise you, in the name of humanity, to obtain a copy of *The Young Doctor's Friend and Guide* and use it, Doctor Wilcox. Learn to use it" (pp. 392–393).

Fischer is a Christ figure. He is a slim blond Jew. He is a "fisher of men." He heals men with his hands and has suffered for it (p. 396). And he has ridden an ass, as he makes evident when he tells Horace about the boy's death, and Wilcox retorts:

"Well, I wish you wouldn't ride me about it. . . . There isn't any need to ride me."

"Ride you, Doctor, on the day, the very anniversary, of our Saviour's birth?"

"*Our* Saviour? Ain't you a Jew?" Doctor Wilcox said.

"So I am. So I am. It always is slipping my mind. I've never given it its proper importance. So good of you to remind me. *Your* Saviour. That's right. *Your* Saviour, undoubtedly *your* Saviour—and the ride for Palm Sunday" (pp. 395–396).

Fischer suffers, not only from Wilcox's prejudice, but also because of his own compassion. A "willingness to oblige" and a "lack of respect for Federal statutes" (p. 395), perhaps those which forbid doctors to aid fugitive criminals without reporting that aid, had caused him great trouble earlier, "on the coast." His compassion is obvious from his tender and sympathetic treatment of the boy, who responds by begging Fischer, in particular, to help him. His education is also obvious. Besides the "certain extravagance of [his] speech which seemed to . . . [Horace] to be of the utmost elegance" (p. 393), there are his attempt to speak to the boy in the latter's own religious vernacular and the quality of his irony, his puns based on Biblical and medical metaphors. I have quoted the Wilcox-as-ass passage above; in another instance Fischer satirically alludes to St. Luke by referring to Wilcox as "the good physician" (p. 395); and, when Wilcox continues to stress Fischer's separateness from the rest of humanity because of his religion, Fischer replies, "You hear him? Having discovered my vulnerable point, my Achilles tendon so to speak, the doctor pursues his advantage" (p. 396).[19]

However, "education" does not of itself fully describe Fischer or adequately indicate his likeness to Christ. His superiority in ability, intelligence, self-confidence, and compassion irritates Wilcox and provokes him to a sar-

castic comment—"You're too damned smart" (p. 396)—
that both reflects Wilcox's own inadequacies and, ironically, defines Fischer's distinctions. The same epithet could
well have been hurled at Christ by his scorning contem-
poraries. Finally, both Christ and Fischer have visited hell
—one to harrow, one to be harrowed:

> "The hell with you," Doctor Wilcox said.
> "All in good time Doctor," Doc Fischer said,
> "all in good time. If there is such a place I shall
> certainly visit it. I have even had a very small look
> into it. No more than a peek, really. I looked away
> almost at once" (p. 396).

The ironic tone of the entire story, in fact, is established at the outset by the title, "God Rest You Merry,
Gentlemen," especially when we recall the full context
of that line:

> . . . Let nothing you dismay,
> Remember Christ our Saviour was born on
>   Christmas Day,
> To save us all from Satan's power when we were
>   gone astray,
> O tidings of comfort and joy. . . .

As Harry Levin has said, "The ironic contrast—romantic
preconception exploded by contact with harsh reality—
is basic with Hemingway. . . ." [20] Instead of the pleasant
home scene such a carol might suggest, where men might
indeed rest themselves merry, we have the harsh carbolic-
tainted atmosphere of a hospital where there is much to
cause dismay, where Satan's power (here ignorance of

bodily functions and too-strict religious fundamentalism) have caused a boy's death, and where the tidings are far from comfortable and joyous.

As Hemingway says in the first paragraph, the Kansas City of the story is much like Constantinople in that both are characterized by dry, dusty, wind-blown hills. It is, in Frederick Hoffman's terms, a landscape as assailant: ". . . The prevailing landscape . . . suggests fear and loss as consequences of the disappearance of a vitally confident and a passionately felt trust. . . . The desert is in the city, the city in the desert. . . . Persons do not recognize each other, since they are not aware of the commitment necessary to spiritual relationship." [21] Fischer is impotent to save the boy's life in this waste land in which there is pain and loss and lack of human contact, and in which the crude and unfeeling like Wilcox ostracize the strange and the different—the hypersensitive boy and the Jewish doctor.

In "The Snows of Kilimanjaro" (1936), Hemingway again uses a wound to indicate sterility, waste, and corruption. In this story, Harry, a writer, is dying from gangrene in his right leg as a result of an unattended, innocuous-seeming scratch of a thorn.[22] As he lies on a cot, watching the vultures and hyenas that sense his impending death, Harry thinks of his life, his career, and his wife. He recalls much that he had experienced that had affected him profoundly, but about which he had never written until he could write about them properly: "Now he would never write the things that he had saved to write until he knew enough to write them well" (p. 54). And when Harry's wife asks, "Don't you love me?" he answers, "No, I don't think so. I never have" (p. 55). Later he recants: "Don't pay any attention, darling, to what I say. I love you, really. You know I love you."

Thus he slips "into the familiar lie he made his bread and butter by" (p. 58). Harry's writing has been slick, facile, and often untrue—like his life—ever since he married for money. Consequently, "each day of not writing, of comfort, of being that which he despised, dulled his ability and softened his will to work so that, finally, he did not work at all" (p. 59). "He had chosen to make his living with something else instead of a pen or a pencil" (p. 60). He had chosen to live by selling himself, his vitality, and he has been castrated by the act and rendered impotent: he has lost the ability to write, he has failed "to work the fat off his soul," and he will die in a few hours. Because he has prostituted himself, there is no redemption for him. His leg wound symbolizes his personal corruption and moral decay, and his death.

Eliot's poem and these works of Hemingway express the disillusionment and the sense of waste and sterility that dominate the literature of the lost generation. Besides theirs, three other works published in the twenties depict maiming and sterility, two in 1928—Aldous Huxley's *Point Counter Point* and D. H. Lawrence's *Lady Chatterley's Lover* [23]—and one in 1929—William Faulkner's *The Sound and the Fury*.

In Lawrence's novel, Sir Clifford Chatterley, Bart., returns to England from World War I paralyzed from the waist down and impotent. The previous year Lawrence had used maiming in its original fertility symbolism in *The Man Who Died;* in *Lady Chatterley's Lover* he employs the wound against the context which Eliot had made prototypical. Lawrence uses Chatterley's disability to represent both the decayed power of the nobility, particularly when it is out of touch with the common people, and the unhealthiness that Lawrence felt was inherent in a mechanized state that transfigured the land and turned men into grimy, unfeeling servants of industrialism.[24] Sir Clifford, no longer capable of sexual creation, devotes himself to intellectual pursuits, to writing and to his business—the family collieries. Lady Chatterley's father says, "As for Clifford's writing, it's smart, but there's nothing in it. It won't last!" [25] As for his business:

> The curious thing was that when this child-man, which Clifford was now and which he had been becoming for years, emerged into the world, he was much sharper and keener than the real man he used to be. This perverted child-man was now a *real* business man. . . . When he was out among men, seeking his own ends, and "making good" his colliery workings, he had an almost uncanny shrewdness, hardness, and a straight sharp punch. . . . In business he was quite inhuman (362–363).

Even Mrs. Bolton, who nurses and mothers Clifford, reacts against this unnaturalness:

> . . . In some corner of her weird female soul, how she despised him and hated him! . . . In the remotest corner of her ancient healthy womanhood she despised him with a savage contempt that knew no bounds (p. 363).

The key words are *inhuman* and *healthy*. In business Clifford is cold, practical, inhuman; his conversations with his friends betray not only his coldness but also theirs, their "belief in the world of the mind" (p. 68), and their theoretical discussions of life as if it were an abstract, mathematical problem. In contrast Lawrence presents us with Mellors, the gamekeeper, warm, alive, sensitive, and—another key word—*tender*. *(Tenderness* was the original title of the novel [p. 13].) As Mark Schorer says in his introduction to the novel, "The basic contrast between life-affirming and life-denying values, between 'tenderness' and the 'insentient iron world' is the sole subject of Lawrence's symbolic amplifications . . ." (p. 32). It is Mellors who represents the natural life of the forest and its inhabitants, who gives life by fathering Connie's child, while Clifford is not only sterile himself but represents the "insentient iron world." For Lawrence was violently opposed to all people who, whether in pursuit of wealth, God, or knowledge, denied their physical beings and thereby denied part of their lives. They were, for him, not fully alive, and so impotence and maiming become viable symbols for him.

Inhumanity is central, too, to *Point Counter Point,* for it is the common failing of nearly all the characters in the novel. One of the central characters, Philip Quarles, a self-portrait of Huxley,[26] was accidentally lamed in childhood. His disability not only prevents him from leading a full life, but also symbolizes that deficiency. Denied complete physical resources, Quarles approaches everything intellectually and unemotionally— even his marriage. What feeling he has for his wife and son, he cannot articulate.

> All his life long he had walked in a solitude, in a private void, into which nobody, not his mother, not his friends, not his lovers had ever been permitted to enter. Even when he held her [his wife Elinor] thus, pressed close to him, it was by wireless, as she had said, and across an Atlantic that he communicated with her.[27]

In Elinor's words, he is "almost human" (p. 93), and so, for one reason or another, is almost everyone in the book with the exception of the Rampions, Huxley's fictional portrait of D. H. and Frieda Lawrence. Walter Bidlake leaves his pregnant mistress whom he doesn't love to chase after Lucy Tantamount, a woman who loves no one, but who indulges in parties, drinking, affairs, and general debauchery for no reason but curiosity. Burlap is a monstrous hypocrite who tries to make love to his wife's best friend after his wife's death, and eventually drives the friend to suicide. Spandrell (whose life and character are distantly based on Baudelaire's) is a compulsive sinner, debaucher, and—ultimately—murderer. Walter's and Elinor's father, John, is an old rake dying of cancer in the home of a wife who keeps repeating her name in an attempt to believe in her own existence. Quarles' son dies of meningitis in minutely described, horrifying scenes, interspersed primarily with details of Burlap's seduction of his frigid landlady. And so on. The novel expresses Huxley's extreme disgust with humanity, and as Jocelyn Brooke says, Huxley's work resembles Eliot's *Waste Land* in that both deal with "broken images." [28] Especially in *Point Counter Point* there are a plethora of such shattered, impotent figures. Lord Edward Tantamount, a cuckold, experiments with newts whose legs he amputates; his brother Charles, born a cripple, spends his days being pulled about the family estate in a donkey cart while he devotes himself to trying to prove logically the existence of God. And Spandrell calls his stepfather "an impotent old fumbler" (p. 99).

Throughout the novel Huxley weaves a theme of emasculation, as these widely separated quotations show: "I was talking about the world, not us. It's tame, I say. Like one of those horrible big gelded cats" (p. 111); "The

cat, an enormous ginger eunuch" (p. 293); ". . . the im-
potent lover" (p. 400). Rampion, arguing with Spandrell
about the spiritual quality of Beethoven's music, says,
"Eunuchs are very spiritual lovers. . . ." And when Span-
drell answers, "But Beethoven wasn't a eunuch,"
Rampion replies, "I know. But why did he try to be one?
Why did he make castration and bodilessness his ideal?
What's this music? Just a hymn in praise of eunuchism.
. . . Couldn't he have chosen something more human than
castration to sing about? . . ." (p. 509).

The incompleteness of the *castrato*—physical and
spiritual—is a theme that is elaborated throughout the
novel. Quarles' mother and wife discuss the effects of his
wound thus: "It raised an artificial barrier between him
and the rest of the world. . . . His poor smashed leg began
by keeping him at a physical distance from girls of his
own age. And it kept him at a psychological distance,
too" (p. 271). Philip's mother has similar thoughts about
her daughter-in-law Elinor as a mother *manquée:*

> Elinor had many excellent qualities. But something
> seemed to be lacking in her. . . . It was as though
> she had been born without certain natural instincts.
> . . . To Rachel the reverence for holy things came
> naturally. It was Elinor's lack of this reverence, her
> inability even to realize that holy things *were* holy,
> which made it impossible for Mrs. Quarles to love
> her daughter-in-law as much as she would have liked
> (pp. 308–309).

Rampion continues the same theme saying that
"mechanical progress means more specialization and
standardization of work, means more ready made and
unindividual amusements, . . . means more intellectualism

and the progressive atrophy of all the vital and funda-
mental things in human nature. . . . [People] live as idiots
and machines all the time, at work and in their lei-
sure. . . ." (p. 357). In fact, Huxley gives Lawrence-qua-
Rampion most of a chapter (34) to denounce the sterility
of modern life:

> ". . . My God, what a horror! No body, no
> contact with the material world, no contact with
> human beings except through the intellect, no
> love. . . ."
> "We've changed that a little. . . ," said Philip,
> smiling.
> "Not really. You've admitted promiscuous forni-
> cation, that's all. But not love, not the natural con-
> tact and flow, not the renunciation of mental self-
> consciousness, nor the abandonment to instinct. . . .
> That's the higher life. Which is the euphemistic
> name of incipient death" (pp. 475–476).

Critics have noticed Huxley's dominant pessimism
in *Point Counter Point* and have praised him for the
novel's tightly controlled musical structure. What has not
been so well noted is how Huxley's disgust and disillusion are echoed throughout the novel by varied but related themes of crippledness, by point-counter-point
juxtapositions of maimed man and man *manqué,* in this
symphonic treatment of the generation's broken images.
William Faulkner's *The Sound and the Fury* (1929)
also deals with decay and destruction, in this case of the
Compson family, representatives for Faulkner of the old
South with its genteel tradition, its honor, and its internal
corruption. The Civil War and the ineptness of the post-
bellum Compsons have cost them most of their property.

What is left is mortgaged so that Quentin may go to Harvard. He commits suicide for twisted reasons of guilt and pride concerning his sister Candace, who afterwards becomes a prostitute. The only males left who bear the once-proud name of Compson are miserly Jason and mentally defective Benjy. Jason has his idiot brother gelded after Benjy's "fumbling, abortive attempt . . . on a passing female child," [29] and so is the last sexually capable male Compson. But Jason, as Faulkner repeatedly tells us, is childless. Thus Benjy's castration symbolizes his own inability to achieve conventional social contact and foreshadows the exhaustion of his family line (as similar deficiencies will provide like symbolism in William Styron's Faulknerian novel *Lie Down in Darkness*). Because the Compsons represent the Old South, their ruin figures its demise in pride, in morals, and in character.

Faulkner again employs castration to signify ruin and desolation in *Light in August* (1932). One of the novel's protagonists, Joe Christmas, is thought to have some Negro "blood" in him. Faulkner never makes clear whether Joe is part black or not, but in the novel the suspicion of mixed races stigmatizes Joe as surely as a more obvious deformity would. A childless farmer named McEachern adopts Joe from the orphanage where his grandfather has placed him. A strict fundamentalist, McEachern does not give the boy any affection, accustoming him to a brutal, loveless world where force rules. Finally, in rebellion, Joe turns on McEachern and kills him.

Fleeing, he seeks for years to find a place for himself in one of the two races in which he might claim membership; but his light skin marks him as an outsider among Negroes, and he feels that his colored ancestry sets him apart from whites, as indeed it does whenever it is discovered. Denied love as a boy, Joe never experiences it in any of his numerous sexual encounters, the last of which, with Joanna Burden, leads directly to his destruction. As Joanna goes through menopause, she fears that she will lose her sexual hold on Joe, and so tries to force him to follow her plans for the future and to make him pray with her—as McEachern had forced him to pray. Joe rebels again and murders Joanna. He is eventually killed by Percy Grimm, a young National Guardsman who achieves through his uniform "a sublime and implicit faith in physical courage and blind obedience, and a belief that the white race is superior to any and all other races. . . ." [30] First Grimm shoots Christmas, then castrates him, gaining "satisfaction from making Joe as unmanly as he is." [31]

Where before emasculation foreshadowed, here it sums up: throughout the novel Joe is a victim of a loveless childhood and of a futile search for personal identity, for peace, for quiet, and for a sense of belonging. His ultimate castration by Grimm merely emphasizes what has crippled Joe all of his life: denial, guilt, and lovelessness have made him unable to love or live. Ironically named for the birthday of Jesus, Joe Christmas is an example of an anti-Christ, one whose experiences make him a paradigm of lovelessness, uncharitableness, and pain. Thus in the 1920s, one poet—T. S. Eliot—and four novelists—Hemingway, Lawrence, Huxley, and Faulkner—created literary works in which maimed characters symbolize sterility and failure.

In the next decade, Nathanael West depicted a landscape of pain and lovelessness similarly characterized by maiming. In *Miss Lonelyhearts* (1933), *A Cool Million* (1934), and *The Day of the Locust* (1939)—three of West's four novels—central figures are maimed: Peter Doyle

(and Miss Lonelyhearts), Lemuel Pitkin, and Tod Hackett. Doyle is a meter reader who walks the city with the
aid of a cane, dragging "one of his feet behind him in a
box-shaped shoe with a four-inch sole. As he hobbled
along, he made many waste motions, like those of a partially destroyed insect." [32] Doyle's wife Fay has already
written Miss Lonelyhearts complaining about her husband, has met the newspaper columnist, and gone to bed
with him. Doyle also meets Miss Lonelyhearts in order
to complain about the difficulty of his own existence. His
plight, his despair, and his crippled state make him representative of all of Miss Lonelyhearts' correspondents, for
at the end of the novel, as the newspaperman runs down
the stairs toward Doyle, "He did not understand the
cripple's shout and heard it as a cry for help from Despe-
rate, Harold S., Catholic-mother, Broken-hearted, Broad-
shoulders,   Sick-of-it-all,   Disillusioned-with-tubercular-
husband. He was running to succor them with love"
(p. 140). Miss Lonelyhearts forces an embrace on Doyle
which the cripple tries to avoid. In their awkward dance,
the gun, which the cripple had brought to shoot the
columnist, "exploded and Miss Lonelyhearts fell, dragging the cripple with him. They both rolled part of the
way down the stairs" (p. 140).

   A Cool Million is a broad, not very funny parody of
the American dream. As Voltaire did to Candide, West
subjects his protagonist, Lemuel Pitkin, to a succession
of misfortunes, including loss of teeth, eyes, leg, scalp,
and—finally—life. Like Candide, Lem witnesses the rape
of his beloved and numerous conflicts and plunderings.
Although at the novel's end he is posthumously hailed as
"the American boy" (p. 255), Pitkin (unlike his Horatio
Alger predecessors) represents an America of dishonesty,
violence, hypocrisy, waste, and pain.

In his final novel, *The Day of the Locust,* West indicates by his title that the land he describes is plague-ridden. It is Hollywood, a locale West knew well as a screen writer. He attacks it as a land of illusion which keeps people hopeful in the midst of want, deprivation, and despair. He writes not of the stars, but of the hangers on—dwarfs, has-beens, never-beens, and never-will-be's. At the novel's grotesque conclusion, a premiere explodes. Thousands of bored, jammed-together onlookers go berserk. They begin to enact the apocryphal vision the protagonist, Tod Hackett, has had for a painting, "The Burning of Los Angeles." In the ensuing riot Tod's leg is broken. In all of his novels West's vision of America is pessimistic, distorted by pain and anger, indignant at wasted lives and unfulfilled promise.

Dramatists, too, use maiming and deformity to signify loss and futility, especially one as sensitive to the symbolic value of maiming as Tennessee Williams. Laura Wingfield, in *The Glass Menagerie* (1945), crippled since childhood, is further denied a normal youth by ill health and painful self-consciousness. She becomes more withdrawn as her mother Amanda increasingly tries to push the girl into the world and into contact with people. Laura retreats into an imaginary world populated by glass figurines—as fragile and as transparent as she— in which her mother's insistent voice is shut out by music from phonograph records left behind by the father who deserted them. When Amanda forces her son Tom to bring a fellow employee home to meet Laura, the gentleman caller turns out to be Jim O'Connor, whom Laura had a crush on in high school.[33] Jim is a victim of the American dream—of self-advancement courses and the power-of-positive-thinking propaganda. He is taking courses in public speaking and radio engineering and has grand plans for his future; but as Tom says:

> He was shooting with such velocity through his adolescence that you would logically expect him to arrive at nothing short of the White House by the time he was thirty. But Jim apparently ran into more interference after his graduation from Soldan [High School]. . . . Six years after he left high school he was holding a job [shipping clerk] that wasn't much better than mine (sc. vi).

Jim tries to infuse Laura with his enthusiasm but fails. He is, as he calls himself, "a stumble-john" (sc. vii), who not only fails to make Laura more self-confident but makes her still less so, a confirmed recluse. While dancing, Laura and Jim bump into the table on which the unicorn stands, knocking it off and breaking it.

> JIM: Aw, aw, aw. Is it broken?
> LAURA: Now it is just like all the other horses.
> JIM: It's lost its—
> LAURA: Horn! It doesn't matter. Maybe it's a blessing in disguise. . . . I'll just imagine he had an operation. The horn was removed to make him feel less— freakish! Now he will feel more at home with the other horses, the ones that don't have horns. . . ." (sc. vii).

Here Laura's glass unicorn, the "star of her menagerie," serves not just as an allegorical representation of Laura, but as a complex symbol for the whole play. By means of it, Williams can suggest not only Laura's sense of estrangement and Jim's impotence, but also—what would otherwise be ludicrous, using a phallic symbol for a girl —Laura's incompleteness and lack of sexual fulfillment.

First, the unicorn serves as a symbol for Laura herself, who feels as much set apart from society as the unicorn was distinct from the horses. The loss of the horn also has obvious Freudian implications for the situation: it suggests in general Laura's present and ultimate infertility, and in particular the fragmented act of love that occurs when Jim kisses her—which makes her radiant— then apologizes, calls himself a stumble-john again, and announces that he is engaged and can never see Laura again—which crushes her. She hands Jim the ruined unicorn as "a souvenir." Finally, as Roger B. Stein points out, the gentleman caller is a savior who does not save, and the broken horn symbolizes "Jim's impotence when he tries to bring Laura into the 'real' world." [34] The world Laura darkens when she blows out the candles at the end of the play is a planet being darkened indeed by the beginnings of World War II.[35] It is a world that denies fulfillment to both crippled Laura and stumble-john Jim and that will soon bring pain to millions.

After that war, and the millions of corpses and cripples it produced, maimed literary characters became an increasingly common symbol for a life of futility and sterility. The technique flourished especially in Europe (see Appendix One), but also in the United States, and, as Williams has already exemplified, frequently in the works of Southern writers. Truman Capote used maiming to suggest fertility in "Among the Paths to Eden"; he used it for the opposite purpose in his first novel, *Other Voices, Other Rooms* (1948). There Edward Sansom's physical paralysis symbolizes the state of all in Skully's landing: the wasted lives of Zoo and Jesus Fever; of homosexual, transvestite Randolph; of Randolph's sister Amy, who marries and spends her life caring for Sansom, the man her brother shot. The paralysis affects most severely Joel Knox, Sansom's son and the protagonist of this story of initiation. Joel's loss in wrestling to tomboy Idabel and his cut buttock foreshadow his emasculation as she takes his sword from him to protect him from a menacing snake, and his acceptance of sexual inversion as he prepares at the novel's end to enter the bedroom of his bewigged and begowned cousin. His maturity bears with it the realization that the decay of Skully's landing and the Cloud Hotel affects all their lives. The pain and disillusion that have blighted the lives of all the characters await him as well.

In 1951 another Southern writer, William Styron, published his impressive first novel, *Lie Down in Darkness*. There are distinct Faulknerian tones in the language and, as I have said, in the themes: the disintegration of a Southern family, rotting in an atmosphere of selfishness, lack of compassion, alcoholism, and incest. The central symbol for this decay is the family's elder daughter, Maudie (who perhaps owes her name to another account of psychological degeneracy told in varying narrative modes, Tennyson's "Maud"). Maudie Loftis is mentally retarded and physically crippled. Her father, Milton, doubts his masculinity in being the parent of such a child. He turns from her and from his wife Helen, who compensates by pouring all her affection on Maudie. When a second child, healthy and beautiful Peyton, is born, she receives all of her father's familial love, and more besides. Helen becomes jealous for herself and for Maudie. And Peyton is torn by the resulting tension: smothered by her father's dependence, infuriated by her mother's rejection and hatred, and made to feel guilty for her sister's inabilities.

A crisis occurs when Maudie falls in love with a construction worker, an Indian, "a short ugly little man with a puny pock-marked face and black raked-back hair." [36] He does magic tricks for Maudie but never speaks to her. Unlike Helen, who feeds her jealousy and martyrdom by using Maudie as a weapon against Peyton and Milton, the Indian asks for nothing, takes nothing but her company, and gives of his tenderness and his magic (in context the two are the same). When his construction job is done, the Indian, Bennie, leaves and takes his magic with him. It is October. "Death was in the air: he [Milton] thought briefly of his father, of Maudie; but wasn't autumn the season of death, and all Virginia a land of dying?" (p. 193). Like Faulkner's Benjy, Styron's Bennie is an *isolato*, an onlooker more than he is a participant; he too loves a strange young girl, scion of a decaying Southern family, but his love is less selfish, less demanding. When he leaves, Maudie, who has no one else to love her for herself, begins to die. Milton seeks to tell Peyton of her sister's fatal illness and, in alcoholic stupor, chases her one fine November day from fraternity house to bar to football game and back again in a grotesque and extremely moving quest. But Maudie succeeds, and dies. Helen blames Milton for his absence from the hospital and for his drinking; she irrationally blames Peyton—because of a long ago incident when Peyton accidentally let Maudie fall and bruise her knee—for the girl's death. In anger and spite and equally irrational guilt, Peyton gives her virginity to a boy to whom she is pinned, the first of a long series of promiscuous adventures in self-punishment that lead to madness and suicide.

Maudie's crippled physical and mental states are not

correlatives just of her family's condition, but of the
South and all of America. In the hospital in which she
dies, Milton meets a successful fellow lawyer and probable
judge-to-be limping from an infected wound caused by
stepping on a rusty roller skate—"How are the mighty
fallen!" The lawyer, Hubert MacPhail, extends his sympathy for Maudie by twice saying "God *damn* tough" (p.
201), then slapping Milton on the knee and inviting him
to their mutual fraternity house for a drink. "It'll do us
both good." At the house, MacPhail, the name is meaningful, displays the same coarseness and insensitivity to
his own son, whose eyes return "a very special sort of
detestation" (p. 205). Dick Cartwright, the boy with whom
Peyton first sleeps, was knocked into thirty feet of water
by his father because he could not, at six years of age,
"handle the sailboat's mainsheet. . . . His father baffled
him, and as a child Dick was torn between love and
hatred" (pp. 233–234). After he and Peyton first make love,
he proves to be impotent.

At Peyton's wedding to Harry Miller, a Jew whose
religion enables Styron to reveal the prejudices of the
Loftis' wedding guests, Virginia aristocracy and bourgeoisie alike, one of the guests is Monroe Hobbie, a crippled dentist whose wife has deserted him. In her final
Molly Bloom-like soliloquy, Peyton thinks of her great-
grandmother: ". . . Grandmother ran like a penguin wad-
dling; she was crippled. . . . She was a Byrd and very
wealthy, but Grandfather spent all the money because he
had no time for figures" (p. 345). So a crippled Byrd, first
of Virginia's fine families, becomes identified for the
reader with the flightless birds of guilt that haunt Peyton
and drive her to her death.

The landscape of the novel is populated with cripples
(besides those already mentioned, Harry's best friend has

a withered arm). It is itself a waste land—"the James
River winding beneath its acid-green crust of scum" (p.
9), Port Warwick built on the land rising out of the
marshes—shadowed by the mushroom cloud of atomic
destruction at Nagasaki, the day before Peyton takes her
life. Maudie is not the novel's central figure; Helen, Milton, and Peyton are. But Maudie represents more clearly,
in the greater simplicity with which we see her, what
afflicts the major characters and the people for whom they
are a microcosm. None of the people in *Lie Down in
Darkness* are whole, secure, content; the hard lack compassion, and those who can love are vulnerable and
broken. It is a massive indictment by Styron of a loveless
and sterile world.

In Styron's most recent novel, *The Confessions of
Nat Turner,* a minor figure again personally represents
the tragedy around him. He is Jeremiah Cobb whom Nat
meets "almost one year to the day before" Cobb, a judge,
sentences him to death.[37] Nat announces two pages later
the crime he will be executed for: "I had for going on
to several years now considered the necessity of extermi-
nating all the white people in Southampton County. . . ."
(p. 48). But Nat determines to make certain exceptions,
according to Ezekial 9:4, "Go through the midst of Jerusalem, and set a mark upon the foreheads of the men that
sigh and cry for all the abominations that be done in the
midst thereof. . . . Slay utterly old and young, both maids
and little children, and women" but come not near any
man upon whom is the mark. . . ."

Cobb is judge in Jerusalem, Virginia (in one of the
book's many coincidences), and Nat describes his face as
"one of the most unhappy faces I had ever seen. It was
blighted, ravaged by sorrow, as if grief had laid actual
hands on the face, wrenching and twisting it into an atti-

tude of ineradicable pain" (p. 49). He appears out of a
"whirlwind of dust" (p. 49), and Nat recalls to mind the
"terrors which had beset him grisly and Job-like. . . ."

A merchant and banker of property and means, chief
magistrate of the county, master of the Southampton
Hounds, he lost his wife and two grown daughters
to typhoid fever on the coast of Carolina, whither,
ironically, he had sent his ladies to recuperate from
winter attacks of the bronchial ailments to which all
three were prone. Shortly afterward his stable, a
brand-new structure on the outskirts of Jerusalem,
burned to the ground in one horrid and almost in-
stantaneous holocaust, incinerating all therein including two or three prize Morgan hunters and many
valuable English saddles and harnesses, not to mention a young Negro groom. Subsequently, the unfortunate man, having taken heavily to the bottle
to ease his affliction, fell down some stairs and broke
his leg; the limb failed to mend properly, and
although ambulatory, he was plagued by a hectic,
mild, irresistible fever and by unceasing pain (pp.
58–59).

Thus Cobb embodies the physical and economic depression that has beset Southampton and the whole of
Virgina. He also represents the physical pain of slavery
that is mankind set against itself. Cobb quotes Scripture
for and against slavery: "Stand fast therefore in the lib-
erty wherewith Christ has made us free, and be not en-
tangled again in the yoke of bondage" (Gal. 5:1); and on
the other side, "Servants be obedient to them that are
your masters" (Eph. 6:5), and "Servants, be subjects to
your masters with all fear" (I Peter 2:18). Yet he de-

nounces such arguments as casuistry, and seems to Nat to
be attuned to Nat's desire to wreak vengeance on the
whites, for he goes on to quote Isaiah 13:6.

> *"Howl ye: for the day of the Lord is at hand; it shall
> come as a destruction from the Almighty.* You're the
> preacher they call Nat, are you not? Tell me then,
> preacher, am I not right? Is not Isaiah only a witness
> to the truth . . . ? Tell me in the honesty of truth,
> preacher: is not the handwriting on the wall for this
> beloved and foolish and tragic Old Dominion?"
> (p. 64).

Cobb recognizes the stupidity of humans' owning humans, the senselessness of it. He bewails the fact but does
no more than try to drink himself into oblivion, as if he
could forget the general pain with his private one. When
Nat appears before him as leader of the slave rebellion,
Cobb's cadaverous face reflects the imminence of his own
death. He can only pity Nat, if it is religious fanaticism
that has led Nat astray, but, in spite of his understanding, he sentences him to hang by the neck until "dead!
dead! *dead!"* (p. 106).[38] Cobb's person and property are as
ravaged as Virginia, which he calls a wasteland:

> "In such a way is our human decency brought down,
> when we pander all that is in us noble and just to
> the false god which goes by the vile name of *Capital!*
> Oh, Virginia, woe betide thee! Woe, thrice woe, and
> ever damned in memory be the day when poor black
> men in chains first trod upon thy sacred strand!"
> (p. 69).

He knows the futility of the system whose justice he administers, and yet like Nat until the very end, he can only despair. Until they and all others repudiate such gods and systems, be they revenge, hate, profit, fear, or whatever for the God of love whom Nat recalls and is called by at the close of the novel, the world will continue to be a sterile place, a waste land.

In 1952 three new authors—Flannery O'Connor, Bernard Malamud, and Ralph Ellison—published first novels in which maimed heroes comment on the world we find them in. In *Wise Blood* (New York, 1952) Miss O'Connor's protagonist, Hazel Motes, finds grace through deliberate ritual tantamount to self-crucifixion. Although he denies Christ, Motes becomes like Him through preaching and suffering that includes blinding himself, wearing barbed wire around his chest, under his shirt, and limping in shoes "lined with gravel and broken glass and pieces of small stones" (p. 221). These acts are penance for his sins; they are acts of atonement which, we are asked and almost made to believe, do indeed bring him at-one-ment with God.

Another approach "to humility through humiliation" [39] is dealt with again in "Good Country People," a story from Miss O'Connor's first collection, *A Good Man Is Hard to Find* (New York, 1955). A one-legged thirty-two-year-old philosophy Ph.D., Joy Hopewell, who in self-revulsion has named herself Hulga, tries to seduce the "good country person" of the story's title, a Bible salesman, so she can take "his remorse in hand and change . . . it into a deeper understanding of life" (p. 186). Joy-Hulga picked her latter name "first purely on the basis of its ugly sound and then the full genius of its fitness had struck her. She had a vision of the name working like

the ugly sweating Vulcan who stayed in the furnace . . ."
(p. 174). Vulcan, of course, was also lame. Instead of seducing and enlightening the Bible salesman, Joy-Hulga
is tricked and taught by him. He steals her artificial leg,
penetrating the shield of reserve and intellectual self-
sufficiency she had erected around her, leaving her "with
only one leg to stand on." Joy-Hulga suffers abasement.
She will be further humiliated by her mother and her
mother's best friend when they discover the circumstances
of her loss. According to Miss O'Connor's theology, such
humiliations prepare one for grace.

For college-educated Julian in "Everything That
Rises Must Converge" and Mrs. Turpin in "Revelation,"
the wounds of others are analogies of their own spiritual
defects. Both are smug and self-satisfied, complacent about
themselves, but condescending and harshly critical of
those around them. Julian, whose last name we never
know but whose given name is that of the scholarly
apostate Roman Emperor, is with his mother when she
suffers a fatal stroke, a symptom of which is the partial
paralysis that causes her to walk "as if one leg were
shorter than the other." [40] Her death plunges Julian "into
a world of guilt and sorrow" (p. 23) where his education
and self-satisfaction are of little comfort. Similarly Claude
Turpin's leg, ulcerated by the kick of a cow, suggests the
character of Mrs. Turpin herself—pompous, self-right-
eous, and seemingly healthy until an attack by one of
O'Connor's demented prophets reveals to Mrs. Turpin
her festering sores of conceit and patronizing charity. For
Flannery O'Connor, a devout Catholic and an artist whose
real theme is always theology, those without grace are
damned, and those who deny their need for grace are surely
so—no wound can be more dangerous.

Another demented prophet appears in "The Lame

Shall Enter First." He is Rufus Johnson, a clubfooted
Negro boy, fourteen years old with an IQ of 140. Sheppard, a social worker, sees great potential in Rufus, and
devotes himself to the boy to the exclusion of his own
son Norton, who ultimately commits suicide. Sheppard's
interest in Rufus is less altruistic than pygmalionesque:
the boy represents a grand opportunity to test his psychological and sociological theories and so prove his own potential, as well as to compensate for the failure in heredity
or childrearing that his son Norton represents to him.
(Critics have noted that these three characters are renewed and reworked appearances of Tarwater, Rayber,
and Bishop from Miss O'Connor's *The Violent Bear It
Away*).[41]

Rufus is undeniably diabolical: he enjoys wrecking
houses and lying, his clubfoot is not only a Platonic manifestation of his warped character but a common analogue
to the Devil's cloven hoof (see note 52); his name (Rufus =
red) and his skin are of the colors most frequently associated with the devil, modern and medieval respectively.
Rufus says that Satan has him in his power (p. 150);
Sheppard sees "the clear-eyed Devil, the sounder of hearts,
leering at him from the eyes of Johnson" (p. 190); the
boy even combs his hair "Hitler fashion" (p. 157).

But Rufus is not entirely evil. He does befriend Norton, and though his talk of heaven and the residence
there of Norton's mother precipitates the boy's suicide in
an attempt to be with her, Rufus assures us that Norton
too is destined for heaven, not having lived long enough
to earn damnation. Moreover, Rufus' rejection of Sheppard's secular theology and Norton's suicide crash through
Sheppard's professional veneer to show him the emptiness
of his life and his need of God.

Sheppard is ironically named. Rufus says, "He thinks

he's Jesus Christ!" (p. 161), and Sheppard does. He sees himself as Johnson's savior and his secular knowledge as much a necessary prosthetic device for Rufus as is the special shoe he buys, both of which the boy rejects. Secure in his own religion, even though it guarantees his damnation, Rufus wants none of Sheppard's atheistic brand.

Miss O'Connor has said, "I suppose the devil teaches most of the lessons that lead to self-knowledge." [42] In this educational sense Rufus is the story's devil. To the extent that Sheppard denies Rufus' religion, and is thus anti-Christ, and to the extent that he is guilty of self-deification, Sheppard assumes that role.[43] But the loss of both boys at the story's end—Rufus to jail, Norton by hanging —strips away his self-erected defenses and prepares him for salvation.

There may well be a question as to whether the wound as Miss O'Connor uses it should be discussed in a chapter devoted to sterility, since it prepares the victim, by showing him his need, for divine grace: the problem is the same in fiction as that in drama of the possibility of a Christian tragedy. Suffice it that a leg wound in the works of Flannery O'Connor does testify to human inability and weakness, the impotence of man to achieve salvation by himself.

Bernard Malamud, whose novels *The Assistant* and *A New Life* were discussed in Chapter Two, used mythic materials quite deliberately in his first novel, *The Natural* (New York, 1952), but to different ends. It is, as Leslie Fiedler has pointed out,[44] an extremely loose adaptation of the Parzival story in which the quest for the Grail has been modernized and transmogrified into a quest for the league pennant by the Knights, a baseball team. Roy Hobbs, the natural talent of the title and the Parzival of

this tale,[45] uses Wonderboy, a bat he has carved out of a
tree split by lightning. He is "Sir Percy lancing Sir Maldemer" (p. 32); he rides the Wonder Bed in the Castle of
Wonders (p. 64; cf. *Parzival*, stanza 567); and he is a
knight "in full armor, mounted on a black charger, . . .
with a long lance as thick as a young tree" (p. 231). The
Fisher King has been demeaned to Pop Fisher, the
Knights' owner-manager; his famous wound, to athlete's
foot on his hands; and the Waste Land, to "a blasted dry
season. No rains at all. The grass is worn scabby in the
outfield and the infield is cracking. . . ." (p. 45). Yet Pop
Fisher's association with vegetation is emphasized when
he says, "I like to stand out in the fields, tending the
vegetables, the corn, the winter wheat—greenest looking
stuff you ever saw" (p. 45).

Roy performs the task of the hero by hitting his first
time up in major league baseball and literally knocking
the cover off the ball. As the chosen hero, he performs
"the freeing of the waters."

> Wonderboy flashed in the sun. It caught the
> sphere where it was biggest. A noise like a twenty-one
> gun salute cracked the sky. There was a straining,
> ripping sound and a few drops of rain spattered to
> the ground. . . . Somebody then shouted it was rain-
> ing cats and dogs (pp. 80–81).

Roy's hitting brings rain and cures Pop's athlete's
foot. But unlike Parzival, Roy never grows up. He never
learns to restrain his impulsiveness, his desire to go after
a bad ball. He never but once (Malamud's version of the
Babe Ruth story of the sick child and the healing home

run) acts altruistically, seeking rather personal glory and fame. When Iris, the earth mother of the novel, and Harriet Bird, Harpy and one of the Erinyes, question him about his motives and the use he will make of the power that hero-worshipping fans grant him, all that Roy wants is to "break every record in the book" (p. 32), to be "the best there ever was in the game" (p. 33). Such statistics are Roy's way of achieving immortality: "If you leave all those records that nobody else can beat—they'll always remember you. You sorta never die" (p. 156). But the impetus is entirely selfish: "The fans dearly loved Roy but Roy did not love the fans" (p. 168).

Malamud also identifies Roy with the Fisher King in two other ways besides his regal name. In daydreams he sees himself "going fishing in a way that made it satisfying to fish . . ." (p. 179). And in love he, like Anfortas, pursues the unfaithful and loveless, the appearance of sex instead of the actual presence of love. He pursues Memo Paris, marked by the "sick breast" of Malamud's unloving women,[46] and characteristic of American materialism at its worst:

> "I am the type who has to have somebody who can support her in a decent way. I'm sick of living like a slave. I got to have a house of my own, a maid to help me with the hard work, a decent car to shop with and a fur coat for winter time when it's cold" (p. 199).

In contrast is Iris Lemon, earth mother and, as her name suggests, fertility goddess. She is a grandmother at thirty-three, impregnated by Roy the only time they make love (by a clear lake, unlike the polluted stream Roy visits with Memo). Her philosophy is expressed by "I don't think you can do anything for anyone without giving up something of your own" (p. 155). Roy never learns this—at least not in the novel.

When Memo becomes more important to him than the league pennant, especially after a food orgy—her attempt to pacify his craving for her—leaves him so weak that he can barely function, he agrees to throw the final playoff game. Then when one hit will win the game for the Knights, Roy finally tries for a hit. But a young pitcher, a natural, strikes him out as he, earlier in the novel, had struck out another hitting champ. So Roy fails the team, Pop, the fans who love and depend on him, and himself. The novel is one of wasted lives, futility, and corruption. The Knights do not achieve their Grail. The Fisher King is not permanently healed. And Parzival, instead of becoming Grail King, suffers and causes suffering, because he remains too natural, too boyish and impulsive, too free of discipline and self-control.

For Ralph Ellison, undoubtedly even more than for Styron, slavery was a crippling condition. Thus in *Invisible Man* (1952), Ellison's unnamed narrator, invisible because he is not seen by others as an individual, meets Brother Tarp in the offices of the Brotherhood (Communist Party) in Harlem. Brother Tarp, too, bears testimony to the inhumanity of his fellows: he is lame.

> ". . . I wasn't always lame, and I'm not really now
> 'cause the doctors can't find anything wrong with
> that leg. They say it's sound as a piece of steel. . . .
> I got this limp from dragging a chain.
>   ". . . Nobody knows that about me, they just

think I got rheumatism. But it was that chain and after nineteen years I haven't been able to stop dragging my leg.[47]

All of the incidents in the novel depict man's cruelty toward and use of other men. The narrator is never treated with simple dignity; the other characters (except Mary) are too busy advancing their own interests to concern themselves with him or his needs. In many instances the basis for self-interest is racial, but not always. Whites and blacks alike deny the narrator his rights, his existence, his manhood. To emphasize that denial, Ellison twice uses the metaphor of castration (pp. 180, 430), for the sterility Ellison is denouncing in *Invisible Man* is not just racial prejudice, but dehumanization and depersonalization of any sort.

Edward Albee uses the same metaphor for the same reason in *The American Dream* (1959, 1960). Grandma explains to Mrs. Barker of the Bye-Bye Adoption Agency Mommy's and Daddy's dissatisfaction with a "bumble" of joy that they had adopted.

> GRANDMA: Weeeeellll . . . in the first place, it turned out that the bumble didn't look like either one of its parents. That was enough of a blow, but things got worse. One night, it cried its heart out, if you can imagine such a thing. . . . But that was only the beginning. Then it turned out it only had eyes for its Daddy.
> MRS. BARKER: For its Daddy! Why any self-respecting woman would have gouged those eyes right out of its head.
> GRANDMA: Well, she did. That's exactly what she did. But then it kept its nose up in the air! . . .

But *then,* it began to develop an interest in its
you-know-what.

MRS. BARKER: In its you-know-what! Well! I hope
they cut its hands off at the wrists!

GRANDMA: Well, yes, they did that eventually. But
first they cut off its you-know-what.[48]

For calling Mommy a name, the bumble has his tongue
cut out. And when it's grown up, Mommy and Daddy are
very disappointed that "it didn't have a head on its
shoulders, it had no guts, it was spineless, its feet were
made of clay. . . ." (p. 101).

The results of such an upbringing are apparent in
Daddy, Albee's version of the castrated American male.
But should we need commentary, it is provided by the
bumble's twin brother whose handsome facade personifies
the American Dream.

> . . . From time to time, in the years that have
> passed, I have suffered losses . . . [this and subse-
> quent ellipses are Albee's] that I can't explain. A
> fall from grace . . . a departure of innocence . . .
> loss . . . loss. How can I put it to you? All right;
> like this: Once . . . it was as if all at once my heart
> . . . became numb . . . almost as though I . . . almost
> as though . . . just like that . . . it had been wrenched
> from my body . . . and from that time I have been
> unable to love. Once . . . I was asleep at the time
> . . . I awoke, and my eyes were burning. And since
> that time I have been unable to see anything, *any-
> thing,* with pity, with affection . . . with anything
> but . . . cool disinterest. And my groin . . . even
> there . . . since one time . . . one specific agony
> . . . since then I have not been able to *love* anyone
> with my body. And even my hands . . . I cannot touch

another person and feel love. And there is more . . .
there are more losses, but it all comes down to this:
I no longer have the capacity to feel anything. I have
no emotions. I have been drained, torn asunder . . .
disemboweled (pp. 114–115).

The disease of lovelessness and inhumanity is now pan-
demic. Without love, concern for others, compassion, the
world we inhabit is indeed waste, and we are all crippled.

The emphasis so far—and rightly so in terms of
quantity—has been on contemporary or near-contempo-
rary fiction. However, authors before those of the present
century have made significant use of lame characters to
suggest sterility and impotence. For example, gout is almost a class sign in English literature, as cripples are an
inevitable consequence of war. Just as authors have used
war wounds symbolically—Jake's emasculation representing the sterility of his era—so has at least one used gout.
In Charles Dickens' *Bleak House* (1852–1853), Sir Leicester Dedlock's debility is of a piece with the decline of his
class and his family. It partakes of the general sense of
malaise suggested in the novel by its title, the fog and
rain that dim most of the proceedings, and even Sir Leicester's family name, Dedlock. Like Clifford Chatterley
after him, Sir Leicester is a member of a class that is
losing its power to control: rotten boroughs are disap-
pearing, and an election can no longer be swung for a few
hundred pounds. The middle classes are ascending in
wealth, in position, and in power, while the nobility must
limp along. The Dedlock fortunes are decreasing; Sir
Leicester's man does not win the local parliamentary seat;
his estate of Chesney Wold is being turned into a swamp
by the rain; he is laid low first by gout and then by paral-

ysis after Lady Dedlock leaves him; and he—the most
noble of the Dedlocks and the least reprehensible—will
die childless. As J. Hillis Miller says:

> The self-enclosure of these characters is not a comic
> and comfortable insulation. . . . It is rather a som-
> ber interment. . . . [There is] a kind of pervasive
> atmosphere of staleness and immobility. And the life
> that is lived in this enclosure may be a physical or
> spiritual paralysis, like that of Grandfather Smallweed
> or that of Sir Leicester who is "like one of a race of
> eight-day clocks in gorgeous cases that never go and
> never went" (Ch. 18).[49]

It should be stressed that Sir Leicester is as crippled physically as he is in forms of social action, particularly politics.

The theme of crippling—of man's mind and spirit,
as well as his body—fascinated Dickens and reappeared
in *Little Dorrit* (1855–1857). The central image of the
novel is Marshalsea Prison, but Dickens is really concerned with all that imprisons. A central character, Mrs.
Clennam, is restricted to a wheelchair, the prisoner "of
her wrathful Calvinist theology and a dark inward sense
of guilt."[50] Another character, a schoolmaster and
blighter of children's minds, is tag-named Mr. Cripples.
Through name, plot, commentary, and imagery, Dickens
condemns all those institutions, public and private, that
maim and pervert men and that sustain the aridity that
makes waste lands.

In this chapter I have tried to show how, by means
of crippling wounds, authors indicate the failure, the in-
competence, or the victimization of certain of their characters. These characters inhabit a world which is usually

bleak, sad, depressing; their lives are grotesque. Perhaps they are best described in this passage about similar grotesques by Paul Rosenfeld in his preface to *The Sherwood Anderson Reader:* [51]

> Almost, it seems, we touch an absolute existence, a curious semi-animal, semi-divine life. Its chronic state is banality, . . . Its manifestation: the non-community of cranky or otherwise asocial solitaries, dispersed, impotent and imprisoned. . . . Its wonders—the wonders of its chaos—are fugitive heroes and heroines, mutilated like the dismembered Osiris, the dismembered Dionysus. . . .

Part 2. Victimizers

Modern novels frequently emphasize the complexity of man. They show that although a man may well be a victim of society or some unreasonable wound, he is as much a victim of his own character and so is not entirely an innocent victim. Even in classical literature, lame Oedipus is a victim of circumstance, but also of his own hubris, and he is a victimizer to the extent that he bears responsibility for the plague that afflicts Thebes. It is perhaps arbitrary to deal separately with characters who function primarily as victimizers, but there are enough of these individuals who cause pain—and enough of them are found in influential roles—to merit their classification into a subgroup of those maimed figures who inhabit, and create, waste lands.

That such characters should be deformed—that they should, in particular, limp—is an ancient notion probably derived from two sources: deformity, from the Platonic concept that a man's character is reflected in his appearance; limping, from the tradition [52] that the Arch Enemy of man, Satan (Hebrew for "the adversary"), has cloven hooves [53] which he can disguise but not entirely conceal should he take human shape. Thus Goethe's Mephisto has no obvious hooves, but does limp (Part I, sc. v, "Auerbachs Keller"): *"Wass hinkt der Kerl auf einem Fuss?"* [54] Artistically, then, it is a small step from Devil to devil or demon, agent of malevolence and evil. Klinschor, the wicked magician in *Parzival,* is a eunuch, castrated for adultery.[55] Shakespeare added lameness to the list of Richard III's deformities that appeared in Holinshed in order to make Richard as diabolical in appearance as in character.

In the nineteenth century Charles Dickens makes obvious use of lameness as a sign of evil with Quilp and Rigaud, the *diaboli ex machina* of *The Old Curiosity Shop* (1840–1841) and *Little Dorrit* (1855–1857) respectively. Quilp, an ugly dwarf, has crooked legs and prefers his liquor boiling hot. Caught in villainy, Sampson Brass, Quilp's pathetic accomplice, complains that he is not responsible, that it is "Quilp, who deludes me into his infernal den, and takes delight in looking on and chuckling while I scorch, and burn, and bruise and maim myself. . . ." [56] Of Rigaud, alias Blandois, alias Lagnier, the official villain of *Little Dorrit,* Dickens says:

Cain might have looked as lonely and avoided. . . .
Miry, footsore, his shoes and gaiters trodden out, . . .
limping along in pain and difficulty; he looked as
if the clouds were hurrying from him, . . . as if
the fitful autumn night were disturbed by him. . . .
He limped on . . . , toiling and muttering. "To the
devil with this plain that has no end! To the devil

with these stones that cut like knives! . . . I hate
you!" [Later] because the man was acquitted on his
trial, . . . the people said . . . that the devil was
let loose.[57]

Meanwhile Rigaud himself sits at the stove, smoking
and warming his feet.

In the twentieth century there appears in James
Thurber's *The 13 Clocks* (1950) a limping diabolical
figure who, for all the lightness with which Thurber
treats him, is actually closer to the archetypal limper than
is Satan himself.

. . . There lived a cold, aggressive Duke, and his
niece [actually a kidnapped girl, no relation], the
Princess Saralinda. She was warm in every wind and
weather, but he was always cold. His hands were as
cold as his smile and almost as cold as his heart. He
wore gloves when he was asleep, and he wore gloves
when he was awake. . . . He was six feet four, and
forty-six and even colder than he thought he was.
One eye wore a velvet patch; the other glittered
through a monocle. . . . His nights were spent in
evil dreams, his days were given to wicked schemes.
. . . Even the hands of his watch and the hands of
all the thirteen clocks were frozen. Travelers . . .
would . . . say, "Time lies frozen there. It's always
Then. It's never Now." [58]

The murderous Duke who limps because one leg has
grown longer than the other—due to his constant practice during childhood of using the same foot to drop-kick
puppies—is quite obviously a winter king, associated with

cold, darkness, and moribund life.[59] His antagonist for
Saralinda's hand, a prince named Zorn of Zorna, is young,
handsome, vital, and even-legged. Zorn, in spite of the
Duke's wicked machinations, wins Saralinda's freedom for
her, as well as her hand in marriage. As he does so, time
is thawed by the princess's warm hand, the thirteen frozen
clocks thaw and strike the hour, "a morning glory that
had never opened, opened . . ." (p. 107), and Zorn and
Saralinda set sail for the Blessed Isles of Ever After. Spring
triumphs over winter once again. A character named Hark
in Thurber's romance says, "There are rules and rites and
rituals, older than the sound of bells and snow on moun-
tains" (p. 98). The eternal cycle of the seasons is as old
as the earth; the ritual enactment of that cycle is almost
as old as man. As I have indicated in previous discussion,
the winter king in such rituals was often represented by
a cloven-hoofed boar. Even in modern literature, those
who seek life, love, or purpose have to contend with those
who pervert, corrupt, defame, and destroy—with enemies
who bear the mark of The Enemy: lameness.

So too in the novels of Bellow and Malamud. Both,
as we have seen, use the ritual imagery of fertility and
the story of the Fisher King with comic deliberateness;
similarly, they consciously use devices associated with the
devil for certain characters. In Bellow's *Herzog* (1964),
Moses Herzog—like Henderson and Bellow's other protagonists—must learn about death and face it in its many
forms in order to live (Dr. Pep's lesson, and also lame
Mr. Benjamin's in Bellow's *The Victim*). Herzog is con-
fronted with a succession of reality instructors from whom
he learns about sex, love, death, and life and his relation
to it. The most gruesome lesson is provided in the courtroom Herzog has visited in search of his lawyer. There

he sees a girl and her lover on trial for murder. The girl
has diabolical attributes—lameness, red hair—and a
wretched existence:

> . . . born lame . . . she had a fourth-grade educa-
> tion, I.Q. 94. An older brother was the favorite; she
> was neglected. Unattractive, sullen, clumsy, wearing
> an orthopedic boot. . . . She was known to have
> violent epileptoid fits of rage; her tolerance for emo-
> tions controlled from the affected lobe was known to
> be very low. Because she was a poor crippled creature,
> she had often been molested, later sexually abused by
> adolescent boys. . . . Her mother loathed her, had
> refused to attend the trial. . . .[60]

The girl even lives in hell: a slum hotel where "you
could smell the misery of it from the street; its black
stink flowed out through open windows—bedding, gar-
bage, disinfectant, roach killer" (p. 236). She and her
lover, a porter in a lunchroom, are on trial for the murder of her three-year-old son, her child by a previous
lover. A relative of the mother testifies that the child was
never clean, that his wife put salve on the boy's cold sore
as the mother would not, that he fed the child when the
mother would not; he described the boy as quiet, unde-
manding, frightened, and with a bad smell (p. 238). The
wife's current lover claims that the boy was a problem
child, that he resisted toilet training and drove his mother
"wild sometimes the way he dirtied himself. And the crying all night!" (p. 239). The medical examiner testifies
that the child suffered from malnutrition, incipient rick-
ets, and already carious teeth. The boy had obviously
been beaten: the scalp was torn, there were unusually
heavy bruises on the back and legs; the bruises were

heaviest in the region of the genitals, where the boy seemed to have been struck by a metal buckle or the heel of a woman's shoe. He also had two broken ribs, one older, the more recent having done lung damage, a ruptured liver, and brain damage. The room clerk testifies that he went to the couple's room to protest the loud noise and the child's crying: he saw the young man lying on the bed, smoking, while the girl threw her three-year old son against the wall. Then the crying stopped.

> The child screamed, clung, but with both arms the girl hurled it against the wall. On her legs was ruddy hair. And her lover, too, with long jaws and zooty sideburns, watching on the bed. Lying down to copulate, and standing up to kill. Some kill, then cry. Others, not even that (p. 240).

This lesson in reality, the barbarous cruelty and the explicit threat to the genitals—many of the women in Herzog's life, especially his wife, Madeleine, are pictured as wielding knives—sickens Herzog, and drives him out of the courtroom. There in the corridor the lesson is duplicated when he stumbles over a middle-aged woman with a cane, a cast on her leg, metal clogs on her foot, and painted toenails. "She did not speak at all but was not ready to let him go off. Her eyes, prominent, severe, still kept him standing, identifying him thoroughly, fully, deeply, as a fool. Again—silently—*Thou fool!*" (p. 240).

Immediately afterward Herzog leaves New York for Chicago, the home of his (second) ex-wife, his daughter June, for whom he is concerned, and his ex-best friend, his wife's lover, Valentine Gersbach. Gersbach, too, has ostensible diabolical qualities, much like the murdering mother. He has red hair, a ruddy complexion, and wears an artificial leg. More to the point he has replaced Herzog in Madeleine's affections and is with June more than her father is. To Herzog, Gersbach is

"On the make everywhere. . . . He's a poet in mass communications. . . . And he makes all sorts of people feel that he has exactly what they've been looking for. Subtlety for the subtle. Warmth for the warm. For the crude, crudity. For the crooks, hypocrisy. Atrocity for the atrocious. Whatever your heart desires.

". . . Is he an Ivan the Terrible? Is he a would-be Rasputin? Or the poor man's Cagliostro? Or a politician, orator, demagogue, rhapsode? Or some kind of Siberian shaman?

". . . With a head like a flaming furnace, a voice like a bowling alley, and the wooden leg drumming the stage" (pp. 214–217).

Gersbach is the prince of social chameleons. In Herzog's own Yiddish, he is a *macher,* and maker, too, of Herzog's wife. When he leaves New York, Herzog blames his life, his misfortunes, his emptiness on Gersbach and Madeleine. He goes to Chicago to kill them, symbolically obtaining his father's pistol on the way. When he comes to his home, he cries for the loss. He spies through the bathroom window, where he sees June:

His child! . . . He melted with tenderness for her. . . . Then a hand reached forward and shut off the [bath] water—a man's hand. It was Gersbach. He was going to bathe Herzog's daughter! . . . Herzog . . . heard him say, not unkindly, "Okay, cut out the monkeyshines," for Junie was giggling, twisting, splashing, dimpling, showing her tiny white teeth. . . . "Now hold still," said Gersbach. He got into her ears with the washrag . . . as she squealed and twisted. The man washed her tenderly. . . . He [Gersbach] was scouring the tub. Moses might have killed him now. . . . He might have shot Gersbach as he methodically salted the yellow sponge rectangle with cleansing powder. There were two bullets in the chamber. . . . [Bellow's ellipsis] But they would stay there. Herzog clearly recognized that. . . . As soon as Herzog saw the actual person giving an actual bath, the reality of it, the tenderness of such a buffoon to a little child, his intended violence turned into *theater,* into something ludicrous (pp. 256–258).

There is sterility, cruelty, lack of love in the world, but unless we beware, we add more. The mother who kills her child is diabolical; Gersbach, in spite of his red hair and missing leg, is not. We see the others in the novel only as Herzog sees them, and eventually we perceive the significance of the novel's opening line: "If I am out of my mind, it's all right with me, thought Moses Herzog." He is not insane, but this initial sentence suggests his egocentricity and masochism. He enjoys suffering, and so creates situations where he can be miserable and pitied. Easy, sensuous sexuality embarrasses him, so that he flees from women he enjoys to women who exploit him. He covets abuse, and so makes both Mady and Gersbach worse than they are, exaggerating the human to the demonic.

In Malamud's *The Fixer* (1966), however, the demonic comes from the denial of the human, the humane. Here Malamud uses various types of lameness to denote sterility. Yakov Bok, a Jewish handyman, leaves the *shtetl,* the rural Jewish ghetto, to seek his fortune in Kiev. Instead he finds misfortune. He is blamed for a murder he did not commit and jailed for two years before he is brought to trial as a religious scapegoat for troubled official Russia in the second decade of this century. His troubles begin when he rescues a drunken Russian who has passed out in the street. "And from him to his daughter with the crippled leg was only one crippled step. . . . And a crippled hop into prison." [61]

In Kiev prison where he will wait two years for trial, Yakov is first thrown into a communal thirty-day cell where one of his fellow prisoners has a clubfoot. On his way to trial at the end of the novel, someone in the crowd hurls a bomb at the armored carriage taking him from the prison. The bomb severely injures a young Cossack guard, "a youth of twenty or so, on a gray mare." He had "youth and good looks, and . . . , as such things go, [is] a free man, give or take a little" (p. 329). After the explosion "the gray mare lay dead on the cobblestones. Three policemen were lifting the young Cossack rider. His foot had been torn off by the bomb. The boot had been blown away and his leg was shattered and bloody" (p. 331). Yakov—whose name is the Russian equivalent of the founder of Israel, Jacob—is himself lamed: by nails coming through his ill-fitting prison shoes, by infection that swells both legs to the knees, by chains in the daytime and by stocks on his bedplank which confine his feet at night. During the latter half of the novel, he limps or literally crawls.

Malamud uses crippledness as a symbol of inhumanity. Many associated with the prison that stands for Russian injustice, and by implication, American injustice as well, bear the stigmata of lameness, from the clubfooted prisoner and Bok, to Kogin and the young Cossack. Kogin, one of the two prison guards regularly assigned to Bok, had a son who committed a senseless crime and was marched to Siberia where he drowned himself in a river. On the night before his trial is to begin, Bok—"his legs . . . swollen and his back teeth, loose" (p. 317)—has hallucinations that his cell is "crowded with prisoners who had lived and died there."

> They were broken-faced, greenish-gray men, with haunted eyes, scarred shaved heads and ragged bodies, crowding the cell. . . . So many prisoners, thought the prisoner, it's a country of prisoners. . . . He beheld long lines of them, gaunt-eyed men with starved mouths, lines stretching through the thick walls to impoverished cities, the vast empty steppe, great snowy virgin forests, to the shabby wooden work camps in Siberia. Trofim Kogin [the guard's son] was among them. He had a broken leg and lay in the snow as the long lines slowly moved past him. He lay with his eyes shut and mouth twitching but did not call for help (p. 317).

What help is there for those crippled by injustice, by inhumanity, by cruelty? (The morning after Bok's nightmares Kogin, the guard, is executed by the Deputy Warden when Kogin prevents him from shooting Bok for spite.)

Malamud, as noted in Chapter Two, writes about man's need for love and the suffering that teaches him that need. One sign marks Malamud's sufferers: lameness —in Pop Fisher's transmogrified athlete's foot, in Sy Levin's pain in the ass, in Frank Alpine's circumcision, and in Yakov Bok's wounds. Two signs mark those who cannot or do not give of themselves in love: red hair, such as that of Gerald Gilley in *A New Life,* the unloving, made-sterile-by-mumps husband of Pauline; and a "sick" breast, denied the male protagonist by a female in the novel, as with Harriet Bird and Memo Paris in *The Natural,* and Avis Fliss in *A New Life.* In contrast, flatchested Pauline Gilley develops breasts in pregnancy after giving herself to Sy Levin; and Iris Lemon, as her name, behavior, and pregnancy indicate, is the fertility goddess of *The Natural.*

In *The Fixer,* Zinaida Nikolaevna Lebedev, Zina, is both crippled and red-haired. She is an only child, the only one to care for her drunken father, Nicolai Lebedev (whom Bok has rescued from the street, in reward for which he has been given a job. Unmarried at thirty, no longer a virgin, Zina is stifled by her circumscribed existence, symbolized, as Yakov's imprisonment is later, by an injured leg. Bok is shy and very deferential among these gentiles and anti-Semites. Somewhat self-educated, a skilled worker, and very polite, though naïve, he attracts Zina, who feeds him lavishly and sets out to seduce him. Entering her bedroom before her preparations are complete, Bok discovers that she is menstruating: "But you are unclean!" Her response is, "But surely you know this is the safest time?" (pp. 52–53). Caution also leads Zina to condemn Bok after his arrest and accuse him of sexual assault. Her selfishness is in direct contrast to Iris Lemon's assertion that "I don't think you can do anything for anyone, without giving up something of your own" (*The Natural,* p. 155). To love means to consider others before self. To consider oneself first, to compound this disregard of others by denying their humanity and dignity, is to foster the world's sterility by one's own demonism. To the extent she does this, Zinaida Lebedev, although she is a minor character in *The Fixer,* embodies its themes as much as Maudie Loftis does those of *Lie Down in Darkness.*

Just as Bok is treated as a scapegoat by Russian officialdom, as a worthless being easily sacrificed to appease mass unrest, so Yakov denies his wife Raisl's individuality and problems, seeing in their childlessness only his own humiliation. His turning away from her and into himself finally forces her to leave him. But after more than two years of unjust suffering, Bok can find in himself the compassion to claim her illegitimate son as his own, easing Raisl's lot and that of the boy. Through his own suffering he has learned to care for and about others.

In this chapter I have made an arbitrary distinction between limping characters in a sterile world, whose wounds symbolize that world, and those who, to a large extent, are responsible for that sterility. Eliot's *The Waste Land* and Huxley's *Point Counter Point* are included in the section on victims, yet the authors obviously intend their characters to be seen as in part responsible for their own predicaments. There are thus victimizers, victims, and self-victimizers—but such fine discriminations are beyond my purpose. What is important is rather how modern writers use maiming to depict the condition of their characters. Thus Clifford Chatterley's narrow class consciousness and warped personality are in large part responsible for his condition even though the immediate cause of his impotence is his war wound. But to just what degree he is responsible for his own condition is a moot point. The wound serves as an objective correlative of his inner faults, just as the wounds of Bok, Zina, and Gersbach symbolize their respective inner selves—as victims or victimizers.

Most of the wounds discussed in the chapter on fertility brought new life only to their bearers, or to those close to them. Brick Pollitt regains his own self-confidence and Maggie's, but nothing is said about the whole of the South; Frank Alpine gains, and perhaps so does Helen, but the world does not. In this chapter, however, the wounds of individuals—the Fisher King, Jake Barnes, Laura Wingfield, Judge Cobb, and Yakov Bok among them—comment on the desolation of their societies. They inhabit a wasteland, but they are not alone. In the view of these writers, this waste land—futile, sterile, loveless—is our world. Only our wounds may be less obvious.

Notes

1. Jessie Weston, *From Ritual to Romance* (New York, 1957); Sir James Frazer, *The Golden Bough*, one-volume abridgement (New York, 1922), pp. 28–29, 371–372, 400–410.
2. Sophocles, *The Oedipus Cycle*, trans. Dudley Fitts and Robert Fitzgerald (New York, 1939), p. 4.
3. T. S. Eliot, *The Complete Poems and Plays* (New York, 1952), pp. 195–196, see also pp. 176, 180–181, 201, 207–208.
4. The source of the Grail motif is not known. A hypothetical one by a Breton conteur named Bleheris has been postulated (cf. Weston, pp. 189–209; also *Parzival*, ed. Helen M. Mustard and Charles E. Passage [New York, 1961], p. xxxiv). The first written source we have is Chrétien de Troyes *Li Contes del Graal* (c. 1175) which was augmented by continuators (Gerbert, Manessier, and Wauchier), modifiers, and translators. Other versions seem independent of Chrétien and may derive from Chrétien's source: *Perlesvaus, Didot Perceval, Peredur, Sir Percyvelle of Galles,* and Wolfram von Eschenbach's *Parzival;* also the *Estoire del Saint Graal, Merlin,* and *Queste del Saint Graal* romances of the "Vulgate Cycle," which were later reworked by Malory for his *Le Morte D'Arthur* (1485); as well as later versions by Alfred Lord Tennyson, *Idylls of the King* (1842–1885), especially "The Holy Grail" (1869), and Richard Wagner's *Parsifal* (1882). These Arthurian romances, as well as the German *Diû Crone,* and the non-Arthurian *Sone de Nansai*—seem-

ingly a reworking of Joseph de Boron's *Joseph d'Arimathie*—all contain a grail of some sort, holy or not, and a maimed knight, usually a ruler known as the Fisher King.

5. Cf. Weston, pp. 22, 122; and *Parzival*, p. 256.
6. Roger Sherman Loomis constructs a sound case for the development of the Fisher King's story from the history of Bran. (Loomis, *Arthurian Tradition and Chrétien de Troyes* [New York, 1949], pp. 64, 170–171, 242–250, 350–355; and 386–387, where he cites the similar conclusions of Heinrich, Nutt, Rhys, Anwyl, Brown, Kempe, Nitze, and Newstead. Also W. T. H. Jackson, *The Literature of the Middle Ages* [New York, 1960], p. 113.) This development includes such variations and innumerable doublets of the maimed king as Bron, Brons, Joseph of Arimethea, Pellinor, Pellehan, "Bliocadran," Gahmuret, Anfortas, Sir Percivale, and Peredur. (See pages cited in Loomis above; see also, and especially, p. 511. For Sir Percivale, *Le Morte D'Arthur*, XIV, x. For Peredur, *The Mabinogion*, trans. Gwynn Jones and Thomas Jones, p. 206. I cannot help but wonder if Tristan's two noisome wounds near his loins, accompanied as they are by widespread lamenting, owe something to the traditional location of the Fisher King's wounds. Cf. Gottfried von Strassburg's *Tristan*, trans. A. T. Hatto [Middlesex, 1960], pp. 7, 133, 138, 341.)
7. *The Mabinogion*, p. 38.
8. Cf. Jessie Weston's and Roger Loomis' belief (pp. 21–22 and 393) that leg wounds in medieval literature are euphemisms for genital injuries—for Percivale in this case, self-castration, as well as the boy in Hemingway's "God Rest You Merry, Gentlemen" and the tutors of Lenz and of Brecht (see Appendix One). Lafcadio in André Gide's *Les Caves du Vatican* (1914) also does penance by stabbing himself in the thigh, but only with a penknife.
9. Edmund Wilson, *Axel's Castle* (New York, 1931), p. 106.
10. See Eliot's note to l. 46 of *The Waste Land*, and l.151, 60–76, 173–214, and 422–433.
11. F. Scott Fitzgerald, *The Great Gatsby* (New York, 1925), pp. 23–24, 149, 118, and 13.
12. Cf. Malcolm Cowley, ed., *Hemingway* (New York, 1944), p. xxi; Carlos Baker, *Hemingway: The Writer as Artist* (Princeton, 1952), p. 90.
13. Ernest Hemingway, *The Sun Also Rises* (New York, 1926), p. 16. Subsequent references to Hemingway's novel will be included in the text.
14. *The Twenties* (New York, 1955), pp. 66–76.

15. April, 1924, *transatlantic review,* pp. 230–234; later in *In Our Time* (New York, 1925).

16. *The Short Stories of Ernest Hemingway* (New York, 1938), p. 94. Subsequent references to Hemingway's short stories in the text will refer to this edition.

17. Critics have noticed Hemingway's concern with suicide in "Fathers and Sons" (1933) and *For Whom the Bell Tolls* (1940), and their interest has intensified since he killed himself in 1961. They have usually dated Hemingway's concern from his father's suicide in 1928, but "Indian Camp" shows his interest in the subject four years earlier.

18. G. Thomas Tanselle, "Hemingway's INDIAN CAMP," *The Explicator,* Vol. XX, No. 53 (Feb. 1962).

19. Of course, Achilles was a sacred king, a fertility figure who was killed at full virility and often at the winter solstice. If Graves is correct in identifying mistletoe with Uranus's severed testicles (*G M,* I, 37–38, 41), then the day of the boy's death gains additional ironic significance.

20. *Contexts of Criticism* (Cambridge, Mass., 1957), p. 150.

21. *The Mortal No* (Princeton, 1964), p. 183.

22. "The Snows of Kilimanjaro" first appeared in *Esquire,* August 1936. Hemingway read French fluently; I wonder if he had read and was influenced by André Malraux's *The Royal Way* (1930), in which a sexually impotent adventurer, Perken, a burnt-out shell of a man, dies of gangrene which results when a Cambodian war spike penetrates under his kneecap.

23. Interestingly, Mark Rampion, a character in Huxley's novel, is based on D. H. Lawrence; he propounds and lives by the philosophy of the full life that Lawrence incorporates into *Lady Chatterley.* (Jocelyn Brooke, *Aldous Huxley* [London, 1954], p. 21; John Atkins, *Aldous Huxley* [New York, 1956], pp. 137 ff.)

24. Cf. *The Mortal No,* p. 417. Hoffman describes the scene of the novel as an "industrial wasteland," a "lost world," and says:

> . . . Clifford Chatterley is . . . an additional thrust at the image of modern hell. His role of the diseased "fisher king" is a parody of Eliot's use of the idea. His paralysis leaves him deprived not only of sexual power but of sensual will, and he behaves like a child going about in a plaything mechanical chair, through which he pettishly exercises control over his universe.

25. D. H. Lawrence, *Lady Chatterley's Lover* (New York, 1959), p. 51. Subsequent quotations from this novel in the text will refer to this Grove Press edition, edited by Mark Schorer.

26. *Point Counter Point* (New York, 1947), Intro. by Harold H. Watts, p. xxi; Atkins, p. 140.

27. Aldous Huxley, *Point Counter Point* (New York, 1928), p. 90. For quotations from this novel in the text, page numbers will refer to this edition. Cf. a similar expression of lovelessness in the earlier novel *Those Barren Leaves* (1925), where the very title suggests infertility. At the opening of Chapter 12, Part III, Miss Thriplow (Mary Thriplow, but distanced in most appearances as Miss Thriplow) records in her notebook: "There are people . . . who seem to have no capacity for feeling deeply or passionately about anything. It is a kind of emotional impotence for which one can only pity them profoundly."

28. Brooke, p. 8.

29. William Faulkner, *The Sound and the Fury* (New York, 1946), p. 18. Significantly, the wound motif is emphasized by a broken leg which the male Quentin Compson suffers, which has to be rebroken when it doesn't set properly (p. 132).

30. *Light in August* (New York, 1950), p. 395.

31. Irving Malin, *William Faulkner: An Interpretation* (Stanford, 1952), p. 56.

32. *The Complete Works of Nathanael West* (New York, 1957), p. 122. All subsequent quotations from West will refer to this edition.

33. That Williams is conscious not only of ancient mythology but also of modern psychiatry is evident from this speech of Tom's at the opening of scene three: ". . . The idea of getting a gentleman caller for Laura began to play a more and more important part in Mother's calculations. It became an obsession. Like some archetype of the universal unconscious, the image of the gentleman caller haunted our small apartment. . . ." *The Glass Menagerie* (New York, 1945). Moreover, Laura does not limp in "Girl in Glass," Williams' own short story on which this play is based. Williams obviously added this physical flaw to Laura so that it might constantly remind the audiences of her plight, an objective correlative for her increasing withdrawal from others, and from life itself.

34. Roger B. Stein, "*The Glass Menagerie* Revisited," *Western Humanities Review*, XVIII (Spring, 1964), 151, 145.

35. *Ibid.*, p. 149.

36. William Styron, *Lie Down in Darkness* (New York, 1951), p. 228. References in the text are from this edition.

37. William Styron, *The Confessions of Nat Turner* (New York, 1967). All subsequent page numbers in the text are from this edition.

38. The words that Cobb speaks at Nat's trial are quoted by Styron from the original *Confessions,* transcribed by Thomas R. Gray and printed by him in Baltimore, 1831, but the conversation Cobb holds with Nat is Styron's invention (as are, probably, the the misfortunes that befall Cobb). I have difficulty reconciling the two speeches; the Cobb who spoke to Nat at the Travis farm would not have had to question Nat's justification for rebelling.

39. Stanley Edgar Hyman, *Flannery O'Connor,* Univ. of Minnesota Pamphlet on American Writers, No. 54 (1966), p. 29.

40. Flannery O'Connor, *Everything That Rises Must Converge* (New York, 1965), p. 22. This volume was published posthumously with a long, reminiscent, and appreciative introduction by Robert Fitzgerald. All subsequent O'Connor short stories referred to in the text are from this volume.

41. Fitzgerald introduction, p. xxi; Hyman, p. 26.

42. Quoted in "Flannery O'Connor's Devil" by John Hawkes, *Sewanee Review,* LXX (1962), 406.

43. Cf. Hyman, p. 26.

44. *No! in Thunder* (Boston, 1960). Cf. Baumbach, *The Landscape of Nightmare* (New York, 1965), pp. 107–111; Richman, *Bernard Malamud* (New York, 1966) pp. 28–49, and Robert Shulman, "Myth, Mr. Eliot, and the Comic Novel," *Modern Fiction Studies,* XII (Winter, 1966–1967), 400–403.

45. He must be Parzival because he does heal Pop Fisher, even if only temporarily. Parzival, too, was a natural, brave from birth and born to become Grail King (cf. *The Natural* [New York, 1952], p. 237, "He coulda been king"), though very much of a fool or simpleton at first (Loomis, p. 239). And the name of Roy Hobbs, it seems to me, means King Lout or King Rustic. (Cf. Baumbach, p. 107.)

46. Cf. footnote 19, Ch. Two.

47. Ralph Ellison, *Invisible Man* (New York, 1952), p. 292.

48. Edward Albee, *The American Dream* (New York, 1963), pp. 99–100.

49. *Charles Dickens* (Cambridge, Mass., 1958), p. 186.

50. Edgar Johnson, *Charles Dickens* (New York, 1952), II, 886.

51. (Boston, 1947), p. xxii.

52. See Stith Thompson, *Motif-Index of Folk Literature* (Bloomington, Indiana, 1956) III, 137–138, 165–166, 321–322; motifs F551, F517, and esp. G303.4.5.

53. The Devil's cloven hooves apparently originate in the Hebrew word for "demon" or "satyr" ("satyr" appears in the New Revised Standard Bible at Lev. 17:7, Is. 13:21 and 34:14) which

literally means he-goat, and demons were so pictured (as Greek satyrs are). "Just as the Arabs degraded the gods of the heathen to *jinn* and attributed to them some of the hairy characteristics of animals, so these satyrs appear to have been originally heathen deities." Earlier on the page appears the statement that "Satan is clearly a development out of the group of spirits which were in earlier days thought to form Jahweh's court, members of which were sent upon errands of disaster to men" (George A. Barton, "Hebrew Demons and Spirits," *Encyclopedia of Religion and Ethics* [New York, 1951], IV, 598); the Devil has retained one of the animal characteristics of that group: cloven hooves.

54. Thomas Mann said that Mephisto "is the genius of *fire*, he has reserved to himself that destructive, sterilizing, annihilating element. The red waistcoat and the cock's feather are the outward signs of his infernal nature. . . . The cloven hoof is replaced by a slight limp" *(Essays,* trans. H. T. Lowe-Porter [New York, 1957], p. 26). Cf. Mann's treatment of Cipolla in Appendix One.

55. Cf. Anton Ehrenzweig, *The Hidden Order of Art* (Berkeley, 1967), pp. 237–244. In this section on fire, which Ehrenzweig sees as symbolic of oral castration, he discusses lame gods of fire: Hephaestus, Logi *(sic),* the Medieval devil, and such related "minor devils" as Klingsor and Prometheus (who stole fire and had to be punished).

56. *The Old Curiosity Shop* (London, 1907), p. 484.

57. *Little Dorrit* (London, 1953), pp. 124, 128.

58. James Thurber, *The 13 Clocks* (New York, 1950), pp. 17–18. Page numbers cited in the text for subsequent quotations from this romance will refer to this edition.

59. Cf. Northrop Frye, *Anatomy of Criticism* (Princeton, 1957), p. 187.

60. Saul Bellow, *Herzog* (New York, 1964), p. 236. Subsequent references will appear in the text.

61. Bernard Malamud, *The Fixer* (New York, 1966), p. 314. Subsequent references will appear in the text.

The archetypal hero-figure stands poised between height and depth, between the Divine and the Devilish, swung forward and upward in reflection of imagination's universal range, hurled back and downward in expression of individual limitation and the restraining censure of the whole upon the part.

—Maud Bodkin
Archetypal Patterns in Poetry, *p. 245.*

4.

Limited
Man

The wounds of the characters to be discussed in this chapter signify their "humanness"—in existential terms, their mortality—their limited powers and abilities juxtaposed with their unlimited hopes, visions, and dreams. The final category then is that of *la condition humaine* —man mortal, imperfect, and desiring more than he can achieve. By *category,* let me repeat, I mean simply those literary figures who are sufficiently similar to be discussed, for convenience, as a group and not some absolutely definable type.

Men are complex and paradoxical; why should symbols which represent them be any less so? As there was overlapping in the previous chapter between victims and victimizers, so will there be in this section. Indeed, according to some authors, to be born is to be a victim. Consequently there may be different but equally valid interpretations of a work of art; *Hamlet* is the greater for its complexity, not diminished because critics cannot agree why Hamlet acts as he does. Thus, although I have mentioned both Oedipus and Jake Barnes before in the context of sterility, I shall discuss them here as examples of limited humanity. For my purpose is more to show how an awareness of the limping hero as such can enrich our comprehension of literature than to provide definitive interpretations.

In mythology pain was often a requisite price for knowledge. Mutilation often accompanied one's ritual initiation into the sacred mysteries of the tribe; it was also the price that many individuals paid for initiation into secret mysteries of nature.[1] Odin gave an eye that he might drink from the Well of Wisdom, then hung nine days crucified on a tree in order to learn the secret of Runes. Smithcraft, too, was considered a sacred mystery, ". . . Every Bronze Age tool, weapon, or utensil had magical properties and . . . the smith was something of a sorcerer. . . . That the Smith-god hobbles is a tradition found in regions as far apart as West Africa and Scandinavia. . . ."[2] The most famous lame smith is, of course, Hephaestus-Vulcan; another is the hamstrung Norse smith Weyland.

Men have made pacts, covenants marked by pain, with God or Devil that assured them greater wisdom or power—from the time of Jacob, who was lamed on becoming Israel, till the time of Adrian Leverkühn in Thomas Mann's *Dr. Faustus,* who paid his soul to the Devil for great musical ability and suffered the slow, torturous death of syphilis. As Mann says:

. . . Certain attainments of the soul and the intellect are impossible without disease, without insanity, without spiritual crime, and the great invalids are crucified victims, sacrificed to humanity and its advancement, to the broadening of its feelings and knowledge—in short, to its more sublime health.[3]

Friedrich Nietzsche and Edmund Wilson have said the same: "It is as though the myth [of Oedipus] whispered to us that wisdom . . . is an unnatural crime, and that whoever, in pride of knowledge, hurls nature into the abyss of destruction, must himself experience nature's disintegration";[4] lame Oedipus, scarred almost from birth, whose knowledge causes the Sphinx to destroy herself, pays for his knowledge through his crimes and his guilt. Wilson, speaking of Philoctetes, says: ". . . genius and disease, like strength and mutilation, may be inextricably bound up together." [5] "The victim of a malodorous disease which renders him abhorrent to society and periodically degrades him and makes him helpless is also the master of a superhuman art which everybody has to respect and which the normal man finds he needs." [6]

At the end of *Philoctetes*, Heracles tells Philoctetes, ". . . You/ Must win, it is ordained, through suffering/ Glory in life." [7] Like Oedipus, Philoctetes possesses special talent, and like Oedipus he suffers. Says the chorus of him, " 'Tis ever a curse for a man to be marked/ Above the common lot" (p. 170):

No other again
Has yet come near
To such misery,
Such endless pain;

Never has been
Such an agony
As the man we have seen
Has suffered here.

This fate he endures,
This wickedness,
Who had done no wrong
By force or fraud
To any on earth
His whole life long,
A lover of truth
and gentleness.

Tis a wonder to know
How patiently
Year after year,
As the days of woe
Dragged slowly on,
He has lingered here,
Listening alone
To the sound of the sea.
(pp. 185–186)

What the Chorus says of Philoctetes might also be said of that other patient sufferer, Job. Both pay grievously for the knowledge their pain brings them.

Ever since the expulsion from Eden, man's lot has been pain. Frye links Philoctetes with Adam:

In many tragedies . . . the central character survives, so that the action closes with some adjustment to a new and more mature experience. "Henceforth I learn that to obey is best," says Adam, as he and Eve go hand in hand out to the world before them. A less

clear cut but similar resolution occurs when Philoctetes, whose serpent-wound reminds us a little of
Adam, is taken off his island to enter the Trojan
war.[8]

If man is to survive, he must adjust, however painfully.

But some refuse to adjust, even at the price of survival. They court disaster for the challenge. On the model
of Prometheus they prove themselves, their worth, in unequal contest with the universe. In the Middle Ages, such
a repudiation of one's place on the great chain of being
was heretical, but some challenged nevertheless. In the
more adventuresome Renaissance, many denied the status
quo—in history: Copernicus and Galileo; in literature:
Marlowe's Tamburlaine and Faustus. After a resurgence
of orthodoxy in the seventeenth century, and a confidence
in right reason in the eighteenth, there was the reawaken-
ing of passionate striving in the nineteenth century that
we associate with Romanticism. But those authors who
approved of this challenge recorded the brevity of their
characters' success or the inevitability of their failure.

Thus it is with Melville and Ahab in *Moby-Dick*
(1851). Ahab is mad with a hubris that Starbuck calls
blasphemy, but Ahab replies:

All visible objects, man, are but as pasteboard masks.
But in each event—in the living act, the undoubted
deed—there, some unknown but still reasoning thing
puts forth the mouldings of its features from behind
the unreasoning mask. If man will strike, strike
through the mask! How can the prisoner reach outside except by thrusting through the wall? To me,
the White Whale is that wall. . . .[9]

Ahab would pit man's puny might against the whale, against the universe. He is man who cannot endure limitation, who cannot adjust to unreasoning power, who is made and doomed to failure in an unequal contest, but who is magnificent in his courage in spite of omens and in the face of death itself.[10] He is heroic in his attempt to force nature to take cognizance of man, to make the cosmos recognize the strength of man's will. And he dies like the gods of Norse mythology—and like Macbeth— in combat with the enemy he has hurt most.

We know that Melville was a voracious reader, and the vast tapestry of his novel contains threads from many mythologies—Oriental, Occidental, and especially Christian. All of these allusions enrich the novel, but some specifically involve maiming and are thus especially germane to this study: the *Pequod* leaves Nantucket on Christmas (VII, 152), the day of the winter solstice and a day appointed for the ritual combat between sacred kings and their successors. "Ahab, like the divine hero Adonis, suffered a 'seemingly inexplicable, unimaginable casualty.' . . . Like the saviour-heroes, Ahab withdrew from the world after being wounded. Only when . . . [he] began to feel the springlike breath from the south [VII, 154] did Ahab return to the world to perform his fated task." [11]

Ahab is not only like ancient Adonis; he resembles, too, the medieval Fisher King. The autumn before the *Pequod* leaves Nantucket there occurs the "inexplicable casualty" mentioned above, a doubling of the wound that deprived Ahab of his leg; as he will again be deprived of it during "The Chase."

> [Ahab] had been found one night lying prone upon the ground, and insensible, . . . his ivory limb hav-

ing been so violently displaced, that it had stake-wise smitten, and all but pierced his groin; nor was it without extreme difficulty that the agonizing wound was entirely cured. Nor . . . had it failed to enter his monomaniac mind, that all the anguish of that then present suffering was but the direct issue of a former woe; and he too plainly seemed to see, that as the most poisonous reptile of the marsh perpetuates his kind as inevitably as the sweetest songster of the grove; so, equally . . . , all miserable events do beget their like (VIII, 229–230).

The shattered leg is only one of many omens of doom. And the groin wound not only presages failure, but its agonizing nature and resistance to cure make it a counterpart to Ahab's other debility which Melville mentions in this same passage: his monomaniac mind, his hubris.

That his quest is mad, that he will not be able to "strike through the mask" and force the cosmos to heed man is symbolized by his own limitations—his great scar and missing leg. But his wound, his "dismasting," has Freudian as well as diabolical implications. The closer he comes to Moby Dick, the more Ahab abjures human relationships: he leaves behind wife and child, does not consider the lives and fortunes of his crew, denies Starbuck's aid and friendship, and finally even deserts Pip— or rather, forces Pip to desert him:

Lad, lad, I tell thee thou must not follow Ahab now. The hour is coming when Ahab would not scare thee from him, yet would not have thee by him. There is that in thee, poor lad, which I feel too curing to my malady (VIII, 316).

Ironically, as he tries to make nature recognize man, Ahab himself becomes both less humane and less human.[12]

Nor is Ahab the only one on the *Pequod* circumscribed in such a fashion—limited in motion and emotion. Perth, the ship's blacksmith, whom Ahab had earlier called "Prometheus, who made men" (VII, 237), had "a peculiar walk . . . , a certain slight but painful appearing yawing in his gait" (VIII, 254). Before he had gone to sea Perth had been a prosperous man with a wife and three children. Because of drink he had lost all—prosperity and family—and, because he had fallen into a drunken stupor in a barn one night and his feet froze, he had lost his toes, too. When Ahab questions his seeming imperviousness to the sparks that fly from his forge, Perth answers, "I am past scorching; not easily can'st thou scorch a scar." "Well, well; no more," replies Ahab. "Thy shrunk voice sounds too calmly, sanely woful to me. In no Paradise myself, I am impatient of all misery in others that is not mad" (VIII, 258). Ahab cannot accept his lot, as Perth now does his, and as Fleece, the other limper of the novel (VII, 15), also does.

Five years before *Moby–Dick* in *Typee* (1846), Melville's first "novel" and first publication of any significance, his protagonist suffered from an injured leg, as he himself endured one at the time he describes. Melville states in the book's preface that it factually recounts four months he spent in the Marquesas after deserting the whaler *Acushnet*. Tommo—a name the narrator assumes for its pronounceability by his Polynesian host-captors—is hampered by a painfully and mysteriously swollen leg. There is no apparent source for the malady (nor is the reason for Melville's sore leg known), yet it plagues Tommo for all but the penultimate period of his sweet incarceration, a period that for Melville was actually closer to one month than four. Many critics have commented on the conflict Tommo undergoes between his desire on the one hand to escape civilization and its problems for the serenity and easy sensuality of Typee; and on the other his puritanical uneasiness among the natives and ultimate fear that he is less guest than captive, fed well only to provide a cannibal feast.

D. H. Lawrence interpreted *Typee* as Melville's semi-conscious return to primitivism that failed:

> . . . He tells of his entry into the valley of the dread cannibals of Nukuheva. Down this narrow, steep, horrible dark gorge he slides and struggles as we struggle in a dream, or in the act of birth, to emerge in the green Eden of the Golden Age, the valley of the cannibal savages. This is a bit of birth-myth, or rebirth myth, on Melville's part. . . . (p. 127).

> We can't go back. And Melville couldn't. . . . Because, in the first place, it made him sick. . . . He had got something wrong with his leg, and this would not heal. It got worse and worse, during his four months on the island.

> . . . But there you are. Try to go back to the savages, and you feel as if your very soul was decomposing inside you (p. 130).

But Tommo-Melville's disappointment at not finding complete contentment in Typee Valley is only one, and the earliest, part of a life-long quest for perfection. Tommo's swollen leg seems, implicitly at least, to be a symbolic recognition of Melville that there are no paradises, that for one reason or another or in one place or another, one's happiness must be limited, tempered, and imperfect. In *Moby–Dick* he makes the statement explicitly:

> For now, since by many prolonged, repeated experiences, I have perceived that in all cases man must eventually lower, or at least shift, his conceit of attainable felicity; not placing it anywhere in the intellect or the fancy; but in the wife, the heart, the bed, the table, the saddle, the fireside, the country (VIII, 172).

Even before the ultimate recognition of evil and reconciliation to it, almost divine acceptance of it, in *Billy Budd,* there is the many-sided examination of evil in *The Confidence Man* (1857).

Guinea and Peg-leg—two cripples—are the first individuals described at any length after the opening of the novel and our meeting with the lamb-like man, and after the *Fidèle*—that "ship of fools" (XII, 17) and microcosm of humanity—has begun its voyage on the Father-of-Waters. Black Guinea is "a grotesque cripple . . . [with] something wrong about his legs," (XII, 10). Peg-leg is a white man "a limping, gimlet-eyed, sour-faced person" (XII, 12) who insists that Guinea's leg-stumps are shams, that he pretends to be a cripple for monetary gain only, and that he may even be a white man in disguise. Indeed Guinea probably is the masquerading confidence man. In a subsequent chapter the one-legged cynic is berating the vanished (or changed) Guinea and those foolish enough to give charity or credence to him or anything else. A similar set of circumstances occurs in Chapter 19.

The whole work is "a riddle wrapped in a mystery inside an enigma." It abounds in shape-shiftings, allusions literary and mythological, and puns. This much is certain: the hardships of life are complex and many, taking various forms; one of mankind's central problems is that of faith (or *confidence*) whether in self, other men, or God. Not to recognize even the existence of these problems is to go crippled in the world, or on the equally shapeshifting river without charts. Not to have any faith is to be cowardly and impotent in one's dealings with men; to expect too much is to court disaster. The middle course is essential, because man, though he can be heroic, is essentially circumscribed.

Two years after Melville had been in the Marquesas and three years before he published *Typee,* his British contemporary Charles Dickens published a view of man's life similar to Melville's and with like symbolism. Although Dickens uses Tiny Tim of *A Christmas Carol* (1843) primarily as an object of pity, a cynosure of emotion, the little cripple is also the story's—and the author's —best known symbol of the painful, blighted lives that struggle to exist in poverty. In spite of the boy's personal warmth, his maiming suggests the effects of the cold, dreariness, loneliness, and want that Scrooge sees on his visits, as opposed to the bustling warmth, love, and plenty of the Fezziwigs. One of the story's original illustrations depicted the scene at the end of Stave II, when out from under the robe of Christmas Present creep Want and Ignorance, "wretched, abject, frightful, hideous, miserable" children created by man's lack of generosity, the very sort of meanness evinced most regularly by skinflint Scrooge.[13] These children are crippled socially, Scrooge spiritually and emotionally, while Tim represents them physically.

The later decades of the nineteenth century continued to produce examples of symbolic maiming in

English-language literature on both sides of the Atlantic, in William Dean Howells' *A Modern Instance* (1882), for example, and Rudyard Kipling's "The Man Who Would Be King" (1888).

The focus of interest in Howells' novel is on the dissolution of unprincipled Bartley Hubbard and the embitterment and gradual desiccation of his impetuous wife Marcia. Although the novel is largely a study of ill-matched characters—particularly dispassionate and egotistical Bartley who provides little security for his volatile wife—these personal deficiencies are reflected by social defects: the puritanical meanness and intellectual dearth in ironically named Equity, Maine; the general decay of profound religious belief; and the frequent lack of morality in places like Boston, centers of commerce not culture, where Mammon receives more tribute than the good Samaritan.[14]

Ben Halleck, college acquaintance of Bartley's and deeply in love with Marcia, is the "good man" of the novel juxtaposed to "wicked" Bartley. Ben is noble, almost beyond belief: he was lamed by a fellow schoolboy's thoughtless prank, but he refuses to blame the culprit, either at the time of the accident or when they meet as adults; yet he considers "his being in love with her [Marcia] when she was another man's wife . . . an indelible stain" (p. 362), and so tortures himself about the morality of asking her to marry him, even after she has been deserted, divorced, and widowed. But Ben is far from perfect—as his deformity implies—even if we accept his extreme moral position (like that of several of Henry James's protagonists) of excessive self-denial and repudiation of anything that might be considered morally tainted. Ben's first flaw, in Howells' eyes, is that his self-denial is not Christian.[15] He is an agnostic, and his becoming a Calvinist minister at the novel's close is an act of moral self-discipline, not a declaration of religious vocation. But neither does Ben have a secular vocation; he finds himself unsuited for everything he turns to, "at odds with life" (p. 164), "estranged" from his parents' religion, his father's leather industry, from Boston society, and from the practice of law. As he tells his sister:

> . . . We're outside of everything, and it makes me mad, because we've got money enough to be inside . . . (p. 165).

> I had the making of a real Harvard man in me; and of a Unitarian, nicely balanced between radicalism and amateur episcopacy. Now, I am an orthodox ruin. . . . I belong nowhere; I'm at odds (p. 165).

Ben's moral dilemma over whether to ask Marcia to marry him is made more agonizing by Marcia's unworthiness. Already too emotional and unreasoning, she becomes, after Bartley's desertion, increasingly manic—hysterical one moment, withdrawn the next. Like Dobbin in Thackeray's *Vanity Fair*, who is too good for Amelia whom he finally wins, Ben would be better off not loving Marcia, let alone questioning the propriety of his feelings. Like Thackeray's novel, *A Modern Instance* lacks a hero. Both its main characters and the society it depicts are corrupted, a condition represented by Ben Halleck's lack of equilibrium in occupation, affection, and gait.[16]

Unlike Ben, who meekly accepted what life had given him, questioning only the morality of his own acts, Kipling's protagonists in "The Man Who Would be King" are more like Ahab: they challenge whatever force has made them travel less than first class. The journalist-narrator frames his story with an account of his first meeting with the protagonists, the men who would be king, but men who, when we meet them, prove to be members of the indigent class known in India as loafers:

> The beginning of everything was in a railway train. . . . There had been a Deficit in the Budget, which necessitated travelling, not Second-class, which is only half as dear as First-class, but by Intermediate, which is very awful indeed.[17]

The Loafer whom the narrator first meets, and a friend of his, show up in the press room some time later. They are Peachey Taliaferro Carnehan and Daniel Dravot, and as Dravot says:

> '. . . The less said about our professions the better, for we have been most things in our time. Soldier, sailor, compositor, photographer, proof-reader, street-preacher, and correspondents of the "Backwoodsman" when we thought the paper wanted one.'
>
> . . . [Carnehan echoes,] 'We have been all over India, mostly on foot. We have been boiler-fitters, engine-drivers, petty contractors, and all that, and we have decided that India isn't big enough for such as us.' (p. 193).

Veritable everymen (by Intermediate status and their plethora of occupations), they have decided to " 'go away to some other place where a man isn't crowded and can come to his own. We are not little men, and there is nothing we are afraid of. . . . Therefore, we are going away to be Kings.' 'Kings in our own right,' muttered Dravot" (p. 194).

From the narrator's maps and books they glean what little the world knows of Kafiristan, in northeastern Afghanistan, and on the next day they set out to conquer and rule. Three years later the narrator learns that they succeeded, for a while. With arms that they smuggled in, and a knowledge of tactics and drilling, they impress the natives and create a formidable though small army; their knowledge of Freemasonry, which has become a mystic religious cult in Kafiristan, convinces the natives that they are gods come on earth. They spread their rule, judge wisely, and teach better farming methods, till one lonely winter Dravot seeks a wife. The girl, believing him to be a god and fearful of what will undoubtedly be a fatal union, bites him when he first tries to kiss her, and draws blood, convincing the priests and assembled natives that Dravot, and Carnehan like him, is "neither God nor Devil but a man!" (p. 223).

Escape from the mob is short-lived for the two. A native loyal to them has his throat unceremoniously cut. Dravot, in spite of a bullet wound in the calf, is forced to march onto a rope bridge across a ravine.

'Out he goes, looking neither right nor left, and when he was plumb in the middle of those dizzy dancing ropes—"Cut, you beggars," he shouts; and they cut, and old Dan fell, turning round and round and round, twenty thousand miles, for he took half an hour to fall till he struck the water, and I could see his body caught on a rock with the gold crown close beside.'

'But do you know what they did to Peachey between two pine trees? They crucified him, Sir. . . . They used wooden pegs for his hands and his feet;

and he didn't die. He hung there and screamed, and they took him down the next day, and said it was a miracle that he wasn't dead' (p. 227).

So reports the narrator's informant, "what was left of a man. He was bent into a circle, his head was sunk between his shoulders, and he moved his feet one over another like a bear. I could hardly see whether he walked or crawled—this rag-wrapped, whining cripple" (pp. 201–202), who is the barely living earthly remains of Peachey Carnehan. His stigmata attest to his identity. So does the horsehide bag from which he removes "the dried, withered head of Daniel Dravot! The morning sun . . . struck the red beard and blind sunken eyes; struck, too, a heavy circlet of gold studded with raw turquoises that Carnehan placed tenderly on the battered temples" (p. 228). The next day Carnehan himself dies, his last words the first stanza of a hymn by Reginald Heber, late Bishop of Calcutta. As usually printed,[18] the hymn is titled, and its first line proclaims, "The Son of God Goes Forth to War." Peachey's version announces that "The Son of Man goes forth to war"; and he changes "A Kingly crown to gain" to "A golden crown," making the parallel closer to his own and Dravot's experiences. Bishop Heber's hymn sings the praises of warriors of meekness and forbearance, of martyrs to the Christian cause, but Kipling's story is an account of a different kind of men, bold, acquisitive, martyrs only to their own hubris.

Like Vulcan, Odin, and Weyland, they pay dearly for their power; like Christ—with whom Carnehan, at least, is identified by his crucifixion and by the hymn he sings before his death—the man who would be king, who would rise above the common lot or urge others to do the same, violates the inertia of nature and invites catastrophe. Man's natural role is limited, neither first class, nor second, but intermediate.

Finding even that niche, narrow as it may be, is problematical if one misdefines it and attempts to fit in somewhere nonetheless. Such is the difficulty of Rickie Elliot, the crippled protagonist of E. M. Forster's *The Longest Journey* (1907). Like Ben Halleck before him and Philip Carey after him, Rickie vainly seeks his proper role and function in life.

The novel opens, as Lionel Trilling notes,[19] with a discussion of appearance versus reality, a dilemma that Rickie dies without solving. Rickie—born Frederick but nicknamed Rickie by his equally lame father for the name's similarity to Rickety[20]—is a romantic. He idealizes people and situations—his wife Agnes, his teaching post at Sawston, his illegitimate half-brother Stephen—investing them with an aura they do not possess. When he becomes aware of their real failings, he is more disappointed, more discouraged, than he ought to be. Desiring what he believes to be a better, finer life, he continues to put his faith in those who are either unworthy—as Agnes is—or incapable of behaving as he believes proper.

Again, in spite of his idealized vision of nature, he does not understand nor fully appreciate nature. He recalls with nostalgia Madingley, the grove near Cambridge where he used to walk. He writes of dryads and speaks of Pan—as did Forster in his short stories—but Rickie obviously does not understand natural forces, either nature herself or men of nature, like Stephen. When Rickie insists on reforming his brother—as he once welcomed Stephen with their mother's picture, not out of love for his half-brother, but because Stephen is identified in his mind with, and is an extension of, his own beloved mother

—Stephen protests against the unreality of such conceptions: "Don't hang on me clothes that don't belong—as you did on your wife, giving her saint's robes, whereas she was simply a woman of her own sort. . . . Tear up the photographs" (p. 303). But Rickie cannot. He confuses illusion with reality; he has, as Forster implies through Rickie's deformity and Ansell's statement, a "diseased imagination" (p. 26). Stephen, on the other hand, is a natural child in many ways: illegitimate, rustic shepherd and farmer, devotee of Demeter—he keeps her portrait—and Dionysus—he's frequently drunk.

Mrs. Failing, Rickie's aunt, warns him to beware the earth. "Going back to her really is going back—throwing away the artificiality which . . . is the only good thing in life" (p. 311). Thus Mrs. Failing (characterized by her name, her insistence on practicality, her coldness, and the congenital family lameness) praises pretense, artifice, illusion—just as her brother, Rickie's father, espoused cynicism and intellectuality at the expense of passion—in contrast to the Demeter-like warmth of his wife. Rickie is aware of this contrast between himself and his brother and is disappointed when Stephen breaks a promise not to drink. He laments, "May God receive me and pardon me for trusting the earth" (p. 318), accepting Mrs. Failing's warning and saying to her at his death, "You have been right" (p. 319).

Afterwards she writes that he was "one who has failed in all he undertook; one of the thousands whose dust returns to the dust, accomplishing nothing in the interval" (p. 319). But this comment is no more true than her warning had been. Twice Rickie has saved Stephen's life—no small feat—though on the second occasion when he pushed his drunken brother off the railroad tracks, the train ran over Rickie's legs, killing him. And his short stories are published, with most of the profits going to Stephen, his wife, and their child, who bears the name of his and Rickie's mother. Rickie was crippled less by his deformed foot than by his intellectualism and distrust of nature, his own impulses, and his brother—in short, by his lack of faith in reality. He believed instead in idealized visions of love, life, marriage, and mother; but his life, in spite of its delusions, was not in vain.

Like Rickie, Philip Carey in W. Somerset Maugham's novel *Of Human Bondage* (1915) has a deformed foot, a clubfoot. But unlike his predecessor, Carey recognizes his other limitations and either adjusts to or overcomes them before his death. His greatest problem, as the title suggests, is *la condition humaine*. The title is taken from Spinoza, from the heading of the "Fourth Part" of his *Ethics:* "Of Human Bondage; or of the Strength of the Emotions." Spinoza's preface to this section begins:

> The impotence of man to govern or restrain the emotions I call "bondage," for a man who is under their control is not his own master, but is mastered by fortune, in whose power. he is, so that he is often forced to follow the worse, although he sees the better before him.[21]

Maugham's novel is about Carey's efforts to overcome this impotence which conditions his ability to deal with his other problems. Carey is tormented about his clubfoot as a child. He is orphaned at nine, and raised by an uncle and aunt who do not understand children in general or him in particular. He makes several false starts toward a profession, loses himself over a mean slut far

beneath him socially and intellectually, and loses a much
better woman because of the other. Finally, after bouts
with extreme poverty, disease, and various occupations, he
finds a profession, a wife, and a place in life—which is to
say, he finds himself.

> He accepted the deformity which had made life so
> hard for him; he knew that it had warped his char-
> acter, but now he saw also that by reason of it he
> had acquired that power of introspection which had
> given him so much delight. Without it he would
> never have had his keen appreciation of beauty, his
> passion for art and literature, and his interest in the
> varied spectacle of life. . . . Then he saw that the
> normal was the rarest thing in the world. Everyone
> had some defect, of body or of mind. . . .[22]

Carey's clubfoot, his lameness, marks the curse under
which all men suffer—the material difficulties of the
world—and an added burden that exists for all sensitive
men—the realization that they must know who they are
and what they should do with their lives, and then act
as they think they should.

Although published in 1915, *Of Human Bondage*
makes no reference to the First World War. And so before
considering in this chapter the literature produced by
that traumatic event, let me mention one more prewar
American work, Edith Wharton's *Ethan Frome* (1911).

Like E. M. Forster, Mrs. Wharton was a student of
Henry James. She was a chronicler of covert impulses and
overt actions against precisely described social settings,
and she measured precisely the distance between what
society expected and what was actually done. Her best-

known works can be divided into two general categories: those that document fashionable New York society, with its less fashionable environs; and those set in rural New England among seemingly simpler, less pretentious people. *Ethan Frome* is one of the latter.

Most artists are, of course, notably concerned with the setting in which they present their characters; Mrs. Wharton no less so. If not beatified by modern interior decorators, she is at least accorded tutelary respect for her *Decoration of Houses* (1897), and her artistic concerns are no less apparent in her fiction. Ethan Frome, her protagonist, is crippled by his environment and his upbringing long before his body is, and Mrs. Wharton emphasizes this relationship in her descriptions of that environment:

. . . When Winter shut down on Starkfield, and the village lay under a sheet of snow perpetually renewed from its pale skies, I began to see what life there— or rather its negation—must have been in Ethan Frome's young manhood.[23]

. . . We came to an orchard of starved apple-trees writhing over a hillside among outcroppings of slate that nuzzled up through the snow like animals pushing out their noses to breathe. . . .And above the fields, huddled against the white immensities of land and sky, one of those lonely New England farmhouses that make the landscape lonelier.

"That's my place," said Frome, with a sideway jerk of his lame elbow. . . . The snow had ceased, and a flash of watery sunlight exposed the house on the slope above us in all its plaintive ugliness. The black wraith of a deciduous creeper flapped from

the porch, and the thin wooden walls, under their
worn coat of paint, seemed to shiver in the wind that
had risen with the ceasing of the snow (pp. 19–20).

Pathetic fallacy, the strongly connotative names—
*Stark*field and Frome, with its suggestion of harsh angu-
larity—and the constant reminders of the season—it is
always winter in the novel, cold, harsh, with a life-killing
frost—all combine to suggest the denial of life. To these
burdens are added the puritanical nature of Starkfield
with its emphases on rectitude and responsibility. Ethan
marries his cousin Zenobia Pierce (whose appearance and
behavior belie the romanticism of her first name), even
though she is seven years his senior and unlovely, because
he is indebted to her for nursing his mother, and because
after his mother's death he fears to endure the solitude
and isolation of the lonely farm by himself. "He had often
thought since that it would not have happened if his
mother had died in spring instead of winter . . ." (Mrs.
Wharton's ellipsis, p. 70).

The only exception to Starkfield's chill is Zeena's
cousin Mattie Silver (whose name suggests her riches).
Mattie comes to live as housemaid with the Fromes, her
father having died before being able to repay some family
funds that he had embezzled. No one else will take her
in because her nearest relations having "ungrudgingly acquitted themselves of the Christian duty of returning good
for evil by giving . . . [Mattie] all the advice at their disposal, . . . they could hardly be expected to supplement
it by material aid" (p. 59). But Zeena "was tempted by
the freedom to find fault without much risk of losing her;
and so Mattie came to Starkfield" (p. 60). The girl provides the only touches of warmth in the novel, and the
only recent ones in Ethan's life: "Her wonder and his

laughter ran together like spring rills in a thaw" (p. 44).

Although he loves her, Ethan cannot escape his poverty, his marriage, his responsibilities. Alone he could perhaps run away from Starkfield, but with Mattie along, he feels that he would need money he does not have; and his personal code will not allow him to ask for it under false pretenses. Nor can he leave Zeena—though he does not love her—with only the farm for support, mortgaged as it is, barely able to provide, and that only through Ethan's enormous efforts. The extent to which his duties weigh upon him become apparent in the scene where Mattie prevails upon him to commit suicide by sledding into a tree.

Immediately before their descent, Ethan is concerned for his horse, standing cold, confused, and hungry. And as they go, Zeena's face appears to him, interposing like a wraith, almost driving him off course. They strike the tree, but Ethan, proper to a fault, has insisted on sitting in front of Mattie, in spite of the greater difficulty of steering, and his tougher body absorbs the brunt of the shock. He is roused from unconsciousness by the pained twitterings of what sounds like a mouse that he wants to help—the wounded animal is Mattie—and by his realization that he must yet feed his horse. Both survive, both terribly crippled; Ethan has failed in dying as he has failed in living.

Life does exist even in Starkfield, as is proved by dances, picnics, the love of Ned Hale and Ruth Varnum, and the warm, pleasant domesticity of the day Ethan and Mattie have when Zeena goes to town to indulge her hypochondria. But it is inaccessible to those who are crippled by convention and standards not of their own devising, by society's codes which the hypocritical avoid, but by which the strong, ironically, are caught. Had he been less strong, less conscientious, Ethan would have had much less of a problem, or none at all; had he been much stronger, more unconventional, he would have been less troubled. But his moral education was such that he spent his strength in a strait-jacket, as crippled as Rickie Elliot or Philip Carey before his body confirms it, though never aware of his social deformity.

Still another pupil of Henry James depicts several cripples, but his purpose, like Howells', is more to indict a society than any individual. Ford Madox Ford in his tetralogy—*Some Do Not . . .* (1924), *No More Parades* (1925), *A Man Could Stand Up—* (1926), and *Last Post* (1928), collectively known as *Parade's End*—discusses not only the life of Christopher Tietjens, but also and especially the times before and after World War I when Edwardian England collapsed irreparably to reveal, as Pound said, "an old bitch gone in the teeth, / . . . a botched civilization." As Ford himself says of *Parade's End,* "My subject was the public events of a decade," "the world as it culminated in the war." [24] And as Robie Macauley says of Tietjens, his nature is "synonymous with the character of an ordered, bounded, harmonious past. . . . He is, in fact, 'the last English Tory.' Mirrored in this 'clear eighteenth-century mind,' the world is an equable and logical mechanism in which God, Man and Nature have a balanced relationship." [25]

The Tietjenses of Groby, one of the largest estates in England, own numerous farms, factories, and collieries. The family is immensely wealthy, and although Christopher, as younger son, is only moderately well off, he has all the advantages of birth. He is a member of the gentry, not just a gentleman but of the "Ruling Classes," one of the "Good People." [26] Beyond that he is educated—so much so that he reads *The Encyclopaedia Britannica* to find errors in it, on the average of seven a page. He works for His Majesty's Imperial Department of Statistics, ordinarily using his brilliance to arrange statistics so as to please the government, not because he cares for the government, but because he enjoys the mental exercise. Socially he is an enormous snob. Morally he is an equally snobbish Anglican saint, against whom others may sin, but whose only retribution is to withdraw further within his holier, smarter, and better-than-thou attitude—all the more irritating to his wife because it is true.

Because he refuses to chide his wife Sylvia for her sins, she is provoked into irritating him more and more in a contest to move him to respond, at least verbally if not physically. But Tietjens—whom Ford makes likable, even admirable in spite of his plaster sainthood—will not play Sylvia's game. When the war comes, and Tietjens' juggling of statistics now means the spending of lives for political purpose, he refuses to play that game as well. All around him the last veneer of Victorian respectability peels away to reveal envy, incompetency, greedy ambition, and seven times seven sins, venial and deadly. When a banker who resents Tietjens' military service and covets Sylvia arranges to discredit Tietjens through checks incorrectly marked "overdrawn," and Tietjens passes it off to his brother Mark as a mistake, Mark is overcome: "It was to him almost unbelievable that a bank could make a mistake. One of the great banks. The props of England.

"By God! he said, 'this is the last of England . . .'" [Ford's ellipsis].[27]

In the four volumes, the examples of collapsing order and values—the confrontation between an idealism associated with the land and the past and a cynical one-upmanship of the present—are too many to enumerate. Most are presented explicitly, as is the incident of the bank check (although use of that financial detail, as Mark points out, has great symbolic weight). But other defects are alluded to symbolically, by laming. That the technique is not unconscious may be inferred from these remarks about *Parade's End* in *It Was the Nightingale:*

> . . . I needed someone, some character, in lasting tribulation—with a permanent shackle and ball on his leg . . . [Ford's ellipsis] (p. 189).

> What preyed most on the mind of the majority of not professionally military men who went through it was what was happening at home. Wounds, rain, fear, and other horrors are terrible but relatively simple matters; you either endure them or you do not. . . . But what is happening at home. . . —that is the unceasing strain! You are tied by the leg (p. 196).

Thus in *Some Do Not* . . . both the old and the new ruling classes of England, those of family and the nouveau riche, are represented as crippled.

> Both of these gentlemen were very lame: Mr. Sandbach from birth and the General [Lord Edward Campion, G.C.B., K.C.M.G. (military) D.S.O., etc."] as the result of a slight but neglected motor accident. He had practically only one vanity, the belief that he was qualified to act as his own chauffeur, and since he was both inexpert and very careless, he met with frequent accidents [as do the rich and careless drivers in *Gatsby*]. Mr. Sandbach ["the Hon. Paul Sandbach, Conservative member for the division and husband of" the general's sister] had . . . a violent manner. He had twice been suspended from

his Parliamentary duties. . . . (III, 74) [pp. 55–56].

Tietjens said that the fault lay with the times that permitted the introduction into gentlemen's company of such social swipes as Sandbach. One acted perfectly correctly, and then a dirty little beggar like that put dirty little constructions on it and ran about and bleated (III, 99) [p. 76].

But the general is little better. Both he and Sandbach are hypocrites, keeping mistresses in private, whereas Christopher, when he finally decides to leave Sylvia, lives openly with Valentine Wannop. Like Sandbach, the general puts dirty constructions on Tietjens' perfectly proper behavior, believing not only that Valentine is Christopher's mistress long before she is, but that other women are as well, that Christopher is living off Sylvia's money and spending it on Valentine, and, worst of all in the general's mind, after the undeniable fact that Christopher is brilliant, Sylvia's accusation that her husband is a Socialist. At one point he even remonstrates against Christopher exclaiming, "Damn it all, it's the first duty of a soldier—it's the first duty of all Englishmen—to be able to tell a good lie in answer to a charge" (III, 94) [p. 72].

Ford applies the mark of maiming to Sylvia, too, when she intrudes on Christopher and Valentine on Armistice night when they have decided to consummate their love. Sylvia stands at the head of the stairs in Christopher's vacant apartment—she has stripped it of furniture as she herself is living at Groby, and had not slept with Christopher for many years even when they did live together—and announces that she has cancer. For further emphasis, she falls the length of the stairs, all to destroy the mood of romance between Christopher and Valentine. "Christopher was not the sort of man who would *like* seducing a young woman whilst his wife lay dying of internal cancer. . . ." But in spite of "a very creditable faint from the top of the stairs and . . . —in spite of practice and of being as hard as nails" [*Last Post*, p. 793], all Sylvia achieves is a sprained ankle. Tietjens gives her no more than superficial attention and then goes off with Valentine. Sylvia is forced to believe that "times changed, the world changed" [p. 785].

One representation of that change—typically bloody —occurs when General Campion recklessly drives in a modern motor car out of his fog-bound driveway and cripples a horse driven surely and carefully—one could expect no less of a true landed gentleman—by Christopher Tietjens. Similarly Valentine, who was educated in the forefront of Victorian tradition by her professor father and who is a fine athlete and excellent Latinist, hurts her leg in a motorcycle accident. In *A Man Could Stand Up—* she must overthrow her Victorian upbringing as she announces to the headmistress of the school where she teaches and to her mother that she is going to live with Christopher. Tietjens must also renounce his past, for it no longer exists, if it ever did.

What he had been before, God alone knew. A Younger Son? A Perpetual Second-in-Command? Who knew. But to-day the world changed. Feudalism was finished; its last vestiges were gone. It held no place for him (IV, 462–463 [p. 668].

Perhaps the strongest expression of this change in life and condition can be seen through Mark—who is the central point of view in *Last Post*—and his objective correlative, the Groby Great Tree. Mark is the eldest son, heir to Groby, indispensable official to the Government Transport Office, and in his brother's opinion, "A 'sound' man: the archetype of all sound men" (III, 161) [p. 127]. Mark and the Groby Tree—over 200 years old, a Yorkshire landmark and symbol of the Tietjens' family [p. 733] —come down almost together. When Mark hears the politically determined terms of the Armistice, he determines never to speak or move again:

> For the betrayal of France by her Allies at the supreme moment of triumph had been a crime the news of which might well cause the end of the world to seem desirable [p. 690].

> He wanted to be out of a disgustingly inefficient and venial world. . . . [p. 740].

> . . . Mark had finished with the Ministry, with the Government, with the nation. . . [sic]. With the world [p. 778].

Doctors conclude that Mark's silence is due to a paralytic stroke, but it is not: it is willful silence—a willful withdrawal from a world that has changed and that he wants no part of—as we know when he speaks twice before he dies, once to Sylvia and once to Valentine. He dies the afternoon he hears that the Groby Great Tree has been cut down by an American to whom Sylvia has leased the estate. "In hauling out the stump . . . the woodcutters had apparently brought down two-thirds of the ball-room exterior wall and that vast, gloomy room, with its immense lustres was wrecked along with the old schoolrooms above it. . . . Christopher's boyhood bedroom had prac-

tically disappeared" [p. 801]. His world gone, Mark goes
with it.

Christopher on the other hand survives—diminished,
but still vital. Although he could take possession of Groby,
he wants no part of it. He is content as a "small producer"
in Sussex (as Ford himself was), with an antique business
besides. He has found happiness with Valentine, who is
about to bear him a child; and his son by Sylvia does not
appear to have been ruined by her. His demesne is greatly
circumscribed: he is poorer, dirtier, busier, and less intellectually engaged—but happier.

In 1924, the same year that Ford published *Some Do
Not . . . ,* Laurence Stallings published his quasi-autobio-
graphical novel *Plumes.* Better known for his collabora-
tion with Maxwell Anderson on *What Price Glory?* (also
of 1924), Stallings was a marine in the First World War
who lost a leg in the battle for Château-Thierry. His protagonist in the novel, who bears the romantic, panache-
like name of Richard Plume, is descended from a family
whose representatives have been wounded in the Revolutionary, Civil, and Spanish-American Wars. Richard has
a thigh mutilated and a knee shattered in the First World
War; after hospitalization and therapy, although he wears
leg braces, he needs crutches or heavy canes to walk. Stallings makes it clear that Richard is not alone in his
plight: there are other crippled veterans looking for jobs
in a new United States. They had gone to war as optimistic boys and returned as cynical, battle-hardened veterans intimately acquainted with death. They had left a
country unsure of its strength or its place in the world,
but they returned to a loud, clamorous, optimistic nation.
They had to adjust to the new society as much as they
did to their own maimed selves. Plume finally gets a job
in a chemical laboratory run by the federal government—

the one agency whose possible bias toward cripples Richard can lay a claim against. His supervisor, Mr. Gary, "a sallow, reed-like young man, with a face that might have worn a crown of thorns, limped from both ankles. . . ." (p. 109). Plume, like Tietjens, wrenches free from his past: he had gone to war because it had been the family tradition that a Plume always fought in the battles of the United States; Richard decides that if his son ever goes to war it will not be because he believes that *dulce et decorum est pro patria mori.*

Another leg-wounded participant in the war was Ernest Hemingway, assistant editor to Ford in publishing *the transatlantic review* in 1924, and author of *A Farewell to Arms,* which Stallings dramatized in 1930. I have discussed Hemingway's *The Sun Also Rises* (1926) in the previous chapter, but it deserves examination here, too. Certainly the world depicted is a sterile one, and the lives of most of the characters are empty and futile. Denied the fulfillment of sexual love, the marriage and children it might bring, Jake Barnes seeks gratification in drinking, fishing, and male companionship; but like Nick Adams in "Big Two-Hearted River," Jake must manage these pleasures very carefully, lest he lose control over them—and himself.

> My head started to work. The old grievance. Well it was a rotten way to be wounded and flying on a joke front like the Italian. . . . In the Ospedale Maggiore . . . that was where the liaison colonel came to visit me. . . . I was all bandaged up. But they had told him about it. Then he made a wonderful speech: "You, a foreigner, . . . have given more than your life. . . . Che mala fortuna! Che mala fortuna!

. . . I lay awake thinking and my mind jumping around. Then I couldn't keep away from it, and I started to think about Brett and all the rest of it went away. I was thinking about Brett and my mind stopped jumping around and started to go in smooth waves. Then all of a sudden I started to cry (p. 31).

In a little while I felt like hell again. It is awfully easy to be hard-boiled about everything in the daytime, but at night it is another thing (p. 34).

Jake lives in a chaotic world not of his own making, and he has been crippled by it. The only order in the world is that which Jake can impose on it. As with Romero, a symbolic counterpart whose life depends on precise, carefully controlled movements, so Jake's existence, his dignity, and his peace of mind depend on the carefully patterned response he can make to life.

. . . In the face of necessities forced upon him by the several levels of isolation (forms of impotence), Jake fashions for himself a pattern of discretion and restraint. . . . Jake must practice a code, must suppress anger and fear, must accept his condition. . . . The wound has forced him into a position where survival and sanity depend upon his balance and self-restraint.[28]

And he does make a patterned response, he does impose order. Like Count Mippipopolous, Jake has "lived very much" and has learned the secret: "to know the values" (p. 60). He has learned to value the friendship of Bill Gorton, with whom he can talk freely, drink freely, and fish, and with whom he can share the beauty of the land, the riches of nature:

> We ate the sandwiches and drank the Chablis and watched the country out of the window. The grain was just beginning to ripen and the fields were full of poppies. The pasture land was green, and there were fine trees, and sometimes big rivers and chateaux off in the trees (p. 87).

> It was a beech wood and the trees were very old. Their roots bulked above the ground and the branches were twisted. We walked on the road between the thick trunks of the old beeches and the sunlight came through the leaves in light patches on the grass. The trees were big, and the foliage was thick but it was not gloomy. . . . "This is country," Bill said (p. 117).

As Philip Young has said, Hemingway richly invokes the beauty of the eternal earth; and since Hemingway does so through Jake's point of view and narration, we are convinced that Jake does value what he sees and experiences: the land, the fishing, the comfort of good fellowship. But most important, and more privately, Jake values artistry like Romero's which, through restraint and control, imposes order on confusion and confers dignity and even beauty on the artist.

> Romero's bull-fighting gave real emotion, because he kept the absolute purity of line in his movements and always quietly and calmly let the horns pass him close each time. He did not have to emphasize

their closeness. . . . Romero had the old thing,
the holding of his purity of line through the maxi-
mum of exposure, while he dominated the bull by
making him realize he was unattainable, while he
prepared for the killing (p. 168).

Thus Jake's personal limitations, as well as the sterility of his world, are symbolized by his emasculation. And
to the extent that each of us is unable to achieve our desires, we all are to some extent impotent, limited, and
restricted. But Jake, like most of us, adjusts, survives, and
finds pleasure and enjoyment where he can; equally important, he learns rules, a code of conduct, by which—
even if he cannot always follow them—he must try to live.

Theologically, limitations have been man's lot since
Adam was driven from Eden, and since then laming has
symbolized man's plight. In the Bible, God says to the
serpent, "I will put enmity between thee and the woman,
and between thy seed and her seed; they shall bruise thy
head, and thou shalt bruise their heel" (Gen. 3:15).[29] And
to indicate the longevity of this condition and its human
ubiquity, characters who symbolize humanity by limping
have frequently been named Adam: Hemingway's Nick
Adams, Wilder's Mr. Antrobus, Isak Dinesen's Adam, and
Robert Penn Warren's Adam Rosenzweig, among others.
Ernest Hemingway's Nick Adams appears in several
volumes of short stories. He is wounded in Chapter VI
of *In Our Time* (1925); in the story "Cross Country
Snow" in the same volume, we learn that he cannot tele-
mark because of his leg. In *Men Without Women* (1927),
the unnamed narrator of "In Another Country" (apparently Nick) is receiving therapy to help him bend a stiff
knee, and other victims of the war are patients in the

same hospital, also receiving aid in an attempt to live normally in spite of their injuries. In *Winner Take Nothing* (1933), in a story significantly titled "A Way You'll Never Be," Nick suffers not only from his stiff leg but also from brain damage, or psychological injuries, sustained when he was wounded. He says to a friend, "Let's not talk about how I am. . . . It's a subject I know too much about to want to think about it any more." [30] The stories about Nick Adams, as I said in the previous chapter, are tales of initiation: Nick encounters the pains of growing up and learns what a man can and cannot do. Philip Young summarizes Nick's career thus:

> A short paragraph reveals that Nick is in the war, tells us that he has been hit in the spine, and that he has made a "separate peace" with the enemy. . . . It would be quite impossible to exaggerate the importance of this short scene, which is to be duplicated by a new protagonist named Frederic Henry in *A Farewell to Arms,* and to serve as climax for all of Hemingway's heroes for at least the next twenty-five years.
> . . . This shell that has caught Nick in the spine is of a piece with the blows he took [as a boy in Michigan]. . . . This wound . . . which is to be the wound which emasculates Jake Barnes in *The Sun Also Rises* and is to hospitalize Lt. Henry in *A Farewell to Arms,* and whose scar Col. Cantwell bears more than thirty years later in *Across the River and into the Trees,* is significant even beyond these facts. From here on in, the Hemingway hero is to be a wounded man, wounded not only physically but . . . psychically as well. . . . [Nick's] experiences have . . . crippled him, as Hemingway was also to show, as surely as his initiation to shrapnel has done.

> . . . The manhood [Nick] . . . attained was . . .
> complicated and insecure, but he was learning a code
> with which he might maneuver, though crippled,
> and he was practicing the rites which for him might
> exorcise the terrors born of the events that crippled
> him.[31]

Nick, Lt. Henry, and Jake Barnes—whose full first name,
significantly, is Jacob—must painfully adjust to life. The
kingdom of which Jake is symbolic ruler—as Jacob was
ruler of Israel—is no promised land of milk and honey,
but is instead a modern waste land [32] where man's life is
circumscribed by pain and loss, and his achievements are
limited by his limited abilities.

War and lameness figure again in Thornton Wilder's
The Skin of Our Teeth (1942), John Knowles' *A Separate
Peace* (1959), and as we saw in Chapter II, Robert Penn
Warren's *Wilderness* (1961). George Antrobus in Wilder's
play about *la condition humaine* is a metaphor for all
men. He is man, *anthropos,* and Adam: "He comes of very
old stock and has made his way up from next to nothing.
It is reported that he was once a gardener but left that
situation. . . ." [33] He is also Noah; a moralist and a lecher;
inventor of the wheel, alphabet, and multiplication tables;
and a ceaseless quester after improvement—material, mental, and spiritual. He and his family endure the glacier,
the Flood, and a war, and he returns from the last event
limping. Wilder's theme is that man faces constant crises,
many of his own making, but that he always survives by
the skin of his teeth. He survives, but he suffers pain,
anguish, and misery, and his lameness is a sign of that
suffering.

Knowles' novel is about two boys in a New England
prep school in the summer, fall, and winter of 1942. They

are approaching manhood, which at another time would mean college and jobs in a secure future, but now boys their own age are going to war and to death. Their school, which has trained thousands of boys in the humanities, is now training them for war. Part of the school is even taken over by the army. Gene, the protagonist of the novel, is an intelligent boy of better-than-average physical prowess, but his best friend Phineas possesses natural grace, daring, as well as great personal magnetism—and Gene is envious. One day when Phineas dares Gene to leap with him from a tree limb into a river, Gene jars the limb, causing Phineas to lose his balance and fall, crushing his leg on the river bank below. Phineas' wound in *A Separate Peace* is as much an unreasonable wound as any in Hemingway's works. For Phineas must learn to cope with his changed state and his hatred of Gene as much, if not more, than with the wound itself. And Gene must deal with his guilt, his love for—and his responsibility to—ungraceful, crippled Phineas. Phineas' shattered leg and its effect on the two boys echoes the way World War II has shattered their lives. The war is not only unreasonable, but it even seems unreal—a nightmare consisting of lurid accounts in the press, radio, and movies, a malicious joke perpetrated by adults, affecting the boys only by the changes it has wrought in their sequestered school. Phineas breaks his leg again and dies as a consequence, but not before he and Gene have come to terms with one another. In the process, Gene learns not to fear himself or others. Through the love, understanding, and sacrifice of Phineas, Gene makes the most important peace of all, with himself, as he grows up.

The final Adam whom I wish to discuss is the limping Adam of Isak Dinesen's "Sorrow Acre" (1942), a story which, like Wilder's play, is a metaphor for life. Dinesen makes distinct parallels between the setting of the story, a Danish farm in the eighteenth century, and the story of creation in the Bible: "The garden and the fields had been . . . [Adam's] childhood paradise"; [34] and when his uncle offers him snuff, Adam replies, "No, thank you, Uncle, it would ruin my nose to the scent of your garden, which is as fresh as the Garden of Eden, newly created." "From every tree of which," said his uncle smiling, "thou, my Adam, mayest freely eat" (p. 39). Adam's uncle is the god of this tale—he has the power of life and death over his peasants—and he teaches Adam that power brings with it responsibility, suffering, even pain. Lame Adam learns that "all that lived must suffer; the old man, whom he had judged hardly, had suffered, as he had watched his son die, and had dreaded the obliteration of his being. He himself would come to know ache, tears and remorse, and, even through these, the fulness of life" (p. 62).

Lameness, then, in these works of Hemingway, Stallings, Wilder, Knowles, and Dinesen that I have discussed in this chapter, signifies that man no longer dwells in Paradise. There is still much that he can enjoy in life, but he must earn his bread by the sweat of his brow, and sometimes his place in life through the bloodshed of others. He must know pain, deprivation, and death. He is unlike the characters in the previous chapter, in that he does not inhabit a land entirely waste and desolate. All is not pain, loss, cynicism, and despair; instead, these novels contain a realistic picture of life as most of us know it and live it. Northrop Frye depicts the condition in this fashion: "As soon as Adam falls, he enters his own created life, which is also the order of nature as we know it. The tragedy of Adam, therefore, resolves, like all other tragedies, in the manifestation of natural law. He enters a world in which existence itself is tragic. . . . (p. 213)."

As I stated before, men react to their recognition of their fate by more or less meekly enduring their lot, as do Ben Halleck, Rickie Elliot, and Ethan Frome; some, like Ahab and the men who would be kings, challenge destiny. William Faulkner writes of the latter sort of man in *Absalom, Absalom!* (1936), the story of Thomas Sutpen's grand design to alter the fate that let him be born poor white trash. Slighted by a Negro butler, Sutpen, then a poor mountain boy, dreams of building a dynasty, with a magnificent mansion set on a large plantation. He ships to Haiti and returns with twenty Negro slaves, with whom he carves a huge plantation out of Mississippi wilderness. He builds his mansion, marries a girl of good family, has children, but then the Civil War comes and the design starts to crumble. One of Sutpen's sons kills another, taxes take most of Sutpen's land, and he is killed by the poor white grandfather of a girl on whom he fathers a baby girl. His children die and his mansion burns. Nothing is left of Sutpen's grandiose schemes: of his mansion only four gutted chimneys rising from the ashes; of his dynasty, only the mulatto grandson of Sutpen's murdered son. Sutpen had gone to Haiti as a virgin, and, during a rebellion there, he received a groin wound that "came pretty near leaving him that virgin for the rest of his life too." [35] His dream to form a dynasty, his desire for a great plantation, and all his work toward both come to naught. His wound foreshadows this inevitable destruction before the forces of history, and under the curse of slavery, as do the wounds of both Benjy and Old Ben—"Benjamin, our last-born, sold into Egypt." [36]

A similar desire for place, for identity, asserts itself in Ab Snopes, in Faulkner's "Barn Burning." Ab is a horse thief and border renegade in *The Unvanquished* (1938), the briefly seen father of that modern *golem* Flem Snopes in *The Hamlet* (1940). He is treated most fully and most centrally in "Barn Burning," where he appears as a ne'er-do-well sharecropper, a Mississippi red-neck with a touch of the demonic about him. He wears a stiff black coat, his "wiry figure . . . [walks] a little stiffly from where a Confederate provost's man's musket ball had taken him in the heel on a stolen horse thirty years ago," and he loves and uses fire "as the one weapon for preservation of integrity, else breath were not worth the breathing." [37] He revenges himself by burning the barns of those he thinks wrong him, and almost every man he ever worked for "wronged" Ab. But Ab cannot change social or economic order just by violating legal order; he cannot make society admit him to a rank in its hierarchy higher than the one he earns by his labor and abilities: his pride and use of violent means are not force enough. Only Flem manages to rise within society's ranks, by playing society's game of acquisitiveness and material self-aggrandizement better than anyone else in Yoknapatawpha County; and Flem is able to do so only because, unlike his father, he never feels any compassion, integrity, or humanity. Socially, economically, he is capable and even dangerous; sexually, like Popeye in Faulkner's *Sanctuary,* he is impotent. We learn this fact from Eula's confession to Gavin in *The Town,* but it was foreshadowed in *The Hamlet*—Labove, the schoolteacher, foresees the husband that earth-mother Eula will have:

> He would be a dwarf, a gnome, without glands or desire, who would be no more a physical factor in her life than the owner's name on the fly-leaf of a book. . . . The crippled Vulcan to that Venus, who would not possess her but merely own her by the single strength which power gave, the dead power of money, wealth, gew-gaws, baubles. . . .[38]

Flem used human greed; he is for many critics the embodiment of modern commercialism that completed the sack of the Old South and its atrophying virtues—an historical process of ruin Faulkner recorded in *Absalom, Absalom!, The Sound and the Fury,* and "The Bear" (1942): "Old Ben, the two-toed bear in a land where bears with trap-ruined feet had been called Two-Toe or Three-Toe or Cripple-Foot for fifty years, [where] only Old Ben . . . had earned a name such as a human man could have worn and not been sorry." [39] Faulkner's prosopopoeia is quite deliberate—old Ben is more human than many men—and Faulkner is explicit about the symbolic value of Old Ben's maimed foot:

> . . . The boy . . . divined what his senses and intellect had not encompassed yet: that doomed wilderness whose edges were being constantly and punily gnawed at by men with plows and axes who feared it because it was wilderness, men myriad and nameless even to one another in the land where the old bear had earned a name, and through which ran not even a mortal beast but an anachronism indomitable and invincible out of an old, dead time, a phantom, epitome and apotheosis of the old, wild life which the little puny humans swarmed and hacked at in a fury of abhorrence and fear, like pygmies about the ankles of a drowsing elephant;—the old bear, solitary, indomitable, and alone; widowered, childless, and absolved of mortality—old Priam reft of his old wife and outlived all his sons.[40]

The bear, like nature which he symbolizes, is still mighty and gigantic, but he is an anachronism, a holdover from the past; and, as the men have maimed the land with their plows and axes, so they have crippled Old Ben with one of their traps. However, through the bear, the old king of the forest, and Sam Fathers, his priest, Ike McCaslin is initiated into the mysteries of woodlore and is taught self-confidence, responsibility, pride, and humility—his woodland heritage—as from his family's ledger books in their commissary store he will learn his "civilized" inheritance of shared guilt for miscegenation, incest, and slavery. Ike will attempt to atone for his grandfather's sins—at least not to incur any more sins himself—in this Genesis of the South that Faulkner tells, but at no time will Ike be as noble or dominating a figure as that crippled patriarch, Old Ben.

Ab Snopes need not have rebelled with violence. He could have suffered and borne his troubles, including his poverty and low station, enduring as Philoctetes and Job had endured. Similarly, Philip Quarles and Laura Wingfield need not have withdrawn into themselves because of their disabilities: Richard Plume, Nick Adams, Jake Barnes, and others adjusted to their plight, why couldn't Ahab and Joe Christmas? This question involves two artistic problems: the author's conception of his character's personality or disposition, and the value that the author places on rebellion for its own sake (the two problems are related insofar as the author creates a passive character or a distinctly rebellious nature, whatever the situation). Are Job and Philoctetes less "heroic" for their passivity than Satan and Prometheus are for their rebelliousness? The problem of interpretation is a weighty one, and one which must ultimately be undertaken by each reader. But by understanding the significance and tradition of the limping hero, the reader may better interpret for himself. The following provides a case in point.

William Styron's *The Long March* (1952) presents us with three views of rebellion: as seen by the authoritarian establishment, by the passionate rebel, and by the involved but relatively objective observer caught between the two. The novella is about life in a Marine training camp during the Korean War, especially as experienced by Lieutenant Culver and Captain Al Mannix, two World War II veterans who have been recalled from civilian life. Their upset and displacement, and a short mortar round that drops on a chow line and kills eight young soldiers, set the tone of the novel, its sense of uneasiness and horrible, futile waste. The balance of the story concerns a thirty-six mile forced march at night which the Colonel, "Rocky" Templeton, hopes will fuse his men into a self-confident, cohesive unit of fighting men.

The march is horrifying. Men collapse from fatigue, and a nail that has come through Mannix's boot cuts deeper and deeper into the Captain's foot. In defiance of Templeton, the embodiment of authority, whose apparent cold-blooded acceptance of eight boys' death as an unfortunate accident revolts him and whose forced march he considers compound stupidity, Mannix deliberately disobeys the Colonel's order to drop out of the march and ride back to the base, dragging his swollen, aching foot as he hobbles along first with, then behind, what remains of his men.

Culver is the story's narrator. He observes for us, he comments. But he is neither man enough to join Mannix in open rebellion against the Colonel nor to quit the march. Styron shows us Culver's thoughts as he realizes that

> . . . he was not independent enough, nor possessed of enough free will, was not *man* enough to say, to hell with it and crap out himself; . . . he was not man enough to disavow all his determination and endur-

ance and suffering, cash in his chips, and by that act flaunt his contempt of the march, the Colonel, the whole bloody Marine Corps. But he was *not* man enough, he knew, far less simply a free man; he was just a marine—as was Mannix. . . .[41]

Eugene McNamara wrote one of the first important articles on Styron's short novel, and his title, "William Styron's *Long March:* Absurdity and Authority," [42] indicates his view of Mannix's revolt. Speaking of Culver, Mc-Namara says that "the choice he thought had to be made between Mannix and Templeton was not a choice between good and evil, but only between two different kinds of men. And Mannix, as much as Culver loves him, is out of date, obsolete, dangerous. 'He was trapped like all of them in a predicament which one personal insurrection could, if anything, only make worse' [p. 56]. The Colonel must be obeyed, not because he is right, but because he is the Colonel" (*M*, p. 270). They are in a state tantamount to war, and obedience without question to orders right or wrong is the only source of order among the chaos.

In examining the novella's metaphoric patterns, Mc-Namara sees Mannix not only as an individualist but as the "old original Adam (or even Satan . . .), filled with pride and defiance. . . ." Colonel Templeton, in Mc-Namara's allegorical vision, is "a 'young ecclesiastic.' . . . He is 'priest-like,' 'tenderly contemplative,' 'a stern father,' and sometimes, flatly, 'the priest.' " The Colonel is a kind of religious leader, "Mannix remains the recalcitrant Old Adam, unconverted, unconvinced, while Culver, like another famous convert who saw the light while on a journey, is converted during the march" (*M*, p. 270).

But if Templeton is the temple, the seat of organ-

ized religion, and Culver the convert to that religion,
Mannix the rebel must be, in this play on names, the
representative of man. He is lame old Adam, and nearly
a cleft-foot, *non-serviam* Satan too, but he is also more:
he is a Christ figure.

Styron describes Mannix, his pain, his suffering, in
these terms:

> The light of dawn, a feverish pale green, had begun
> to appear, outlining on Mannix's face a twisted look
> of suffering. His eyes were closed (p. 93).

> Mannix's perpetual tread on his toe alone gave to
> his gait a ponderous, bobbing motion which re-
> sembled a man wretchedly spastic and paralyzed. It
> lent to his face too . . . an aspect of deep, almost
> prayerful passionate concentration—his eyes thrown
> skyward and lips fluttering feverishly in pain—so
> that if one did not know he was in agony one might
> imagine that he was a communicant in rapture, offer-
> ing up breaths of hot desire to the heavens (pp. 113–
> 114).

> His face with its clenched eyes and taut, drawn-down
> mouth was one of tortured and gigantic suffering
> (p. 119).

Mannix's favorite expletive is "Jesus," even specifically,
at times, "Christ on a crutch!" (p. 33). Mannix is a Jew;
he is Old Adam and the Second Adam, the Son of Man:
Jesus. The nail that pierces his foot parallels the crucifixion too closely to leave any doubt. Moreover as Caiaphas, high priest of the temple of Jerusalem, denounced
Jesus, so "the Colonel looked at him steadily for a mo-

ment, coldly. Mannix was no longer a simple doubter but the heretic, and was about to receive judgment" (p. 109). Note Styron's use of the definite article: *the* heretic; limping anti-Christ and lame,[43] scourged, thorn-crowned, speared, and crucified Christ have become one (Mannix was badly lacerated by mortar fragments during World War II and is also a mass of scars from head to swollen foot). The scene at the end of the novel between the maimed Jewish captain, who is wearing only a towel as a loin cloth, and the Negro maid, "the two of them communicating across that chasm one unspoken moment of sympathy and understanding" (p. 120), emphasizes Mannix's relationship with Christ and shows that Mannix is not just a personal rebel but a spokesman for the individual worth and human dignity of all people who have endured centuries of pain and persecution.

Styron was obviously concerned to universalize his story, to make it more than just an account of a particular contemporary event. He describes a tableau between Templeton and Mannix in the operations tent, saying that "in the morbid, comfortless light they were like classical Greek masks, made of chrome or tin, reflecting an almost theatrical disharmony" (p. 29). The march is an exodus: "Panic-stricken, limping with blisters and exhaustion, and in mutinous despair, the men fled westward, whipped on by Mannix's cries. . . . Dust billowed up and preceded them, like Egypt's pillar of cloud. . . ." (p. 99). Like ancient sacred heroes, many of whom—including Christ—served as scapegoats, Mannix "was unable to touch his heel to the ground even if he had wanted to" (p. 110).[44] Styron also says of Mannix, "He only mutilated himself by this perverse and violent rebellion" (p. 101), a comment that might apply to Hephaestus, Prometheus, and even Christ.

Mannix is a heretic and Templeton is a priest, but it is important to see Mannix's heresy in terms of Christ's, and to see Templeton as someone like Dostoyevsky's Grand Inquisitor. Templeton does represent order, and like the Grand Inquisitor's, his system is ultimately less painful than Mannix's; for Templeton does not force the men to march as Mannix does—the Colonel has provided trucks on which they can ride. And as McNamara has pointed out, Templeton's concern at times is paternal in nature. The conflict between Mannix and Templeton, then, is not merely the rebellion of an inferior against a superior, nor even that, as McNamara titles his article, of absurdity versus authority; Mannix and Templeton are "mighty opposites." They represent stable social order and the rebel who wants to change that order—a rebel whose actions in mild form produces progress, and in the extreme, anarchy—who wants to change things for the better or just to alter them for the sake of change.

Styron does not answer the question, which is more valuable, an orderly system or a rebel willing to challenge it; the answer of course involves knowing whether the rebel can indeed improve the system. One may consider Mannix's rebellion as a personal *non serviam* or a public proof of man's incontrovertible will and indomitable spirit in spite of pain. But however one decides, one must see Mannix as a descendent of Old Adam and Satan and Second Adam, as representative man, limited and limping.

The final group of works I wish to examine contains dramas in which laming symbolizes *la condition humaine,* such as *They Knew What They Wanted* (1924) by Sidney Howard (Tony's two broken legs suggest his social inept-ness and perhaps something of impotence, for his wife

Amy's child has been begotten by Joe, the foreman on his ranch); or *Dead End* (1935) by Sidney Kingsley. In the latter play, Gimpty is an architect who after six years of education cannot find employment in Depression America, and who watches the tenement slums in which he grew up warp others mentally and socially, as he is warped physically. Kingsley's title, *Dead End,* describes Gimpty's foot, as well as the street the characters live on and the destiny that awaits them. Even the play's epigraph, from Thomas Paine, underscores the protagonists' limitations: "The contrast of affluence and wretchedness is like dead and living bodies chained together." Another example from the Depression where crippling serves to figure financial limitations is Clifford Odets' *Awake and Sing* (1935): although Moe lost his leg in the First World War, it symbolizes his and the other characters' inability to dominate their environment, worrying as they do about money, love, pregnancies, politics, fulfillment, and even a place to live. The only Paradise they know is grandfather Jacob's record of Caruso singing "O Paradiso," and even that, like the lives of all of them, like Moe's leg, is shattered. And yet they try.

So does Peter Coen, whose problems are less financial than religious. Coen—Coney as he is called in Arthur Laurents' play, *Home of the Brave* (1945)—is an hysterical paralytic who cannot walk because of the guilt he experiences in reaction to the relief he felt when his friend Finch was shot and he himself escaped physical injury; and his guilt is particularly deep-seated because he associates it with his religion. Coney is a Jew who has known anti-Semitism, as a boy in Pittsburgh and in the Army:

[Coney tells his friend] I told you I heard something in the middle of the night once. Some drunken bum

across the hall from my aunt's yelling: Throw out
the dirty sheenies! . . . That was us. But I just
turned over and went back to sleep. I was used to it
by then. What the hell! I was ten. That's old for a
Jew. When I was six, my first week in school, I
stayed out for the Jewish New Year. The next day
a bunch of kids got around me and said: "Were you
in school yesterday?" I smiled and said, "No." They
wiped the smile off my face. They beat the hell out
of me. I had to get beat up a coupla more times before I learned that if you're a Jew, you stink. You're
not like other guys. You're—you're alone. You're—
you're something—strange, different. . . . Well god-
damit, you make us different, you dirty bastards!
What the hell do you want us to do? [45]

Now, guilty about leaving Finch, Coney thinks that
the prejudice of others is justified because of the revulsion
he feels against himself. His doctor tries to convince him
that all men, Jews and Gentiles, experience relief in battle
at not getting shot, that he is not particularly cowardly
or inconsiderate because he is a Jew. Coney is crippled
as much by the prejudice with which he has been incul-
cated as he is by the shock of Finch's death; like Joe
Christmas, he has been alienated and emasculated by society. A chance remark of his sergeant reveals to Coney
what the doctor had told him, psychologically convinces
him of what he had known but had not been able to believe: all men feel relief at survival; all men are alike.
Coney regains the use of his legs, shakily. He has con-
quered the prejudice that crippled him, but it has left
its mark upon him, and it still exists to maim others.

Tennessee Williams' plays have appeared in each of
the two preceding chapters because his conscious manipu-
lation of Greek mythology makes them outstanding ex-

amples of the use of the archetype of maiming. The same is true of *Sweet Bird of Youth* (1959). The play takes place in the Royal Palms Hotel on Easter Sunday, and Williams' stage directions call for a cyclorama as a backdrop on which there should be "nonrealistic projection . . . , the most important and constant being a grove of royal palm trees": [46] the sacred grove and the day of sacrifice of the sacred king. The constant theme of the play is castration: the local political machine has a young Negro castrated "to show they mean business about white women's protection in this state" (p. 90); Heavenly Finley, the girl friend of the protagonist Chance Wayne, is "cleaned and cured, . . . spayed like a dawg" (p. 103); Chance is going to be gelded by Tom Finley, Heavenly's brother; and the Princess Kosmonopolis "is really equally doomed. She can't turn back the clock any more than can Chance" (p. 122), her latest lover.

Chance is an Adonis-figure, not only because of his good looks, as Henry Popkin suggests,[47] but also because of Williams' emphasis on castration, which we have seen is part of the ritual worship of Adonis, reputedly prince of Cyprus, and his Phrygian counterpart Attis. The Princess refers specifically to Cyprus at one point (p. 104), and the narcotic she and Chance share is hashish—not Oriental opium, Mexican marijuana, or South American cocaine, but hashish, specifically of Moroccan growth. *Hashish* is an Arabic word, and "the style [of the set] is vaguely 'Moorish' " (p. 17); Williams is constantly suggesting the Mediterranean and the Middle East. Furthermore, part of the second scene of Act II is played in the Palm Garden of the hotel, and the gardens of Adonis should be familiar alike to readers of Frazer (pp. 341–347) and Weston (p. 47) or Spenser, Shakespeare, and Milton.[48] Although most have seen no more in Chance Wayne's name than that his opportunities are rapidly diminishing, one should recall that one of Frazer's favorite terms for a vegetation deity who presides over the cycle of nature is the "waxing and waning god."

One final point on the identification between Chance and Adonis. The play is set on Easter Sunday, yet several times (pp. 41, 47, 120, 122) Williams specifies a musical theme entitled "The Lament"—even though earlier in the play (p. 18) a church choir has supplied "The Alleluia Chorus." But Easter is a time of celebration, of glorification, of the Resurrection, so "The Lament" is out of place unless it is specifically for the impotent characters of this play. Yet Williams' use of symbols is rarely so narrow; they usually add mythic overtones and a sense of eternal recurrence. And "Lamentations" and "Laments" have been a part of the ritual of Adonis (cf. Frazier, 326; Weston, 37, 39–40) which extends in the form of pastoral elegy down to and beyond Shelley's "Adonais."

Not only is Chance's name symbolic, but so is the Princess's. In the original version of the stage play, she was Ariadne del Lago, the Princess Pazmezoglu.[49] Like the mythical Ariadne, she offers a route of escape to the sacred hero. During the run of the play, and in subsequent published versions, Williams changed her name to Alexandra del Lago, the Princess Kosmonopolis. Alexandra is a name Williams had used before, for Alexandra Whiteside of *Battle of Angels* (1940); it is a variant of Cassandra, and like Cassandra's, the Princess's advice and warnings to Chance go unheeded; and she is afflicted with the disease that castrates all in the "kosmonopolis," the state of the universe—age.

But even if Chance is equated with mythic Adonis, whose rituals were celebrated at times now associated with Christ (Frazer, 340, 346–349; Weston 46–47), and Easter is a time of resurrection for them both, we are still left with the question Kenneth Tynan asked in his review of the play (*New Yorker*, March 21, 1959, p. 99): Does castration equal resurrection? For Williams, in this play at least, the answer is yes, and a line from Williams' "Desire and the Black Masseur" explains why: ". . . Atonement [is] the surrender of self to violent treatment by others with the idea of thereby clearing one's self of his guilt." [50]

Chance has guilt—for his mother's lonely death, Heavenly's venereal disease and hysterectomy, and his own wasted life: like Harry of "Snows of Kilimanjaro," he has sold himself, his youth, his vitality. If he were not castrated by Tom Finley, he would be by age. So although Williams may not have prepared us to believe that Chance really desires atonement, there is no other explanation for his willing submission to castration. By refusing to flee with the Princess, by waiting for emasculation at Tom Finley's hands, Chance is showing greater strength, greater determination, greater manliness than he has ever done with his dreams of fame and fortune in Hollywood. However, Chance achieves only a very personal and psychological resurrection, at-onement only with himself (or perhaps with the audience, too), as he ironically gains in manliness at the moment he faces the loss of his manhood. Like Jake Barnes, he finally learns that one cannot capitalize forever on ephemeral good fortune, but that one—although crippled—must find within one's self reason, purpose, and method for continuing to live.

The theatre of the absurd also deals with *la condition humaine,* but its protagonists are doomed, not just to failure, but to ignoble, unheroic defeat. They cannot win, and most cannot even make grand gestures. Their defeats, for the most part, are pitiable but not tragic. Their achievements are of endurance only.

Samuel Beckett has built many of his plays and novels around "crippled, legless, paralyzed heroes," [51] mostly impotent, socially and sexually. In *Waiting for Godot* (1952 [original French publication], 1954 [first English or American edition]), Estragon is tormented by too-tight boots; in *Endgame* (1957, 1958), "a blind old man, Hamm, sits in a wheelchair. Hamm is paralyzed, and can no longer stand. . . . In two ash cans that stand by the wall are Hamm's legless parents, Nagg and Nell"; [52] in *Molloy* (1951, 1959), the title figure suffers stiffening in one leg, shortening of the other, and loss of toes; in the same novel, Moran is also crippled and suffers the loss of his son while searching for Molloy; in *The Unnameable* (1953, 1959), Mahood (manhood?) is a one-legged dervish; in *Malone Dies* (1951, 1959), bedridden Malone still clutches half a crutch, his last mode of transportation— and MacMann (son of man?), a character invented by Malone, moves by rolling along the ground; in *Eleutheria*, an unpublished play, the protagonist lies in his bed until the very end of the play; in *Act Without Words* (1957, 1958), a man is stranded on the desert, completely immobile as the play ends; in *Embers* (1959), the protagonist sits at the seashore throughout the play, musing; and in the ironically titled *Happy Days* (1961), Winnie is buried up to her breasts in the first act, up to her neck in the second. When not physically hobbled, most of Beckett's characters are extremely immobile; and, in the plays where they can or do move, their locus is very limited: *Endgame* takes place in one small room; Krapp never leaves his room. Their solitary state or age or physical condition makes normal sexual intercourse impossible—as in *Malone Dies:* "The spectacle was then offered of MacMann trying to bundle his sex into his partner's like a pillow into a pillow-slip, folding it in two and stuffing it in with his fingers. . . . Both were completely impotent." [53]

The crippled characters have usually been maimed in bicycle accidents: Nagg and Nell lost their legs in the wreck of their tandem bicycle, Molloy and Moran were injured while on bicycles, and so on. Hugh Kenner, in his study of Beckett, explains that Beckett's conception of a perfect man consists of a Cartesian philosopher on a bicycle.

> [He would be a] Cartesian Centaur, with body and mind in close harmony: the mind set on survival, mastery, and the contemplation of immutable relativities. . . , the body a reduction to the uncluttered terms of the quintessential machine. From the Beckett canon it is . . . clear that M. Godot, . . . [the] solving and transforming paragon, does not come today, but perhaps tomorrow, and that meanwhile the Molloys, Morans, and Malones of the world must shift as they can, which is to say, badly. Cartesian man deprived of his bicycle is a mere intelligence fastened to a dying animal. The Cartesian Centaur was a seventeenth-century dream, the fatal dream of being, knowing, and moving like a god. In the twentieth century he and his machine are gone, and only a desperate élan remains. . . .[54]

Man in the twentieth century, says Beckett, is an almost helpless cripple striving to make his way in an absurd universe: man cannot be, know, or move like a god; he can never perceive everything, he can move only clumsily, and all that he can do, limited man that he is, is endure. That is *la condition humaine*.

Miss Bodkin has said that the archetypal hero-figure is caught between what he is and what he would be; I have added that his dilemma, which is simply the human predicament, is frequently marked in literature by a maiming wound, and we have seen how such a wound adds to our understanding of Oedipus, the various Adams, Jake Barnes, Sutpen, and Ahab. Indeed, Ahab applies both halves of the description, aspiration and limitation, to himself: "Oh, oh, oh! how this splinter gores me now [as it did on Nantucket beach, too]! Accursed fate! that the unconquerable captain in the soul should have such a craven mate" (VIII, 350)!

Notes

1. Northrop Frye, *The Anatomy of Criticism*, p. 193.
2. Robert Graves, *The Greek Myths*, I, 87–88; Cf. Sir James Frazer, *The Golden Bough*, p. 86. Cf. also the mystical attributes that surrounded the mason's craft in the earliest days of freemasonry.
3. "Introduction," *The Short Novels of Dostoevsky* (New York, 1945), p. xv.
4. Friedrich Nietzsche, *The Birth of Tragedy*, trans. Francis Golfing (New York, 1956), p. 61.
5. Edmund Wilson, *The Wound and the Bow* (Cambridge, Mass., 1941), p. 289.
6. *Ibid.*, p. 294.
7. Sophocles, *Electra and Other Plays*, trans. E. F. Watling (London, 1953), p. 211. Subsequent quotations will be annotated in the text with page references to this edition.
8. Frye, p. 220. It is perhaps significant that the isle on which maimed Philoctetes spent ten years of festering exile was Lemnos, the fiery volcanic isle associated with Hephaestus, the one on which the god's legs were supposed to have been broken. It might also be noted that Philoctetes' father Poeas, navigator for the Argonauts, disabled Minos' bronze helot Talos by shooting it in the heel; that Philoctetes killed Paris by shooting him in the heel with Heracles' arrows after Paris had killed Achilles in similar fashion; and that Achilles' tutor Cheiron (cf. John Updike's *The Centaur* [1963] and another centaur Pholus were

also killed by Heracles' arrows, in the foot and knee, respectively. (GM, I, 318).

9. Herman Melville, *Moby–Dick or, The Whale* (New York, 1963) VII, 204. The edition referred to is the reissue by Russell & Russell of Melville's works in 16 volumes; *Moby–Dick* occupies vols. 7 & 8. All subsequent quotations in the text from Melville will refer to this edition.

10. To fly in the face of omens, as Ahab does, blasphemously to seek "vengeance on a dumb brute" (VII, 204), no doubt courts destruction. And there are parallel bits of pattern in Melville's grand design which show how close to self-destruction Ahab's quest is: Ahab and Moby Dick are much alike. They are both loners, although their kind are gregarious. Both are wounded in the "leg": Ahab lost his to Moby Dick and limps on an ivory leg carved from a sperm whale's jaw; Moby Dick has three holes punctured in his starboard fluke (doubtless by whalers), "harpoons lie all twisted and wrenched in him," and "he fantail[s] a little curious . . . before he goes down" (VII, 202). Both have wrinkled brows (VII, 202, 228, 247). And both are badly scarred, Ahab by the livid white scar that marks the right (the starboard) side of his face (VII, 152–153), Moby Dick by a crooked jaw VII, (202, 228).

11. Richard Chase, *Herman Melville* (New York, 1960), p. 44. On the same page, Chase quotes from W. H. Auden's poem "Herman Melville," describing Ahab as that "rare ambiguous monster" who "had maimed his sex."

12. Cf. D. H. Lawrence, *Studies in Classic American Literature* (London 1924), p. 124: "Melville . . . cannot accept humanity. He can't belong to humanity. Cannot." (Subsequent quotations from Lawrence in the text will be from this, the Phoenix edition.) Richard Chase, *op. cit.*, comes to similar conclusions as to Ahab's lack of humanity.

13. Scrooge is associated with the themes of cold and want in terms that suggest the chilling qualities of a winter king:

> [Scrooge is] hard and sharp as flint, from which no steel had ever struck out generous fire. . . . The cold within him froze his old features, nipped his pointed nose, shrivelled his cheek, stiffened his gait; made his eyes red, his thin lips blue. . . . A frosty rime was on his head, and on his eyebrows, and his wiry chin. He carried his own low temperature always about with him; he iced his office in the dog-days, and didn't thaw it one degree at Christmas. (*Christmas Books* [London, 1954], p. 8).

As Dickens' biographer, Edgar Johnson has noted ("A Christmas Carol," *Saturday Review*, 50 [Dec. 30, 1967], 13, 42.):

> The story is an attack on the business rapacity that was making nineteenth century England into a wasteland of satanic mills and industrial slums. . . .
> Scrooge . . . is the personification of the economic man. . . . His business philosophy and his way of life have crushed all natural affection, deformed and stunted all the warmer impulses of humanity. . . . [He is] a mere moneymaking machine, as hard and sharp as flint, as frozen as the internal ice that clutches his shriveled heart. Misled by a false conception of self-interest, Scrooge has crippled himself into bleak sterility.

14. Cf. Lionel Trilling, "W. D. Howells and the Roots of Modern Taste," *The Opposing Self* (New York, 1955), p. 82: *A Modern Instance* depicts "a change in the American character, a debilitation of the American psychic tone, the diminution of moral tension. Nothing could be more telling than Howells' description of the religious mood of the 'seventies and 'eighties, the movement from the last vestiges of faith to a genteel plausibility, the displacement of doctrine and moral strenuousness by a concern with 'social adjustment' and the amelioration of boredom."

   Cf. also William M. Gibson in his introduction to the Riverside Edition of *A Modern Instance* (Boston, 1957), p. xiii: Howells' "novel was to dramatize outwardly the effect upon a marriage of the social callousness of his age and the disruptive potential in the passional relation of the sexes." All subsequent quotations from *A Modern Instance* in the text will refer to this edition.

15. Cf. Richard Foster, "The Contemporaneity of Howells," *New England Quarterly*, XXXII (March, 1959), 58, who speaks of Ben as "charity crippled—charity without the informing sanction of religion."

16. Ben's self-doubts and the entire last section of the novel, excluding the trial scene, are esthetically dissatisfying, as if Howells himself had had trouble resolving the problem he had created. Critics as varied as Oscar Firkins *(William Dean Howells* [Harvard, 1924, reissued New York, 1963] pp. 71, 101–102), Everett Carter ("The Palpitating Divan," *English Journal*, XXXIX (May, 1950), 238), and Edwin H. Cady, have commented on the weakness of the ending, Cady *(The Road to Realism* [Syracuse, 1956] pp. 208–210) going so far as to suggest

that the illness which interrupted Howells' completion of the novel was psychosomatic, that the problem was too close to home to be solved easily and comfortably (p. 211). If so, perhaps Ben Halleck's wound is a projection of Howells' own.

17. The story was first collected in *The Phantom 'Rickshaw and Other Stories* (1888), which was then put into the *Wee Willie Winkie and Other Stories* volume of subsequent collected editions. The quotation appears on p. 183 of the Mandalay Edition (New York, 1925) to which all other quotations in the text will refer.

18. *The Hymnal: Army and Navy,* ed. Ivan L. Bennet (Washington, D. C., 1942), p. 416.

19. *E. M. Forster* (New York, 1964), p. 77.

20. E. M. Forster, *The Longest Journey* (New York, 1922), p. 34. All subsequent quotations in the text will refer to this edition.

21. Benedict de Spinoza, *Ethics*, trans. W. H. White, rev. A. H. Stirling, James Gutmann ed. (New York, 1949), p. 87.

22. W. Somerset Maugham, *Of Human Bondage* (New York, 1915), p. 756.

23. Edith Wharton, *Ethan Frome* (New York, 1911, 1939), p. 7. Subsequent quotations in the text will refer to this, the Scribner, edition.

24. *It Was the Nightingale* (London, 1934), pp. 187, 195.

25. *Parade's End*, intro. Robie Macauley (New York, 1950), p. viii.

26. *It Was the Nightingale*, p. 199.

27. Ford Madox Ford, "Some Do Not . . . ," *The Bodley Head Ford Madox Ford* (London, 1963), III, 272. This edition is the standard one of *Parade's End*, but it follows a wish of Ford's not to include the last volume, *Last Post*. Thus subsequent reference in the text will have page numbers in parentheses for the Bodley Head ed., in brackets for the complete four-in-one volume by Knopf, ed. Robie Macauley—where the quotation cited appears on p. 218.

28. Frederick J. Hoffman, *The Twenties* (New York, 1955), p. 82.

29. C. G. Jung refers to this passage from Genesis in a case study which demonstrates the psychic, as well as the literary, presence of lameness as a symbol ("Mind and Earth," *Contributions to Analytical Psychology*, trans. H. G. & Cary F. Baynes [London, 1928] pp. 102–107). Jung records that a young man suffered from severe attacks of pain near his heart, from a choking sensation, and from acute pains in his left heel. There was nothing organic to account for these symptoms. Dream analysis revealed that the young man, an army officer, had been jilted by a girl he loved and that he had repressed his true feelings,

which were now making themselves manifest as literal heart-ache and a lump in the throat *(globus hystericus)*. When he gave vent to his feelings about the loss of the girl, the officer's heartache and choking disappeared, but the pain in his heel persisted. Subsequently the patient dreamed of being bitten in the heel by a snake and becoming paralyzed. Jung interpreted the dream, and the man's previous pain, in this fashion:

> [By rejecting him,] the girl gave him a wound that crippled him and made him sick. . . . [Moreover] he had been the darling of a somewhat hysterical mother. She had sym-pathized with him, marvelled at him, and humoured him in such an exaggerated way that he never found his right place in school, where he became almost effeminate. Then later, turning suddenly to the masculine side he went away to the army, where he was able to cover his inner weak-ness by a display of "manliness." Thus, in a way, his mother had lamed him (p. 104).
>
> Apparently he [the patient] had once heard of the heel-bite of the snake [in the Bible], but had given it no thought and it was soon forgotten. Yet something in him deeply unconscious heard it and did not forget, bringing it again to the surface at a suitable moment (p. 105).
>
> It seems as though this hypothetical deeper layer of the unconscious—of the collective unconscious, as I shall now speak of it—had translated experiences with woman into the bite of a snake, and had thereby generalized them into a mythological *motif* (p. 106).

Cf. also Robert Graves' *The White Goddess*, p. 276.

30. *The Short Stories of Ernest Hemingway* (New York, 1938), p. 407.

31. Philip Young, *Ernest Hemingway* (New York, 1952), pp. 12–13, 51–52.

32. Even the Fisher King, preeminently associated as he is with sterility, does not escape at least one very different interpreta-tion. Urban T. Holmes, Jr., reads Chrétien's *Contes del Graal* as an allegory of the conversion of the Jewish Temple to Christianity, with the Grail Castle as Solomon's Temple, and the maimed Fisher King as lame Jacob, religious leader of his people ("A New Interpretation of Chrétien's *Conte del Graal*," *University of North Carolina Studies in the Romance Lan-guages and Literatures*, VIII [1948], 7–36; originally published in *Studies in Philology* XLIV [1947], 453–476).

33. Thornton Wilder, *Three Plays* (New York, 1957), p. 111.

34. *Winter's Tales* (New York, 1957), p. 34. All subsequent quota-tions from this source in the text will refer to this edition.

35. William Faulkner, *Absalom, Absalom!* (New York, 1951), p. 254.

36. *The Sound and the Fury* (New York, 1946), p. 19.

37. "Barn Burning," *Collected Stories of William Faulkner* (New York, 1950), pp. 5, 7–8.

38. William Faulkner, *The Town* (New York, 1957), p. 331.
——, *The Hamlet* (New York, 1940), p. 118.

39. *Go Down, Moses* (New York, 1942), p. 230; cf., "The big old bear with one trap-ruined foot . . . had earned for himself a name, a definite designation like a living man" (p. 193).

40. *Ibid.*, pp. 193–194. Interestingly, Priam, whom Faulkner mentions in this passage, was originally named Podarces, "bear-foot"; he was renamed Priam, "redeemed," when his sister Hesione ransomed him from slavery. And Ike McCaslin's full first name is Isaac—the son of Abraham, father of Jacob.

41. William Styron, *The Long March* (New York, 1962), p. 102. All subsequent quotations from this book will be noted in the text.

42. Eugene McNamara, "William Styron's *Long March:* Absurdity and Authority," *Western Humanities Review*, XV (1961), pp. 267–272. Subsequent quotations from this article in the text will be marked *M* to distinguish them from quotations from Styron.

43. Cf. Robert Graves' *King Jesus*, mentioned in note 4, Chapter II.

44. Cf. the discussion of the sacred foot in Chapter I; also Frazer, pp. 576–580, 592–595; and Maud Bodkin, *Archetypal Patterns in Poetry* (London, 1934), p. 21: "Our exaltation in the death of Hamlet is related in direct line of descent to the religious exultation felt by the primitive group that made sacrifice of the divine king, . . . and by the communion of . . . [his] shed blood, felt . . . life strengthened and renewed." The passage from Frazer shows the ritual scapegoat nature of Christ, as the Bible shows Him fulfilling that role politically and psychologically; as for His sacred foot, in the passage referred to in the note above, Graves repeats the phrase from Matthew 4:6 and Luke 4:11, "Lest you strike your foot against a stone," altering it to read, "Lest you strike your sacred foot against a stone."

45. Arthur Laurents, *Home of the Brave* (New York, 1946), p. 28.

46. Tennessee Williams, *Sweet Bird of Youth* (New York, 1962), p. 16. All subsequent references to this play in the text will refer to this edition.

47. "The Plays of Tennessee Williams," *Tulane Drama Review*, IV 1960), pp. 45, 48.

48. Spenser: *Colin Clout*, 1, 804; *The Faerie Queene*, II, x, 71–74;

III, vi, The Argument and cantos 29–39. Shakespeare: *I Henry VI*, I, vi, 6. Milton: *Paradise Lost*, IX, 11. 439–440.

49. *Esquire*, April 1959, p. 115.
50. *One Arm* (n.p., 1948), p. 85.
51. Martin Esslin, *The Theatre of the Absurd* (Garden City, 1961), pp. 42–43.
52. *Ibid.*, 27; in *Avant-Garde: the Experimental Theatre* (Berkeley, 1962), p. 45. Leonard Pronko mentions a Professor Lamont who suggests that Hamm is the wounded Fisher King, Clov is Parsifal, and the Holy Grail is a jar of dry cookies. Pronko disagrees with this view because he feels that the Fisher King is a scapegoat, suffering for others, while each of the characters in *Endgame* suffers only for himself. He does say, however, that he thinks the idea pregnant.
53. Samuel Beckett, *Malone Dies* (New York, 1956), p. 89.
54. Hugh Kenner, *Samuel Beckett* (New York, 1961), pp. 124, 132.

> *I stretched thy joints to make thee even feet,*
> *Yet still thou run'st more hobbling than is meet;*
> *In better dress to trim thee was my mind,*
> *But nought save homespun cloth in the house I find.*
> *In this array, 'mongst vulgars may'st thou roam;*
> *In critics' hands beware thou dost not come. . . .*
> *—Anne Bradstreet*
> *"The Author to Her Book"*

5.

Conclusion

The literary history of the limping figure, thus, begins in fertility sacrifices around the Mediterranean, where the maiming foreshadowed not dearth but plenty, and involved the preservation and transmission whole of the stuff of life. It proceeds to include the inverse of this symbolism, that of the Fisher King, whose wound, like the Devil's deformity, presages sterility and futility. Modern use includes that of the crippled figure's representation of man's lot as similarly crippled—incomplete, imperfect, and restricting. Authors like Dickens probably used maiming intuitively because of its visual rightness for their purposes; students of anthropology from Eliot through Saul Bellow have obviously chosen to maim their protagonists with full consciousness of the tradition within which they were working. As readers, it behooves us, for a more complete comprehension of the works we read, to be aware of that tradition also.

By insisting on the significance of characters' wounds, I hope that I have not distorted any of the texts I have examined. Obviously, I have scrutinized these works primarily from one critical vantage point and have not explicated them completely. But I never intended to do so. No application of a single critical theory to a given text (not even a quadripartite analytical method such as Dante's) will reveal all of a work's complexities. To do so, a close reader must use all of the critical tools at his disposal—close textual analysis, patterns of rhetoric and symbolism, studies of historic and social contexts, and biographical and psychoanalytical information among them. Had such thoroughgoing analysis been my goal, I would have selected a work, or an author's works, and subjected them to such multifaceted scrutiny. Rather, my purpose has been to identify a new tool for criticism, to polish an unknown or not fully realized facet, and thus add to our understanding of a given text. Sometimes such added understanding must be limited. In *Lady Chatterley's Lover*, although Clifford's role as a sterility figure is essential to the novel, Clifford is not the book's dominant character. In *Moby-Dick,* identifying Ahab as a limping hero is only to announce the obvious. And Eliot's Fisher King and the wounded protagonists of Hemingway have already received much critical attention. However, I think that the limping heroes in Styron's *The Long March,* in Malamud's novels, and in Williams' plays add essential, informing dimensions which, if overlooked, alter our understanding of the works in which they appear.

Clearly an author does not create a major work of art simply by including in its cast of characters a maimed figure. The presence of a limping hero in a piece of fiction tends to universalize it, but such an attempt can seem too easy or obvious. In Hemingway's *The Old Man and the Sea*, Santiago's cry, " 'Ay,' . . . just a noise such as a man might make, involuntarily, feeling the nail go through his hand and into the wood" (p. 107), is an underlining of Christ symbolism that is already quite apparent; in the same way, I think Robert Penn Warren's use of Adam Rosenzweig's deformity in *Wilderness* is too blatant. Thus, our recognition of limping heroes as such and their function in literature will augment our understanding, but maimed figures do not, by their mere presence, tell us anything about the quality of the works in which they appear.

I have tried to collect as many literary limpers as I could, as I read of them, or as they were pointed out to me—and so not especially systematically. It is difficult to number them exactly: are Thammuz, Attis, and Adonis three distinct figures, or only different names for one; are Horus and Harpocrates two or one? It does not matter; the numerical incidence of these characters, though no proof, does indicate the ubiquity of limpers and their particular density in the iconography of certain periods. Since the Classical Age, in which he originated as a literary figure, the limping hero has been most prominent in the Middle Ages and since the second half of the nineteenth century, for reasons which were noted in the introduction. There certainly have been limpers in literature at other times, but by and large they do not appear to be symbolic.

For example, there are lame characters in English Renaissance drama: Richard III, Brainworm, Rafe Damport, Cassio, and many gout-stricken elders (Falstaff included). How Richard's diabolical nature is augmented by his maimed condition I have already mentioned. Ben

Jonson might have intended the same for Brainworm (*Every Man in His Humour,* 1598) when the latter masquerades as a crippled veteran, but except as a trickster or *diabolus ex machina*—a character who turns the wheels of a creaky plot—Brainworm is not particularly devilish; he certainly does not cause sterility—just the opposite. Rafe Damport (*The Shoe-Maker's Holiday,* 1599) is a veteran of the wars who actually has been lamed. Thomas Dekker might have used Rafe, as Stallings uses Plume, as an example of a maimed man who must readjust to his old life and has great difficulty in doing so. Certainly Rafe has cause since he cannot find his wife, who at the time is being persuaded into a new marriage by a London gentleman. But Dekker does not dwell on Rafe's wound, nor on his difficulties except as they contribute suspense to the play. Rafe's lameness is no more than a "ruptured duck"—his badge of service. It would seem that most English Renaissance playwrights are not concerned with symbolism; beyond surface details there will, at most, be allegory: Nymph Eliza for Queen Elizabeth in George Peele's *The Arraignment of Paris* (1584), or the general indictment of human failings which are particularized in Johnson's plays.

Shakespeare is an exception. Michael Cassio's wound may be symbolic. We know that those left to rule at the end of Shakespeare's plays are not the grand figures, for good or bad, that their predecessors were. Malcolm is a lesser man than Macbeth, Albany than Lear, Fortinbras than Hamlet, Aufidius than Coriolanus, Ferdinand than Prospero, and Cassio than Othello. Shakespeare seems to be saying that greatness frequently leads to disorder, resulting in the orderly but mediocre inheriting the earth (a conclusion not far distant from either Nietzsche's or Bradley's about tragedy). And so perhaps Cassio's missing

leg at the end of *Othello* marks him as just such a man—
great neither in goodness nor evil, of moderate abilities
and personal magnetism—a limited man.

Oliver Goldsmith's "The Disabled Soldier" (1760),
like the character of Rafe Damport, is simply an adver-
tisement of British pluck and fortitude, highly dubious in
this soldier's case, considering his catalogue of woes and
the sorry life he has to look forward to, Goldsmith's pan-
egyric notwithstanding. Toby and Tristram Shandy pose
something of a problem, as usual (*Tristram Shandy*, 1759–
1767). Difficult as it is to separate innuendo from anything else in this "novel," Uncle Toby was wounded in
the groin by a cannon ball, much to the Widow Wadman's displeasure; and Tristram's "nose" suffers from
heredity, forceps, and window sash. Both are probably
impotent, so the Shandy family line is at an end. Indeed,
the novel ends on an instance of impotence: that of the
Shandy's bull. Yet Sterne treats the Shandys' disabilities
almost entirely for humor and as entirely personal (non-
symbolic); there is material for both tragedy and symbolism but Sterne develops neither.[1] Thus it is not until the
nineteenth century that symbolism flourishes and increasingly features maimed figures. Gout no longers serves
simply to denote—as it did with Falstaff—that a person is
well fed. As noted in Chapter III, I think we may see
symbolism as Dickens uses it in *Bleak House,* for we
know that there are several patterns of symbolism at work
in that novel: the fog and mud, Krook's junk shop known
as the Court of Chancery, Miss Flite's caged birds, the
disease that reveals the common humanity of all, and so
on.

The examples discussed in the chapter on fertility—
The Man Who Died, Brick Pollitt, Adam Rosenzweig,
Mary O'Meaghan, Sy Levin, Frank Alpine, Dr. Pep, and

Henderson—are, with the addition of the little lame balloon man, the only examples I know of maimed figures who denote fertility in twentieth-century literature. The remaining modern limpers either signify sterility or impress upon us man's limitations in contrast to his infinite desires. As Northrop Frye says, ". . . in the twentieth century, on the whole, images of descent"—images associated with hell, pain, death, or quests for "dark truths"— "are . . . in the ascendent." [2] The disillusionment that affected those who lived through the Great War and its aftermaths produced in one decade five great and influential works of art built around maimed figures who symbolized the sterility of the age or the restricted abilities of man: *The Waste Land* (1922), *The Sun Also Rises* (1926), *Point Counter Point* (1928), *Lady Chatterley's Lover* (1928), and *The Sound and the Fury* (1929). Since then limpers have continued to proliferate in novel, poem, short story, and play—especially in Theatre of the Absurd and in that European post-war literature called *Trümmerliteratur* or *Kahlschlagprosa* (literature of devastation).[3]

For writers who describe an era of disappointment, depression, despair, even self-disgust—whether their protagonists rise above such conditions or not—a maimed individual has been a particularly apt symbol.

Notes

1. That there is no symbolism, according to Earl R. Wasserman (*The Subtler Language* [Baltimore, 1959]) is the point, and is another instance of the "powerfully energetic impotence . . . [which] hangs over Sterne's novel" (p. 171). Since the public myths of the Neo-Classical age had been demolished, and the personal ones of Romanticism had not yet been invented, Wasserman feels that the Shandys' language is discursive only,

that each rides his own linguistic hobby horse, and that—without symbols—no real communication takes place. Each character lives in his own world, incidents—like Bobby's death—have different meanings for each, and nothing unites the characters' world, just as no organizational pattern unites Sterne's preeminently discursive novel.

2. "New Directions from Old," *Myth and Mythmaking*, ed. Henry A. Murray (New York, 1960), p. 127.

3. The terms are taken from Albert Soergel and Curt Hohoff, *Dichtung und Dichter der Zeit* (Düsseldorf: August Bael, 1963), II, 810. See Appendix One.

European Literature

In the previous chapters, I sought to trace the lineage and development of the limping hero, primarily in English language literature, even though his provenance in western literature is from lands around the eastern end of the Mediterranean in ages long before there was an English language. Now I intend, not to outline, but to indicate briefly some of the appearances of the maimed figure in European literature. Since my training has been primarily in the literature of Great Britain and America, with the addition of a few classics from other sources, I know of far fewer examples, but these (as well as a few Asian instances—see Meng Tsao-Yu and Zaman Khan in Appendix Two)—indicate that my general categories and treatment could well be applied to this whole body of literature.

The first instances of limping heroes I know of are in the mythology of the Middle East, divine or divinely linked characters like Attis, Jacob, and Oedipus. In Norse mythology, too, Weyland the smith, mentioned in "Deor" and the *Nibelungenlied,* is lame like Hephaestus, as are many of the metal-mining or metal-working Teutonic dwarfs such as those in the *Volsungasaga* and *Thiddriksaga*. Robert Graves, as quoted in Chapter Four, declares that lame smith-gods are a tradition from West Africa to Scandinavia (*The Greek Myths*, I, 87–88). A possible source of their deformity could be their work with fire, and conflation of their attributes with those of the Devil; their subterranean habitat would also aid this identification, as would their demonic characteristics. Certainly that contemporary of the Fisher King, Klinschor, the eunuch wizard of *Parzival*, has distinct devilish qualities.

The Fisher King, as I said in Chapter Three, was not the only maimed literary figure of the Middle Ages whose wound presaged disaster. In *The Mabinogion*, Bran's wounded foot precedes his death and the desolation of Ireland and Wales. In one version, Diarmuid's death occurs when he is gored in the thigh by a boar; in another, he is tricked by Finn mac Cool and steps on a boar's bristle, piercing his vulnerable heel. Each of Tristan's thigh wounds is ominous: the first precedes and causes his initial meeting with Isolt; the second is the occasion of his sending for her, and dying when betrayed by his wife before Isolt reaches him. With equally dire consequences, the feet of Oisin, Cuchulainn, and Math figure in Celtic and Cymbric mythology (Chapter One).

During the Renaissance, as Richard III evinces, the deformity of the Devil was the most common literary use of lameness. (Marlowe seems unaware that Tamburlaine meant, literally, Timur the lame; he does, however, get humor from Dr. Faustus' apparent loss of a leg in Act IV of *Dr. Faustus* [1589].) In 1641 Luis Vélez de Guevara published a novel entitled *El diablo cojuelo, The Little Crippled Devil*. A friend of Cervantes and author of over one hundred plays, which had an influence on Calderón and the whole tradition of heroic drama, de Guevara is best known for this novel, and through a French version of it by Alain René le Sage entitled *Le Diable boiteux,* or

Asmodeus, The Devil Upon Two Sticks (1707). Asmodeus is a small, crippled devil who is freed from the imprisonment of a sorceror by a student named Don Cleofas. The latter is fleeing from a young woman who wants to force him into marriage. In gratitude for his freedom, Asmodeus takes Don Cleofas on a tour of Madrid, revealing to him the joys and miseries, fortunes and misfortunes of those they encounter. Throughout, there is much social criticism and satirical deflation of hypocrisy. En route through Madrid, Asmodeus assumes the form of Don Cleofas to rescue a young noblewoman, and at the conclusion of the novel she marries Don Cleofas—in gratitude and, through the devil's help, love. Asmodeus identifies himself as the diabolic deity of lovers, as Cupid, no less, whose function he performs in the novel. Thus, in spite of his shape, ugly appearance, and title, he would seem to be a figure of fertility.

In the eighteenth century, limpers in English literature seem singularly unsymbolic, and so are they also in German literature of the same period. Karl Moor of Friedrich von Schiller's *Die Raüber* (*The Robbers*, 1771) denounces the century as castrated (*"Pfui, Pfui über das schlappe Kastraten-Jahrhundert . . ."* I, ii), but although this early example of German *Stürm und Drang*, this early Romantic, laments the absence of true men in the era, heroes of stature, Schiller does not symbolically objectify Karl's metaphor in the play. Three years later, Jakob Michael Reinhold Lenz has his protagonist Laüffer, in *Der Hofmeister* (*The Tutor*, 1774), castrate himself in remorse for having seduced and, as he mistakenly believes, having caused the suicide of one of his pupils. The self-mutilation is not treated as a dramatic climax; in fact relatively little is made of it. Nor does Lenz comment seriously through the act of mutilation on sexual desire in general or on the nature of teachers, as Brecht did much later.

Two decades later, Heinrich von Kleist wrote *Der zerbrochene Krug* (*The Broken Jug*, written 1806, first

produced 1808; actually *pitcher* would be a better translation than *jug*). The comedy concerns the comeuppance
of a lecherous, old, clubfooted judge named Adam, who
tries to seduce a virtuous maiden named Eve. The ploy
Richter (Judge) Adam tries to use to overcome Eve's
scruples, and keep her silence, is his threat to have her
fiancé Ruprecht drafted into military service and shipped
to the Orient. Almost caught in Eve's second-floor room
by Ruprecht, Adam leaves through her window, with Eve's
scratches on his face. In his haste to depart, he breaks the
pitcher of the play's title and also gets momentarily caught
on the trellis against the wall. Ruprecht is unable to see
Adam's face, but is able to land blows on his head before
the judge breaks loose, losing his official wig and injuring
his leg when he lands. The next day Eve's mother appears
in court to sue Ruprecht, whom she had found in Eve's
room, for the valuable broken jug. Though Adam is only
too happy to find Ruprecht immediately guilty, a judicial
examiner who is fortuitously present insists on a fair trial
and justice. Ultimately the physical evidence—Adam's
scratched face, the wig found outside Eve's window that
fits his bruised head, and the odd-shaped footprints leading to his door (which a neighbor identifies as those of the
Devil)—and Eve's testimony make it plain who the culprit
was. But again, as throughout this Age of Reason, the
author does not seem to imply that his theme is applicable
to any besides those in the play. He makes no use in the
play of the fact that it is Adam who tries to seduce Eve,
that Richter Adam has more than a bit of the old Adam
in him and is, in fact, identified with the Devil, or that
justice was corrupt and self-serving.[1] The judge's clubfoot
is nothing more than a stage device to make him all the
more repulsive as a suitor to Eve, and to make his footprints readily identifiable.

   Also in the early nineteenth century, we have in
Germany Goethe's grand opus *Faust* (1808, 1831), with

its limping Mephisto. Then there are few limpers until the flourishing of symbolism and symbolic maimed figures in midcentury, as in Melville's *Moby-Dick* (1851), Dickens' *Bleak House* (1852-1853), and the use of Arthurian material for Wagner's *Lohengrin* (1850), *Tristan und Isolde* (1865), and *Parsifal* (1882)—a return to the "matter of Britain" paralleled by Tennyson's "Morte d'Arthur" (1842) and *Idylls of the King* (1859–1888), by the Pre-Raphaelites, and by Edward Arlington Robinson's *Merlin, Lancelot,* and *Tristram* (1917, 1920, 1927).

Before, during, and after World War I, maimed figures appeared in profusion to represent their authors' view of life as sterile or, at best, severely limited. Only one example I know of suggests fertility: in Franz Werfel's play *Bockgesang* (*Goat Song*, 1921), the unseen creature— half goat, half man—who represents primitive, irresistible, Dionysiac energy. All the other crippled characters, though they may be energetic, are not divinely so, and their capabilities are severely restricted.

In Frank Wedekind's *Der Marquis von Kieth* (1900), Kieth is a lame, rough-skinned, horse-stealing opportunist whose talents are not quite equal to either his schemes or his opponents. When financially and socially ruined, Kieth rejects escape through either retreat to an asylum or suicide. He concludes that "life is a roller coaster"; he's been beaten, knows his limitations, and is down on his luck, but refuses to give up. In *Hidalla, oder Karl Hetmann der Zwergriese* (*Hidalla, or Karl Hetmann, the Dwarf-giant,* 1903), Wedekind spins a tragic fable of a crippled dwarf who preaches a Nietzschean theme of perfect man through eugenics; unfortunately, Hetmann's own deformities exclude him from anything but verbal participation in his own scheme, while the world uses him, commits him to the asylum Kieth avoided, and finally drives him to suicide.

The famous expressionist playwright Georg Kaiser

dealt with physical versus mental limitations in *Rektor Kleist (Headmaster Kleist,* 1905), whose protagonist is mentally competent but physically deformed and sexually impotent. In Kaiser's drama *Der gerettete Alkibiades (Alcibiades Saved,* 1920), Socrates is a hunchback who, in battle, picks up a thorn in his foot. Kaiser's Socrates, a source for the Brecht character and story cited in the introduction of this book, is thus twice crippled, and confounds expectations by not doing what is expected of him, avoiding ostentation and praise, and emphasizing intellect over action—not through rational choice, but forced to by pain and fear of embarrassment.

Similarly trapped is Franz Kafka's Gregor Samsa, in "The Metamorphosis" (1915). Gregor is forced into a job as traveling salesman, which he loathes, in order to support himself and his father, mother, and sister. Dominated and used by his father, trapped by his senseless, scurrying job, Gregor metamorphoses into an insect of human proportions. Crawling from his room to explain to his firm's chief clerk why he missed his morning train, Gregor causes the clerk to flee in revulsion, his mother to faint, and his father to drive him back. In his disgust, the father does not see that Gregor is now wider than he had been before, and in his haste to have his son out of his sight, propels him into his room, injuring Gregor's left side and the legs on that side, damaging one severely. Later Gregor's father immobilizes him again by injuring his back with a thrown apple.

Gregor's position can be described by a series of constricting, concentric circles. The outermost, society, restricts him with what is to him a demeaning job. His father forces that choice on Gregor in spite of his own savings and ability to work. After Gregor's metamorphosis, his range of motion and choice is limited still farther, at most to his room and sometimes to a corner under the couch, lest he discomfit his family by his disgusting appearance. His sister is the last to turn from him, but when she too does, he dies, only to be dumped out by the unsentimental charwoman, leaving the Samsas to go their own ways.

In 1922, Ernst Toller wrote his expressionistic drama *Hinkemann*, literally "limping man," though sometimes translated, for no reason I know, as *Brokenbrow*. Eugene Hinkemann is not actually lame—in fact his physique and general appearance are excellent—but like Jake Barnes, he was emasculated by a war wound. Afraid of losing his wife when all that he can provide—besides love and his need of her—is food and shelter, Hinkemann takes the only job he can in the shattered economy of postwar Germany, a fake strongman who bites rats' throats and drinks their blood for the titillation of the public. Says the showman who hires him: "The public likes *blood*. Plenty of it. . . . Spells success in my business." Then when introducing Hinkemann, the showman calls him "the strong man of the Empire. . . . Devours live rats and mice before the very eyes of our esteemed public. The hero of the civilized world." [2] Hinkemann presumably, like Toller himself, had gone to war with youthful enthusiasm and dreams of militaristic glory, but returns disillusioned, broken in body, and pessimistic in outlook. For Toller, who wrote the play during a five-year jail term for political activism, the rats Hinkemann bleeds alive symbolize the common men who are bled in war and daily life by the capitalists who profit by their labors. Less Communist than apostle of brotherhood, though jailed as a Communist, Toller mocks the too-simple answers of the Communist spokesman in the play, Unbeschwert (light of conscience). Hinkemann tells him:

> What a change there'd have to be before you could build a better world. You fight the bosses; . . . but you're every bit as bad as they are:

Men stand alone;
A great pit opens where there is no help,
And in the sky there is no happiness,
The trees are thick with mockery
And the waves make fun of me.
There is a choking darkness, without love.
No help for me, no help.   (p. 179)

The play began with Hinkemann's killing, to put out of its misery, a bird that had been blinded to make it sing better; it ends with Hinkemann, who has threatened to commit suicide, failing to do so. His wife, Margaret, ashamed of having deceived him, does commit suicide. And Hinkemann, who has defined living as "only being hurt and wanting to go on" (p. 191), is left alone, unloved, unmanned.

In 1923, Ettore Schmitz, a Triestine paint manufacturer, witnessed the publication of the third novel, *La coscienza di Zeno (The Confessions of Zeno),* by his nom de plume and alter ego Italo Svevo. The novel is much less pessimistic than the works of Kafka and Toller just discussed, and Zeno's wounds are psychosomatic. Cast in form of quasi-self-analysis—"fictional" confessions by Zeno to his analyst—Zeno's pains, cramps, and maladies assume special significance. His lameness begins with a chance meeting with a friend, crippled with rheumatism, who informs him that fifty-four muscles are involved in every step one takes. Valetudinarian that he is, Zeno is fascinated: "I could not of course distinguish all its fifty-four parts, but I discovered something terrifically complicated which seemed to get out of order directly I began thinking of it. I limped as I left the café, and for several days afterwards walking became a burden to me. . . ." [3] Thereafter Zeno limps when he discovers that he has a rival for the affection of the girl he desires (pp. 106–110), is smitten in hip and arm when the same rival ridicules him before the girl (p. 133), suffers a pain in his side (like Levin's pain in *A New Life*) when deceiving his wife with his mistress, and at the end of the novel, having despaired of the psychiatrist, is still seeking relief from his miseries from a physician (p. 391).

The explanations for Zeno's hypochondria are clear. One day in swatting a fly he only injures it, and later he sees it standing awkwardly on one maimed leg, trying to clean its wings with its hind legs, falling over, and repeating the process.

> . . . In cleaning its wings so persistently the insect showed that it did not know which was the wounded limb. Secondly, its persistent efforts showed that it assumed health to be the portion of everyone, and that though we have lost it we shall certainly find it again. These errors are quite excusable in an insect which only lives for one season and has no time to learn by experience (p. 103).

But Zeno is a man, much older, much wiser. He assumes that health is not the portion of everyone. To the contrary, he says that "life is like a little disease" (p. 410). Such a disease is not, as P. N. Furbank says, just "an embodiment of the moral order, following its own obscure purposes, always ready at its own chosen time to intervene and punish him," [4] although Zeno does punish himself, as he does with his mistress, when no one else seems about to do so. Rather Zeno's pains are an expression of his view of man's limited possibilities in life: "The law of nature does not confer the right to be happy, on the contrary, it condemns us to pain and suffering" (p. 346). And not only is Zeno willing, like his namesake the Stoic philosopher, to endure such pain, but when he has no physical woes to confirm his expectations, he invents some.

Nor is this hypochondria depressing, for Zeno is a delightful character. His statement "as I looked back over my life and my malady, I felt that I loved and understood them both" (p. 395) may not be entirely true for Zeno, but it approaches the truth for us. Zeno accepts his human limitations, which he sees in terms of poor health, and because of this acceptance, triumphs in his own small way and enjoys his life.

Another triumph of sorts occurs in Bertolt Brecht's *Mann ist Mann (Man Equals Man,* 1926). This complex, expressionistic play criticizes British imperialism in India, while demonstrating—the point of the title—that soldiers, men, are interchangeable, and that with sufficient, proper conditioning, any man can replace any other. A secondary plot theme involves Sergeant Fairchild, nicknamed "Bloody Five," "the Devil of Kilkoa," "the human typhoon," because "once in a while he takes someone who gives him the wrong name at roll-call, wraps him in six square feet of canvas, and rolls him under the feet of his elephants." [5] Bloody Five is the toughest man in the army, a terror to his men and a source of pride to himself, until it rains—then he turns completely sensuous, visiting whore houses and disregarding the military till the rain ceases, much to his subsequent shame. To preserve his name and reputation, and to be sure of maintaining self-control, Bloody Five castrates himself:

Here's a rope. Here's an army pistol. . . . Rebels are always shot. It's as simple as that! "Pack your bag now, Johnny!" No girl in the world will ever cost me a penny again! That's it. It's as simple as that. I needn't even take my pipe out of my mouth. I hereby assume my responsibilities. I must do it— to remain Bloody Five. Fire! (pp. 139–140)

The playwright's own reaction to Fairchild's self-mutilation is ambiguous. The social educator admires the act of self-discipline, rational control over irrational impulse, but the artist is shocked by this violent act of repression, especially when committed in defense of a name, an image.[6]

Brecht's reaction to violence, his sense that it is necessary for social change in a corrupt world, becomes less ambiguous with time. In 1929 he saw produced, to the accompaniment of music by Paul Hindemith, *Das Badener Lehrstück vom Einverstandnis* (the title is translated by Martin Esslin as *The Didactic Play of Baden on Consent;* a translation of the play by Gerhard Nellhaus was entitled simply *The Lesson*).[7] The play itself deals with the historical necessity for death and sacrifice; the cause for bloodshed is explained in a "comic interlude" entitled "Does Man Help Man?" The answer—demonstrated by having two clowns dismantle a third, sawing off one leg, then the other, unscrewing an ear, removing the arms, and finally the head—is No. Finally in *Der Hofmeister* (1950), Brecht revised Lenz's play of the eighteenth century to attack Germany's teachers as emasculated and gutless. When sexually competent, Brecht's Laüffer is harassed, abused, and poorly paid. Like Bloody Five, he castrates himself to remove temptation and protect himself professionally; after his mutilation he is socially accepted and even encouraged to marry the second of his pupils whom he has seduced, or who has seduced him. Brecht's satire is against the social system that encourages docility and lack of personal freedom—an ironic attack considering Brecht's own political affiliations, but within the play such meaning is obviously his intent. A similar attack on personal weakness, weakness symbolized by the artificial leg of still another tutor, occurs in Halldór Laxness' *Independent People* (1934–1935). The unnamed tutor who seduces Sola is tubercular, a drunkard, and a parasite who begs his living much of the time. Unlike Sola and her father, who are strong enough to endure Iceland's hardships, the tutor is not an independent person. A third European with Communist affiliations, André Malraux, published at this time *The Royal Way* (1930), in which Perken's inner corruption and lack of sustaining values are symbolized by his gangrenous, rotting leg.

Brecht's *Lehrstück* in 1929 is only one of several German works dealing with maiming in that year, the year of Hemingway's wounded Lt. Henry in *Farewell to Arms*, of castrated Benjy in Faulkner's *The Sound and the Fury*, of crippled Lord Chatterley in the first public edition of Lawrence's *Lady Chatterley's Lover*. Beside Brecht in Germany, that year, there was Alfred Döblin, whose stream-of-consciousness novel *Alexanderplatz Berlin (Berlin Alexanderplatz* in most English versions) follows the proletarian existence of Franz Biberkopf—furniture maker, cement worker, pimp, thief, and newsboy—against the background of Berlin. Franz's impotence in Book I is symbolic of his self-delusion and lack of self-control; and these hidden, private deficiencies are objectified by Franz's later loss of an arm and then subsequent complete loss of rationality and commitment to an asylum. Insanity, impotence, castration, and death are constant symbols in German authors' portraits of their own country.

Still another German author to use maiming was Thomas Mann. As early as 1897, Mann had suggested social incapacity through physical deformity in *Der kleine Herr Friedemann (Little Herr Friedemann)*. Johannes Friedemann's "pigeon breast, humped back, disproportionately long arms, . . . with the strut deformed people often have" [8] make him extremely cautious in opening his life to anyone else, repulsive to the one person he turns to for love. Rebuffed, he drowns himself. In Mann's *Buddenbrooks* (1901), the family, which gives the novel its name and represents Germany's wealthy burgher class, progressively decays, losing morals, wealth, influence, health, happiness, and even members. The second last of the male Buddenbrooks, Christian, limps because of severe neuritis and is confined by his wife to a mental institution. The last male Buddenbrook, Hanno, suffers from decaying teeth—an objective correlative in several of Mann's works for spiritual decay—and dies of typhoid, "a form of dissolution, the garment, as it were, of death." [9] Thus we see Mann's use of maiming to indicate sterility; in 1929 appeared the first of two works in which he used it as a specific symbol of diabolism.

In "Mario and the Magician" (1929), Cipolla, the magician of the title, is a perverted mesmerist. Although there is no explicit evidence that the story is allegorical rather than symbolic, Cipolla is a Fascist demagogue whose career, even prophetically, parallels Mussolini's in some ways.[10] Cipolla is a Platonic portrait of evil whose malignancies are made manifest in his rotten teeth, his hunchback, his lameness, and his homosexuality. Moreover, Cipolla's excessive drinking and smoking serve as the fuels for his infernal power. In the story, Mann reinforces limping as a sign of evil—self-centered, destructive evil—by describing how a local boy, Fuggerio, has his toe pinched by a crab:

[Fuggerio was] a repulsive youngster whose sunburn had made disgusting raw sores on his shoulders. He outdid anything I have ever seen for ill-breeding, refractoriness, and temper and was a great coward to boot. . . . A sand-crab pinched his toe in the water, and the minute injury made him set up a cry of heroic proportions—the shout of an antique hero in his agony—that pierced one to the marrow and called up visions of some frightful tragedy. Evidently he considered himself not only wounded, but poisoned as well.[11]

Later Fuggerio makes the townspeople feel that a national indignity is done to them when the narrator's eight-year-old daughter takes her bathing suit off to rinse it clean on the public beach. Thus Mann reduces the plight of wounded Achilles and poisoned Heracles to that of a boy whose toe is pinched by a crab, and Italian super-patriotism to an incident about a nude child, a bitterly satiric comment on Fascist megalomania and Mussolini's plans for restoring to Italy the grandeur of the Roman Empire. He also has Cipolla shot by Mario, a waiter, whom the magician publicly ridicules.

Again, in the thirteenth chapter of *Dr. Faustus* (1947), Mann uses lameness as a sign of demonism for Schlepp-fuss, Adrian Leverkühn's theology instructor at Halle. Schleppfuss, who dresses in black, has pointed teeth, and is remembered by the novel's narrator as dragging one foot when he walked, is an *advocatus diaboli* who impresses on Leverkühn the nature of evil and the role of women as tempters. For Leverkühn, there are two women who are important in his life: Hanne—the earth mother and stable-girl whose bare feet were caked with dung and who introduced the great composer-to-be to polyphony in music through the singing of rounds—and the Leipzig whore who gives him the syphilis that inspires and destroys him.[12] There is a somewhat similar case in the composer Herr Kuhn in Herman Hesse's *Gertrud* (1910), whose crippled leg is an incentive to his creativity in music.

After the second world war, as after the first, many mutilated victims appeared in the literature of the times as symbols of maimed survivors of the conflict and of the land itself laid waste. Among the first to develop this practice was the short-lived Wolfgang Borchert. His story "Three Dark Kings"[13] is a modern telling of the Gift of the Magi. The nameless Joseph and Mary of this tale, and their new-born infant, live in a freezing postwar ruin.

The Magi are three wanderers—old soldiers, wounded, homeless, without shelter or food—who are drawn, not by a star, for the sky is devoid of moon or stars, but by the little family's pitiful fire. No gold, frankincense, and myrrh have they to offer as gifts, but only two yellow bonbons, some tobacco, and a wooden donkey that took seven months to carve. One of the three soldiers trembles constantly from shell shock, one has no hands, and the donkey-carver's feet are badly swollen due to hunger-caused edema. These are dark kings, indeed, fit for a dark nativity in a desolate age. But yet these men give what they can and share the little family's fire. On this bleak Christmas day, against "Joseph's" refrain that he wishes he had someone to punch in the face, the actual humanity of these people stands out like the little fire, a spot of light and warmth amidst waste and ruin.

Borchert's fame, however, rests on his play *Draussen vor der Tür* (*Outside the Door*, 1947).[14] In this expressionistic drama, originally written for radio, Beckmann returns to Germany from the Russian front where "he has waited outside in the cold for a thousand days. And as entrance fee he's paid with his knee-cap" (p. 78). He tries suicide by drowning—"I couldn't bear it any longer. This limping and lumping it" (p. 85)—but the river wants no part of him and throws him back. A woman takes him in, shares her absent husband's clothes, and is willing to share her bed, too, with Beckmann, only to have her husband, a one-legged corporal, return. Says Beckmann, "I want a night's sleep without cripples" (p. 91); "Shall I go on living? Shall I go on limping . . . ?" (p. 122). Finally Beckmann comes to realize that he, too, is less than whole; like those who deny him, he has murdered, as well as being driven to self-murder.

The same realization pervades Heinrich Böll's novel *Der Zug war pünktlich* (*The Train Was on Time*, 1949).[15] The protagonist, Andreas, who has been wounded in the leg long before the novel opens and who later dreams ominously of being legless (pp. 39–40), is on his way from leave in Paris to the Russian front. At the train's last stop, in Lvov, he meets a whore who confesses to him that she spies on her German clients for the Polish resistance. Like Beckmann (whose first name we never know, just as we never learn Andreas' last name), the girl says, ". . . It's all so senseless. Everywhere innocent people are being killed. Everywhere—and by us too" (p. 113). She promises to lead Andreas and his companions to safety, to "a place where we can live in freedom" (p. 140), then takes them in the car of a German general with whom she was to have spent the night to where they all, she included, are machine-gunned by partisans.

Böll's book of short stories, *Wanderer, kommst du nach Spa . . .* , (1950) [16] is ironically titled, for most of the stories deal with people who were war-wounded; sickness unto death seems normal, not health resorts. Of the stories, those specifically concerning leg wounds are the title story, "On the Bridge," "The Farewell," "My Expensive Leg," and "Lohengrin's Death." None of the protagonists of these expressionistic tales has a name except Grini (Lohengrin) Becker of the last named, and his fate is fairly typical, as is Böll's irony in his choice of the boy's romantic name. Grini nearly loses both legs when the moving train from which he is stealing coal (to sell on the black market) runs over him. While he worries about his hungry younger brothers and whether he will have to tell hospital authorities where his father and older brother are, he dies of loss of blood and an overdose of anaesthetic; meanwhile the tired and overworked doctor wonders if his colleague has been arrested with the streptomycin which they have been denying patients to sell on the black market.

No famous knight-errant here, rather an ill-fated grimy urchin. The closest we come to chivalry is in "On the

Bridge," where a crippled war veteran refuses to include
certain pedestrians, especially one pretty girl, in his count
of traffic across the bridge. Reacting against mechanization
and unhuman precision, the counter preserves the girl's
individuality, and asserts his own, by not making just
a statistic of her. But his personal act does no violence
to the status quo: his figures are recorded with a certain
percentage allowed for error.

Postwar Germany, says Böll, is a convalescent ward:
many of the injured are ambulatory, though all bear
scars of havoc. Today when we think of holocaust literature, we tend to think only of the victims of Belsen,
Auschwitz, and Buchenwald. Böll reminds us that all of
Germany—German soldiers, too—suffered.

Friedrich Dürrenmatt, the Swiss playwright, treats
the same theme in his radio play *Stranitzky und der
Nationalheld* ("Stranitzky and the National Hero," 1952).
Stranitzky, a former soccer champion, is a legless veteran
who is pushed around on a wagon by another former
athlete, blinded in war. They are visited by the head of
their mythical state, who comes to their part of the country only because leprosy has broken out in the capital.
Stranitzky speaks to him for the veterans, who, as victims
of politics, want to rule, but Stranitzky's words go cen-
sored over the radio and television, making his followers
believe that he has deceived them; and they turn on him.
In flight, he and his blind source of mobility fall into a
canal and drown. Against strange sound effects, absurd
events, devices used for shock, Dürrenmatt depicts an
inferno of sickness and injury, deception and mistrust,
and lack of concern.

In his most famous play, *Der Besuch der alten Dame
(The Visit of the Old Lady,* 1956), Dürrenmatt again in-
vestigates deceit and lack of compassion. The play tells
of the return to her hometown by the richest woman in
the world, Claire Zachanassian. Nearly forty years before,

Claire and Anton Ill were lovers. When she became pregnant by him, he bribed two friends with a bottle of schnapps to swear before a judge that Claire was a whore, that they had slept with her many times. So, free from her, Ill married the daughter of the well-to-do town grocer, and Claire became the whore she was accused of being. Her child died, but in the whore house she met, then married, the billionaire Zachanassian. For years preceding the action of the play she has so manipulated the economy of the area that the town, Güllen, has become bankrupt. Now she will restore the town and bestow a fortune on each of its citizens besides, in return for one thing: justice—the death of Anton Ill. The townspeople protest that justice, their honor, cannot be purchased, but two acts later, they kill Ill.

Dürrenmatt's bitter satire on the availability, at a price, of honor and justice is accompanied throughout by appropriate symbolism. *Güllen* means sewage, liquid waste. The pun on Ill's name, bilingual though it is, is obvious; and his two friends who swore falsely at Claire's trial have been tracked down by her and have been punished by being blinded and castrated. Claire, a *diabola ex machina,* has demonic red hair and a limp—she lost her left leg in an automobile accident, her right hand in an airplane crash; both have been replaced by artificial limbs.[17] The immediate causes of crippling here are modern and mechanical; the ultimate ones are age-old: selfishness and lack of love.

A final short story is the last nondramatic example I want to cite in this brief survey. In Ilse Aichinger's "Der Gefesselte" ("The Bound Man," 1953), a man is attacked and robbed by thieves who leave him so tied that he can move his limbs only slightly. He hobbles along and soon he learns to do so with such grace that a circus hires and exhibits him. In spite of his bonds, his move-

ments become so deft and graceful that he wins respect
and even love. But when he faces a wolf in a stunt that
the circus has arranged, the woman who cares for him
slashes his ropes in fear for his safety, and he moves blun-
deringly and awkwardly, so much so that, although he
could subdue a wolf while bound, he must now shoot
the wolf to save himself. Miss Aichinger's parable is open
to several interpretations, one of which would undoubtedly
be that when man recognizes his limitations and adjusts
his life accordingly, he can act well, as Jake Barnes does
(or even courageously, as Hemingway defines it: grace
under pressure). When he ignores his bonds or struggles
against them, when he pretends that he is not limited,
man can only flounder about awkwardly.

This view of man's state as ultimately crippled also
informs much of absurdist drama. We have seen it expressed in the plays of Beckett, in his lame, legless, and
immobile characters. The same sense of malaise, of maiming as a symbol of, at best, limitation, at worst, futility
and sterility, occurs in the plays of Arthur Adamov and
Boris Vian.

In Adamov's *La Grande et la petite Manoeuvre*
(1953), the main character, known simply as *le mutilé*
is "a legless, armless cripple on a pushcart, [who] is kicked
into the road by the woman he adores, to be crushed by
the crowd." [18] A compulsive masochist, *le mutilé*
hears inner voices, in response to whose commands he
loses his limbs. In contrast to *le mutilé* is *le militant,* a
political activist who seeks to overthrow the cruel dicta-
torship of the land in which both characters live. But
eventually *le militant* admits that, in spite of the nobility
of his intentions, he has caused terror and death, even
the death of his own child. The small actions of *le mutilé*
in the play are dwarfed by those of *le militant,* whose
revolutionary activities are symbolic of the plight of

humanity itself, causing evil in the name of good. Both
le mutilé and *le militant* are, as Esslin says, crippled by
their "incapacity for love" (pp. 57–59).

Another of Adamov's plays, significantly titled *Tous
Contre Tous* (1953), also deals with politics, love, and
death. In a country where foreign war refugees are all
easily marked by a limp, the play's protagonist,

> . . . Jean Rist, loses his wife to one of the refugees
> and becomes a demagogue ranting against them. For
> one brief moment he is in power, but when the wheel
> of political fortune turns and the persecutors become
> the persecuted, he escapes arrest by assuming a limp
> himself and pretending to be a refugee. He lives in
> obscurity, upheld by the love of a refugee girl. When
> there is another upheaval and the refugees are again
> persecuted, he might perhaps escape death by de-
> claring his true identity. But in confirming that he is
> the well-known hater of refugees, he would lose the
> love of the girl. He refuses to do so, and goes to his
> death.[19]

"Shibboleth" has been transformed into a limp, and
people are still judged by externals; *Tous Contre Tous*
deals with prejudice as did *Light in August* and *Home
of the Brave,* with those forces of suspicion and ruthlessness that do indeed make "all against all."

Finally, Boris Vian objectified this ruthlessness in
his absurdist drama *Les Bâtisseurs d'Empire (The Empire
Builders,* 1959).[20] The characters of Vian's play, presumably the empire builders of the title, are obviously members of the bourgeoisie. Although we never learn Father's
occupation, if any (we also never learn his last name),
the only empire we can associate him with is that of the
middle class, for instead of building an empire, aggrandiz-

ing territory, we see the family losing ground as it moves ever-higher in a tenement into ever-smaller apartments. The stimulus for their retreats is a noise just outside their circle of existence, an ominous sound "that is frightening to hear but difficult to describe. A deep reverberating noise with overtones of shrill throbbing" (pp. 7–8). The only actions Father takes to accompany the family's withdrawals are to make empty, bombastic speeches; to repress any memory of when things were better, in order better to accommodate himself to what is; and to hastily nail up each new entry way to prevent the source of the noise from entering—in fact Father's speedy self-seclusion on two occasions shuts out first his daughter, then his wife.

Father does not repress all his hostility, however. In each successively smaller apartment the family encounters, waiting, what is identified in the dramatis personae as a "schmürz"; "It is completely wrapped up in bandages, and dressed in rags. One of its arms is in a sling. It is holding a walking stick in its free hand. It limps, bleeds, and is ugly to look at" (p. 8). And frequently, in whatever-sized abode, Father beats, kicks, chokes, or even shoots the schmürz, dispassionately, as one might pick lint off a sleeve while talking. Obviously, the schmürz—whose name derives from the German word for pain—is a scapegoat, a symbol of suffering. For although the schmürz that last confronts Father dies just before the end of the play, others appear at the very end, after Father's apparent demise while saying, "I didn't know . . . Forgive me . . . I didn't know . . ." (p. 76, Vian's ellipses). One's suffering may end, particularly upon realizing one's self-involvement and seeking forgiveness, but humanity's pain continues.

These examples from European literature, obviously not balanced nationally, do indicate the international ubiquity of the limping hero. They also confirm the truism that artists the world over use like symbolism for like

situations. And, finally, they show how the maimed figure
—especially in the literarily self-conscious twentieth century—can indicate fertility or its opposite, but how, after
two devastating world wars, he most often stands for the
latter: sterility or human limitation.

Notes

1. The only scholar whom I found to disagree is Jack D. Zipes,
   The Reader's Encyclopedia of World Drama, ed. John Gassner
   and Edward Quinn (New York, 1969), p. 88. Zipes believes that
   Kleist "renders an original interpretation of paradise and original sin. Adam and Eve are expelled from paradise, not because
   they eat from the tree of knowledge, but because they refuse
   to acknowledge what they know." However, Eve's refusal to
   testify ("acknowledge") is only temporary, and when Richter
   Adam is expelled at the end, she is restored to her lover Ruprecht, presumably a paradise of sorts.
2. *Hinkemann,* trans. Vera Mendel, *Seven Plays* by Ernst Toller
   (London, 1935), pp. 166, 168. All subsequent quotations from
   this play will be taken from this edition.
3. Italo Svevo, *The Confessions of Zeno,* trans. Beryl de Zoete
   (New York, 1930), p. 102. All subsequent quotations or references will be to this edition.
4. P. N. Furbank, *Italo Svevo* (Berkeley, 1966), p. 180.
5. Bertolt Brecht, *Seven Plays,* ed. Eric Bentley (New York, 1961),
   "A Man's a Man," trans. Eric Bentley, p. 99. Subsequent quotations from this play refer to this edition.
6. See Martin Esslin's discussion of this ambivalence in *Brecht:
   A Choice of Evils* (London, 1959), pp. 218, 221–222.
7. Bertolt Brecht, *The Lesson,* trans. Gerhard Nellhaus, *The Harvard Advocate,* CXXXIV (February 1951), 2–9.
8. Thomas Mann, "Little Herr Friedemann," *Stories of Three
   Decades,* trans. H. T. Lowe-Porter, (New York, 1936), p. 4. This
   story was originally published in 1897, then collected in 1898
   in Mann's first published volume, a collection of short stories
   bearing this story's title.
9. Thomas Mann, *Buddenbrooks,* trans. H. T. Lowe-Porter (New
   York, 1953), pp. 590–591.
10. Cf. Henry Hatfield, *Thomas Mann* (New York, 1962), pp. 90–91.

11. Thomas Mann, "Mario and the Magician," *Death in Venice,* trans. H. T. Lowe-Porter (New York, 1954), pp. 141–142.

12. Schleppfuss, of course, means "dragging foot." Significantly, too, the narrator learns of Leverkühn's visit to the whore in a letter in which Leverkühn tells "what is afoot betwixt me and Satan," how he was led to the whorehouse by a guide with "diabolical pronunciation," a "small-beer-Schleppfuss," whom the narrator terms Adrian's "betrayer." (Thomas Mann, *Doctor Faustus,* trans. H. T. Lowe-Porter [New York, 1948], pp. 141, 142, 148.)

13. *Das Gesamtwerk* (Hamburg: Rowohlt, c. 1948, pub. 1949), pp. 228–230. In the translation *The Man Outside,* (see n. 14) this story is titled "The Three Dark Magi."

14. David Porter has translated *Draussen vor der Tür* as *The Man Outside,* intro. by Stephen Spender (Norfolk, Conn., 1952). All quotations in the text are taken from this edition.

15. Heinrich Böll, *The Train Was on Time,* trans. Richard Graves (New York, 1956). All references in the text are to this edition.

16. Heinrich Böll, *Wanderer, If You Come to the Spa,* trans. Mervyn Savill (London, 1956). All references are to this edition.

17. Maurice Valency's adaptation of Dürrenmatt's play, titled *The Visit* (1958), unfortunately obscures much of the symbolism. Ill is renamed Schill—another pun perhaps, but certainly with a different meaning—Claire's broken bones are allowed to mend, not be replaced, and the castration of Koby and Toby is alluded to but not made explicit.

18. Martin Esslin, *The Theatre of the Absurd* (New York, 1961), p. 58. Quotations in my text are from this edition. I am indebted for knowledge of Adamov and Vian to Mr. Esslin's book.

19. *Ibid.,* p. 63.

20. Boris Vian, *The Empire Builders,* trans. Simon Watson Taylor (New York, 1967). References will refer to this edition.

Appendix Two
The Hospital

Achilles. From Greek myth, *Aethiopis* (9th century B.C.),
to H. D.'s *Helen in Egypt* (1961).

Acrisius. Greek myth.

Adam. "Sorrow Acre" (1942), Isak Dinesen.

Adam, Richter. *The Broken Jug (Der Zerbrochene Krug)*
(1806, 1808), Heinrich von Kleist.

Adams, Nick. *In Our Time* (1925), Ernest Hemingway.
Also *Men Without Women* (1927), and *Winner Take
Nothing* (1933).

Adonis. Greek myth.

Aeneas. *Iliad,* Homer.

Adgistis. Phrygian myth.

Ahab. *Moby-Dick* (1851), Herman Melville.

Alpine, Frank. *The Assistant* (1959), Bernard Malamud.

Amahl. *Amahl and the Night Visitors* (1951), Gian Carlo
Menotti.

Ancaeus of Arcadia. Greek myth.

Anchises. Greek myth.

Andreas. *The Train Was on Time* (1949), Heinrich Böll.

Andrews, Todd. *Floating Opera* (1956), John Barth.

Androcles' Lion. *Androcles and the Lion* (1916), George
Bernard Shaw; also Aulus Gellius (2nd century A.D.).

Antrobus, Mr. *The Skin of our Teeth* (1942), Thornton
Wilder.

Asa. I Kings 15:23 and II Chron. 16:12.

Asinius. *The Golden Ass* (before 114), Apuleius.

Asmodeus. *Le Diable Boiteux* (1707), Alain René Le
Sage. Also called *Asmodeus; or, The Devil on Two
Sticks,* based on *El diablo cojuelo* (1646), Luiz Vélez
de Guevara.

Attis. Phrygian myth.

Axelrod, Moe. *Awake and Sing* (1935), Clifford Odets.

Barnes, Jake. *The Sun Also Rises* (1926), Ernest Hemingway.

Barnwell, Saxe. *Accident* (1964), Elizabeth Janeway.

Barrow, Clyde. *Bonnie and Clyde* (1967), David Newman
and Robert Benton.

Bata. "Two Brothers," Egyptian myth.

Becker, Grini. "Lohengrin's Death" (1956), Heinrich Böll.

Beckmann. *Draussen vor der Tür (Outside the Door)*
(1947), Wolfgang Borchert.

Ben, Old. *The Bear* (1942), William Faulkner.

Benjamin, Mr. *The Victim* (1947), Saul Bellow.

Berthalet, Paul. *Lili* (1954), Helen Deutsch.

Biberkopf, Franz. *Berlin Alexanderplatz* (1929), Alfred
Döblin.

Bliocadran. *Li Contes del Graal.*

Bloody Five (Blutiger Fünfer, alias Sgt. Fairchild). *Mann
ist Mann* (1926), Bertolt Brecht.

Bok, Jakov. *The Fixer* (1966), Bernard Malamud.

Bows, Mr. *Pendennis* (1849–1850), William Thackeray.

Boyle, Johnny. *Juno and the Paycock* (1924), Sean O'Casey.

Brainworm. *Every Man in His Humour* (1598), Ben
Jonson.

Bran (Ban) the Blessed. Welsh myth.

Brown, Father James. *The Living Room* (1953), Graham
  Greene.
Buddenbrooks, Christian. *Buddenbrooks* (1901), Thomas
  Mann.
Bumble. *The American Dream* (1959, 1960), Edward
  Albee.
Bundren, Cash. *As I Lay Dying* (1930), William Faulkner.
Burns, Anthony. "Desire and the Black Masseur" (1948),
  Tennessee Williams.
Butt, Father. *Portrait of the Artist as a Young Man* (1916),
  James Joyce.
Byrd, Grandmother. *Lie Down in Darkness* (1951), Wil-
  liam Styron.
Caldwell, George. *The Centaur* (1963), John Updike.
Campion, General Lord Edward. *Some Do Not* (1924),
  Ford Madox Ford.
Cantwell, Colonel Robert. *Across the River and Into
  the Trees* (1950), Ernest Hemingway.
Carey, Philip. *Of Human Bondage* (1915), W. Somerset
  Maugham.
Carmanor. Greek myth.
Carnehan, Peachey. "The Man Who Would Be King"
  (1888), Rudyard Kipling.
Cassio, Michael. *Othello* (c. 1602-1603), William Shakes-
  peare.
Chatterley, Clifford. *Lady Chatterley's Lover* (1928), D. H.
  Lawrence.
Cheiron. Greek myth.
Chester Good. *Gunsmoke*.
Christmas, Joe. *Light in August* (1932), William Faulkner.
Cipolla. "Mario and the Magician" (1929), Thomas
  Mann.
Clark, G. S. *The Affair* (1959), C. P. Snow.
Clennam, Mrs. *Little Dorrit* (1855-1857), Charles Dickens.
Cobb, Jeremiah. *The Confessions of Nat Turner* (1967),
  William Styron.

Combalus. Syrian myth.

Compson, Benjy and Quentin (m). *The Sound and the Fury* (1929), William Faulkner.

Coney, Peter Coen. *Home of the Brave* (1945), Arthur Laurents.

Creighton. *Nigger of the Narcissus* (1897), Joseph Conrad.

Crouchback, Guy. *Sword of Honour* (1965), Evelyn Waugh.

Daley, Tom. *The Weight of the Cross* (1951), Robert Bowen.

Damport, Rafe. *The Shoemakers' Holiday* (1599), Thomas Dekker.

Darley. *Justine* (1957), Lawrence Durrell.

Davy. "Leg" (1934), William Faulkner.

Dedlock, Sir Leicester. *Bleak House* (1852-1853), Charles Dickens.

Deo Gratias. *Burnt-Out Case* (1961), Graham Greene.

Devil. Myth.

Diarmuid. Irish myth.

Dionysus. Greek myth.

Dixon, Forrest. *Hail, Hero!* (1968), John Weston.

Doyle, Peter. *Miss Lonelyhearts* (1933), Nathanael West.

Dravot, Daniel. "The Man Who Would Be King" (1888), Rudyard Kipling.

Duke of Coffin Castle, The. *The Thirteen Clocks* (1950), James Thurber.

Einhorn, William. *Adventures of Augie March* (1953), Saul Bellow.

Elliot, Rickie. *The Longest Journey* (1907), E. M. Forster.

Engstrand, Jacob. *Ghosts* (1881, 1883), Henrik Ibsen.

Estragon. *Waiting for Godot* (1952, 1954), Samuel Beckett.

Eurydice. Greek myth.

Falstaff. *Henry IV, Part II* (1597-1598), William Shakespeare.

Fewkoombey, George. *Dreigroschenroman* (1934), Bertolt Brecht.

Finklestone, Baro. *Back to China* (1965), Leslie Fiedler.

Fisher King, The (Anfortas). Medieval romance.

Fleece. *Moby–Dick* (1851), Herman Melville.

Freeman, Freddie (Captain Marvel, Jr.). American comic book character.

Friedemann, Herr. "Little Herr Friedemann" (1897), Thomas Mann.

Frome, Ethan. *Ethan Frome* (1911), Edith Wharton.

Gama, King. *Princess Ida* (1884), William S. Gilbert.

Garland, Able, père et fils. *The Old Curiosity Shop* (1840-1841), Charles Dickens.

Gersbach, Valentine. *Herzog* (1964), Saul Bellow.

Giles, alias Billy Bocksfuss. *Giles Goat-Boy* (1966), John Barth.

Gimpty. *Dead End* (1935), Sidney Kingsley.

Ginsfarb. "Death Drag" (1932), William Faulkner.

Gordon, Lee. *Lonely Crusade* (1947), Chester Himes.

Goriot, Père. *Père Goriot* (1834), Honoré de Balzac.

Guinea. *The Confidence Man* (1857), Herman Melville.

Hackett, Tod. *The Day of the Locust* (1939), Nathanael West.

Halleck, Ben. *A Modern Instance* (1882), William Dean Howells.

Hamm. *Endgame* (1957, 1958), Samuel Beckett.

Harpocrates. Egyptian myth.

Harry. *The Snows of Kilimanjaro* (1936), Ernest Hemingway.

Hazen, Corporal Samuel. *The Searching Wind* (1944), Lillian Hellman.

Heegan, Harry. *The Silver Tassie* (1928), Sean O'Casey.

Helmbrecht Schlingdasgeu. *Meier Helmbrecht* (c. 1250), Wernher der Gartenaere.

Henderson, Eugene. *Henderson the Rain King* (1959), Saul Bellow.

Henry, Lt. Fred. *A Farewell to Arms* (1929), Ernest Hemingway.

Hephaestus. Greek myth.

Heracles. Greek myth, Apollodorus.

Himmo Farah. *Himmo: King of Jerusalem* (1969), Yoram Kaniuk.

Hinkemann, Eugene. *Hinkemann* (1922), Ernst Toller.

Hobbie, Monroe. *Lie Down in Darkness* (1951), William Styron.

Holt, Edward. *Edward, My Son* (1948), Robert Morley and Noel Langley.

Hopewell, Hulga. "A Good Man is Hard to Find" (1955), Flannery O'Connor.

Hop-Frog. "Hop-Frog" (1849), Edgar Allen Poe.

Horney, Tom, and friend. "Two Legs for the Two of Us" (1951), James Jones.

Horus. Egyptian myth.

Hummel. *The Centaur* (1963), John Updike.

Iambe. Greek myth.

Idmon. Greek myth.

Iphiclus. Greek myth.

Jacob. Genesis 33:25–32.

Jesus Christ. Christian myth.
    Also Robert Graves' *King Jesus* (1946).

Jim, Nigger. *The Adventures of Huckleberry Finn* (1885), Mark Twain.

Johnson, Rufus. "The Lame Shall Enter First" (1965), Flannery O'Connor.

Jordan, Robert. *For Whom the Bell Tolls* (1940), Ernest Hemingway.

Joyce. "England, My England" (1922), D. H. Lawrence.

Julian. *Tiny Alice* (1964, 1965), Edward Albee.

Kelly, Connie. "Champion" (1924), Ring Lardner.

Kelway, Robert. *The Heat of the Day* (1949), Elizabeth Bowen.

Khan, Zaman. "The Soldier" (1966), Krishan Chandar.

Kieth, Marquis von. *The Marquis von Kieth* (1900), Frank Wedekind.

Kleist, Rektor. *Rektor Kleist* (1905), Georg Kaiser.

Klinschor. *Parzival* (c. 1205), Wolfram von Eschenbach.

Knowles. *Nigger of the Narcissus* (1898), Joseph Conrad.

Koby. *Der Besuch der alten Dame* (1956), Friedrich Dürrenmatt.

Kogin, Trofim. *The Fixer* (1966), Bernard Malamud.

Kuby, Thomas. *The Financier* (1912), Theodore Dreiser.

Kuhn, Herr. *Gertrud* (1910), Hermann Hesse.

Lafcadio. *Les Caves du Vatican* (1914), André Gide.

Läuffer. *Der Hofmeister* (1950), Bertolt Brecht.
 Also *Der Hofmeister* (1774), Jacob Michael Reinhold Lenz.

Lebedev, Zinaida Nikolaevna. *The Fixer* (1966), Bernard Malamud.

Levin, Seymour. *A New Life* (1961), Bernard Malamud.

Little Lee Roy, "Keela the Outcast Indian Maiden." *A Curtain of Green* (1941), Eudora Welty.

Llew Llaw Gyffes. Welsh myth.

Loby. *Der Besuch der alten Dame* (1956), Friedrich Dürrenmatt.

Loftis, Maudie. *Lie Down in Darkness* (1951), William Styron.

Lucius. *Golden Ass* (before 114), Apuleius.

McCallum, Buddy (Virginius, Jr.). "The Tall Men" (1941), William Faulkner.

MacDowall, Gertie. *Ulysses* (1922), James Joyce.

Machine, Frank and Sophie. *Man with a Golden Arm* (1949, 1950), Nelson Algren.

MacMann. *Malone Dies* (1951, 1959), Samuel Beckett.

MacPhail, Hubert. *Lie Down in Darkness* (1951), William Styron.

Magwitch. *Great Expectations* (1860-1861), Charles Dickens.

Mahood. *The Unnameable* (1953, 1959), Samuel Beckett.

Malone. *Malone Dies* (1951, 1959), Samuel Beckett.

Mannix, Al. *The Long March* (1952), William Styron.

Martin. "The Return," Guy de Maupassant.

Math. Welsh myth.

McBride. *The Confessions of Nat Turner* (1967), William Styron.

Meehan, R. E. *Finnegans Wake* (1939), James Joyce.

Meng Tsao-yu. "Molten Iron" (1967), Tsu Hsi-Nin.

Mephibosheth. II Samuel 4:4.

Mephisto. *Faust* (1808), Goethe.

Mink, Ann. *Call It Sleep* (1934), Henry Roth.

Molloy. *Molloy* (1951, 1959), Samuel Beckett.

Monygham, Dr. *Nostromo* (1904), Joseph Conrad.

Mopsus. Greek myth.

Moran. *Molloy* (1951, 1959), Samuel Beckett.

Motes, Hazel. *Wise Blood* (1952), Flannery O'Connor.

Mountolive, David. *Mountolive* (1958), Lawrence Durrell.

Moyer, Ken. "Expect the Vandals" (1958), Philip Roth.

Munitis. Greek myth.

Mutilé, Le. *La Grande et la petite Manoeuvre* (1953), Arthur Adamov.

Nagg and Nell. *Endgame* (1957, 1958), Samuel Beckett.

Narwitz, Rupert. *The Fountain* (1932), Charles Morgan.

Nauplius the Argonaut. Greek myth.

Nell, Little (Mr. Nell). "God Rest You Merry, Gentlemen" (1900), Stephen Crane.

Neroni, Madeline Vesey. *Barchester Towers* (1857), Anthony Trollope.

Novotny. "Novotny's Pain" (1962), Philip Roth.

Oedipus. Greek myth, Sophocles.

O'Meaghan, Mary. "Among the Paths to Eden" (1963), Truman Capote.

Ordway, Tom. *The Ordways* (1965), William Humphrey.

O'Shaugnessy, Sergius. *Deer Park* (1955), Norman Mailer.

Osiris. Egyptian myth.

Ostenburg, Countess Rosmarin. *The Dark is Light Enough* (1954), Christopher Fry.

Pan. Greek myth.

Paris. Greek myth.

Peg-Leg. *The Confidence Man* (1857), Herman Melville.

Pellehan. *Morte D'Arthur,* Thomas Mallory; after the *Suite du Merlin.*

Pellinor. *Morte D'Arthur,* Thomas Mallory.

Pep, Dr. "Dr. Pep's Sermon" (1949), Saul Bellow.

Percivale. *Morte D'Arthur,* Thomas Mallory.

Peredur. *The Mabinogion* (1949), ed. by Gwyn Jones and Thomas Jones.

Pérez, Thomas. *The Stranger* (1942), Albert Camus.

Periphetes. Greek myth.

Perken. *The Royal Way* (1930), André Malraux.

Perth. *Moby–Dick* (1851), Herman Melville.

Peyrac, Joffrey de. *Angélique* and *Angélique and the King,* Sergeanne Golon.

Philoctetes. Greek myth, Sophocles.

Phineas. *A Separate Peace* (1959), John Knowles.

Pholus. Greek myth.

Pinedo, Luis. *Muertes de perro* (1958), Francisco Ayala.

Pitkin, Lemuel. *A Cool Million* (1934), Nathanael West.

Plume, Noah and Richard. *Plumes* (1924), Laurence Stallings.

Pollitt, Brick. *Cat on a Hot Tin Roof* (1955), Tennessee Williams.

Popeye. *Sanctuary* (1931), William Faulkner.

Portia. *Julius Caesar* (1599–1600), William Shakespeare.

Posa, Baroness Erika von. *Attendance List for a Funeral* (1966), Alexander Kluge.

Quarles, Philip. *Point Counter Point* (1928), Aldous Huxley.

Quilp. *The Old Curiosity Shop* (1840-1841), Charles Dickens.

Quirt, Sgt. *What Price Glory* (1924), Maxwell Anderson and Laurence Stallings.

Ra. Egyptian myth.

Ralph. *Lord of the Flies* (1954), William Golding.

Revalière, M. "The Cripple," Guy de Maupassant.

Richard III. *Henry VI, Part II* and *Part III,* and *Richard III* (1590-1593), William Shakespeare.

Rico (Sir Henry Carrington). *St. Mawr* (1925), D. H. Lawrence.

Rigaud, alias Lagnier, alias Blandois. *Little Dorrit* (1855-1857), Charles Dickens.

Rivers, Reno. *Leafy Rivers* (1967), Jessamyn West.

Rosenzweig, Adam. *Wilderness* (1961), Robert Penn Warren.

Samsa, Gregor. *The Metamorphosis* (1915), Franz Kafka.

Sandbach, Paul. *Some Do Not* (1924), Ford Madox Ford.

Sansom, Edward R. *Other Voices, Other Rooms* (1948), Truman Capote.

Sarah. *The Hustler* (1959), Walter Tevis. (Henry, the Negro janitor in the novel, also limps.)

Sawyer, Tom. *The Adventures of Huckleberry Finn* (1885), Mark Twain.

Schearl, David. *Call It Sleep* (1934), Henry Roth.

Schleppfuss. *Dr. Faustus* (1947), Thomas Mann.

Schmürz. *Les Bâtisseurs d'Empire* (1959), Boris Vian.

Seal, Basil. *Basil Seal Rides Again* (1963), Evelyn Waugh.

Sengstack, Abner. *The Financier* (1912), Theodore Dreiser.

Shandy, Toby. *Tristram Shandy* (1759-1767), Laurence Sterne.

Silver, Mattie. *Ethan Frome* (1911), Edith Wharton.

Smith, Mr. *Das Badener Lehrstück* (1929), Bertolt Brecht.

Smith, Perry. *In Cold Blood* (1965), Truman Capote.

Snopes, Abner. "Barn Burning" (1939), William Faulkner. Also *The Unvanquished* (1938), and *The Hamlet* (1940).

Snopes, Byron. *Sartoris* (1929), William Faulkner.

Socrates. "Socrates Wounded" (1948), Bertolt Brecht. Also "Der gerettete Alkibiades" (1920), Georg Kaiser.

Stranitzky. *Stranitzky und der Nationalheld* (1952), Friedrich Dürrenmatt.

Sutpen, Thomas. *Absalom, Absalom!* (1936), William Faulkner.

Talos (Bronze). Greek myth.

Talos (Daedalus' nephew). Greek myth.

Tantalus. Greek myth.

Tantamount, Charles, Lord Gattenden. *Point Counter Point* (1928), Aldous Huxley.

Tarp, Brother. *Invisible Man* (1952), Ralph Ellison.

Telephus. Greek myth.

Thammuz. Mesopotamian myth.

Thubby. *The Ferret Fancier* (1965), Anthony C. West.

Tietjens, Sir Mark and Sylvia. *Last Post* (1928), Ford Madox Ford.

Tiny Tim. *A Christmas Carol* (1843), Charles Dickens.

Tlepolememus. *The Golden Ass* (before 114), Apuleius.

Tommo. *Typee* (1856), Herman Melville.

Tony. *They Knew What They Wanted* (1924), Sidney Howard.

Tristan. *Tristan* (c. 1210), Gottfried von Strassburg.

Turpin, Claude. "Revelation" (1965), Flannery O'Connor.

Ulysses. Greek myth.

Uranos. Greek myth.

Uraz. *The Horsemen* (1968), Joseph Kessel.

Van Rensburg, Albert. *Manor House* (1964), Johannes Meintjes.

Vulcan. The Latin Hephaestus.

Wayne, Chance. *Sweet Bird of Youth* (1959), Tennessee Williams.

Wegg, Silas. *Our Mutual Friend* (1865), Charles Dickens.

White, George. "Happily Ever After" (1920), Aldous Huxley.

Whiteside, Sheridan. *The Man Who Came to Dinner* (1939), George S. Kaufman and Moss Hart.

Williams, Jake. *The Confessions of Nat Turner* (1967), William Styron.

Wilson, Scratchy. "The Bride Comes to Yellow Sky" (1898), Stephen Crane.

Wingfield, Laura. *The Glass Menagerie* (1945), Tennessee Williams.

Winnie. *Happy Days* (1961), Samuel Beckett.

Weyland. "Deor," *Nibelungenlied, Volsungasaga.*

Wren, Jenny (Fanny Cleaver). *Our Mutual Friend* (1865), Charles Dickens.

Zachanassian, Claire. *Der Besuch der alten Dame* (1956), Friedrich Dürrenmatt.

Zeno. *Confessions of Zeno* (1923), Italo Svevo.

Zeus, Cretan. Greek myth.

UNNAMED

"Bound Man." Ilse Aichinger (1953).

Boy in "God Rest You Merry, Gentlemen" (1933), Ernest Hemingway.

Crippled, red-haired girl in *Herzog* (1964), Saul Bellow.

Cripple, "hoary" and "hateful" who directs Childe Roland in Browning's poem "Childe Roland to the Dark Tower Came."

Disabled Soldier. "On the Distresses of the Poor; Exemplified in the Life of a Common Soldier" (1760), Oliver Goldsmith.

Donkey carver. "Die drei dunklen Könige" (1948), Wolfgang Borchert.

Der Einbeinige. *Draussen vor der Tür* (1947), Wolfgang Borchert.

Indian father. "Indian Camp" (1925), Ernest Hemingway.

Julian's mother. "Everything that Rises Must Converge" (1965), Flannery O'Connor.

Lame boy. "The Pied Piper of Hamelin," the folktale and Robert Browning's poem of the same title.

Lame man. Acts 3:2.

Little Lame Balloon Man. "In Just—" (1924), E. E. Cummings.

Loveless lame girl. "Seeds" (1921), Sherwood Anderson.

"The Leg." (1953), Karl Shapiro.

Man who castrates self. *The Sound and the Fury* (1929), William Faulkner.

The Man Who Died. "The Man Who Died" (1928), D. H. Lawrence.

Old cripple. "The Old Cripple," Guy de Maupassant.

Policeman. "The Last Laugh" (1924), D. H. Lawrence.

Refugees. *Tous Contre Tous* (1953), Arthur Adamov.

New England wine-maker. "Black Music" (1934), William Faulkner.

One-legged sailor. *Ulysses* (1922), James Joyce.

Stranger. *Independent People* (1934-1935), Halldór Laxness.

Stranger. *The Oldest God* (1926), Stephen McKenna.

Traveler, If You Come to the Spa . . . (1950), Heinrich Böll; characters in

"Traveler, If You Come to the Spa . . ."

"On the Bridge"

"The Farewell"

"My Expensive Leg"

"Lohengrin's Death"

Woman with cane and cast. *Herzog* (1964), Saul Bellow.

Index

Because of the large number of names involved, this index is arranged simply in alphabetical order. No attempt has been made to align authors with their texts, although, of course, their names will usually be mentioned together on the same page. Page numbers in italics indicate references to footnotes, and names that appear in Appendix Two are not included in this general index, nor are secondary sources.

Abraham, *184*
Absalom, Absalom! (Faulkner), 163, 165, *184*
Achilles, 3, 6, 15, 16, 21, *30, 120, 179*
Acrisius, 21
Across the River and into the Trees (Hemingway), 159
Act Without Words (Samuel Beckett), 177
Acushnet, 132
Adam (Biblical), 128-129, 158, 160-162, 168-169, 171, 179

Adam (Isak Dinesen), 158, 161-162
Adams, Nick, 70-72, 155, 158-160, 166
Adam, Richter (Judge), 198, *216*
Adamov, Arthur, 213, *217*
Adams, George, 71
Adams, Dr. Henry, 70-71
"Adonais" (Shelley), 175
Adonis, 7, 17, 19-20, 22-24, *29-31, 51, 55, 130,* 174-175, 189
Aegeus, 26

Aeneas, 24
Aeneid (Virgil), 21, *30*
Agdistis, 19
Ahab, 3, 129-132, 137, 163, 166, 179, *180*, 188
Aichinger, Ilse, 212-213
Aigremont, Dr. (pseud. Siegmar Baron von Schultze-Gallera), *28*
Albany (*of King Lear*), 190
Albee, Edward, 101-103
Alcibiades Saved (Kaiser), 200
Aldous Huxley (Atkins), *120, 121*
Aldous Huxley (Brooke), *120, 121*
Alexanderplatz Berlin (Döblin), 206
Alpine, Frank, 48-55, *62*, 191
Amazons, 58
Amelia (Amelia Sedley, *Vanity Fair*), 137
American Dream, The (Albee), 101-103
"Among the Paths to Eden" (Capote), 42, 88
Amy (of *They Knew What They Wanted*), 172
Ancaeus of Arcadia, 22
Ancaeus of the Calydonian boar-hunt, 22
Anchises, 24, *30*
Ancient Mariner, 57
Anderson, Maxwell, 6, 154
Andreas, 209-210
Androcles' lion, 7
Anfortas, 100, *119*
Ansell, Stewart, 142
Antaeus, 13
Antrobus, George, 158, 160
Aphrodite, 18, 24-25, *30-31*, 54-55
Apollo, 22, *26*
Apollodorus, 16-17, 21

Apuleius, 34, *60*
Ariadne, 175
Aristophanes, 26
Aristotle, 14-17, *28*
Arnewi, 57
The Arraignment of Paris (George Peele), 190
Artemis, *31*, 41
Ashley, Brett, 69-70, 155
Asinius, 34
Asmodeus, 197
Asmodeus, The Devil Upon Two Sticks (Le Sage), 196-197
The Assistant (Malamud), 44, 48, 59, *62*, 98
Atkins, John, *120, 121*
Atreus, 21
Attis, 19-20, 26, *29, 30*, 51, 55, 174, 189, 195
Auden, W. H., *180*
"Auerbach's Keller" (Goethe), 107
Aufidius, 190
"The Augsburg Chalk Circle" (Brecht), *9*
"The Author to Her Book" (Anne Bradstreet), 187
Awake and Sing (Clifford Odets), 172
Axelrod, Moe, 172

Badener Lehrstück vom Einverstandnis, Das (Brecht), 205
Baker, Carlos, *119*
Balaam the Lame (i.e. Jesus), *60*
Barker, Mrs., 101-102
"Barn Burning," (Faulkner), 163-164, *184*
Barnes, Jake, 4, 69, 70, 126, 155-158, 160, 166, 176, 179, 201, 213
Barton, George A., 21, *29, 62, 123*
Bata, 18

Les Bâtisseurs d'Empire (*The Empire Builders*), 214-215, *217*
Baudelaire, 80
Baumbach, Jonathan, *61, 62,* 68, *122*
Baynes, H. G. and Cary, *9*
"The Bear" (Faulkner), 165
Beatrice (Dante's), 47
Becker, Grini, 210
Becket, Thomas à, 64
Beckett, Samuel, 177-178, *185,* 213
Beckmann, 209
Beethoven, Ludwig van, 81
Belli, Ivor, 43-44
Bellow, Saul, 55-59, *62,* 109, 187
Bendigeidfran (Blessed Bran), 65
Bennet, Ivan L., *182*
Bennie (the Indian), 90
Mr. Benjamin, 109
Bentley, Eric, *216*
Beowulf, 17
Berlin Alexanderplatz (Döblin), 206
Der Besuch der alten Dame (Dürrenmatt), 211
Bettelheim, Bruno, 21, *29,* 54, 55, *62*
Biberkopf, Franz, 206
Bidlake, John, 80
Bidlake, Walter, 80
Big Daddy (Pollitt), 40, 42
Big Mamma (Pollitt), 42
"Big Two-Hearted River" (Hemingway), 155
Billy Budd (Melville), 134
Bird, Harriet, *61,* 100, 116
Blanche (Du Bois), 39
"Bliocadran," *119*
Bleak House (Dickens), 104, 191, 199
Molly Bloom, 91
Bober, Helen, 50-55, *62,* 118

Bober, Morris, 48-52
Bockgesang (*Goat-Song* by Werfel), 199
Bodkin, Maud, 5, 125, 170, 178, *184*
Bok, Raisl, 117
Bok, Yakov, 116-118
Böll, Heinrich, 210-211, *217*
Mrs. Bolton, Agnes, 78
Borchert, Wolfgang, 208-209
"The Bound Man" (Aichinger), 212-213
Bradstreet, Anne, 187
Brainworm, 189-190
Bran (Bendigeidfram), 65
Branwen, 66
Brass, Sampson, 107
Brecht, Bertolt, 7, *9, 118,* 197, 200, 204-205, 206, *216*
The Broken Jug (Heinrich von Kleist), 197
Bron (Bran), 65
Brokenbrow (see Hinkemann)
Brooke, Jocelyn, 80, *120, 121*
Brother Tarp, 101-102
Buchanan, Tom and Daisy Fay, 68
Buddenbrooks (Mann), 206, *216*
Buddenbrooks, Christian, 207
Buddenbrooks, Hanno, 207
Budge, E. A. Wallis, 27, *28, 29, 30*
Bundren, Cash, 3
Burden, Joanna, 84
Burlap, 80

Cady, Edwin H., *181-182*
Cagliostro, 112
Caiaphas, 169
Cain, 107
Calderón de la Barca, 196
Campbell, Joseph, 5, 18, *62*
Campion, Lord Edward, 150-152

Candide, 85
Cantwell, Colonel Robert, 159
Capote, Truman, 42, 59, *61*, 88
Carey, Philip, 141, 143-144, 148
Carmanor of Lydia, 22
Carnehan, Peachey Taliaferro,
  138-140
Carter, Everett, *181*
Cartwright, Dick, 91
Cassandra, 175
Cassio, Michael, 189, 190
Castor, 21
Cat on a Hot Tin Roof (Ten-
  nessee Williams), 39, 42, 59,
  61
Caves du Vatican, les (Gide),
  119
Cellini, Benvenuto, 26
The Centaur (Updike), 55, *179*
Cervantes, Miguel de, 196
Chase, Richard, *180*
Chatterley, Sir Clifford, 77-79,
  104, 117, 188, 206
Chatterley, Constance, 78, 79
Cheiron, 3, 21, *30*, *179*
Chiang-yuan, 10
Chrétien de Troyes, *118*, *183*
Christ, *32*, 35, 38, 46, 51, 55,
  56, *60*, 64, 73-75, 84, 95, 98,
  140, 169-171, 175, *184*, 189
A Christmas Carol (Dickens),
  135, *179*
Christmas, Joe, 83-84, 166, 173
Cipolla (of "Mario and the Ma-
  gician"), *123*, 207-208
Clennam, Mrs., 105
Cleofas, Don, 197
Clov (of *Endgame*), *185*
Cobb, Jeremiah (Judge Cobb),
  92-95, 118, *122*
Coen, Peter, 172-173
Cohn, Robert, 69
Coleridge, S. T., 57
Colin Clout (Spenser), *184*

*The Collected Letters of D. H.
  Lawrence, 60*
*Collected Stories of William
  Faulkner, 184*
The Complete Poems and Plays
  (Eliot), *118*
*The Complete Works of Na-
  thanael West, 121*
Compson, Benjy, 83, 90, 163,
  206
Compson, Candace, 83
Compson, Jason, 83
Compson, Quentin (m.), 83, *121*
The Confessions of Nat Turner
  (Styron), 92-95, *121*
The Confessions of Zeno
  (Schmitz), 202-204, *216*
The Confidence Man (Melville),
  134-135
Conrad, Joseph, 57
A Cool Million (West), 84-85
Copernicus, Nicolaus, 129
Corinthians (1, 14:1; 1, 13:1), 45-
  46
Coriolanus, 190
Cornford, Francis, 26
La coscienza di Zeno (Schmitz),
  202
Cowley, Malcolm, *119*
Crates, 15
Cripples, Mr., 105
Cronus, 18, 22, 25
Cross, Tom Peete, *28*
"Cross Country Snow" (Heming-
  way), 158
Cuchulainn, 196
Culver, Lt., 167-169
cummings, e. e., 33
Cupid, 197
Cybele, 19-20, *30*, 54-55

Daddy (of *The American
  Dream*), 102-104
Dahfu, 58

Damport, Rafe, 189-191
Dante, 47, 188
The Day of the Locust (West), 84, 86
de Boron, Joseph, *119*
de Guevera, Luis Vélez, 196
de Zoate, Beryl, *216*
Dead End (Kingsley), *172*
Death in Venice (Mann), *217*
The Decoration of Houses (Wharton), 145
Dedlock, Sir Leicester, 104-105
Dekker, Thomas, 190
Demeter, *31*, 142
"Deor," 195
"Desire and the Black Masseur" (Tennessee Williams), 176
Devil, 8, 97, 107, *122*, *123*, 126, 139, 187, 196, 198
Le Diable boiteux (le Sage), 196
The Dialogues of Plato, 28
Diana, 41
Diarmuid, 16, 17, 22, *30*, 196
Dickens, Charles, 104, 105, 135, *181*
The Didactic Play of Baden on Consent (Brecht), 205
Didot Perceval, 118
Diehl, Paul, 27
Dieterich, Albrecht, *31*
Dinesen, Isak, 158, 161-162
Diodorus Siculus, 29
Diogenes of Apollonia, 28
Diogenes Laertius, *28*
Diomedes, 24
Dionysus, 7, 12, 20, 26, 29, *31*, *32*, 106, 142
"The Disabled Soldier" (Goldsmith), 191
Diû Crône, 118
Dobbin, Capt. William, 137
Döblin, Alfred, 206
Dr. Faustus (Mann), 126, 208, *217*

Dr. Faustus (Marlowe), 196
Don Quixote, 57
Donahue, Francis, *61*
the donkey-carver ("Three Dark Kings"), 209
Dostoyevsky, Fyodor, 171
Doyle, Fay, 85
Doyle, Peter, 84-85
Draussen vor der Tür (Borchert), 209, *217*
Dravot, Daniel, 138-140
the Duke (of *The 13 Clocks*), 108-109
Dürrenmatt, Friedrich, 211-212, *217*

Easter, 36
Egyptian Two Brothers, 18
Ehrenzweig, Anton, *123*
El Diablo Cojuelo (de Guevera), 196
Electra and Other Plays (Sophocles), *179*
Eleutheria (Beckett), 177
Eliot, T. S., 65-68, 77, 80, 84, 117, *118*, *119*, *120*, 187-188
Elizabeth I, 190
Eliot, Agnes, 141
Elliot, Rickie, 141-143, 148, 163
Ellison, Ralph, 95, 101-102, *122*
Embers (Beckett), 177
The Empire Builders (Vian), 214
Endgame (Beckett), 177, 185
Ephesians (6:5), 93
Epitome (Apollodorus), 21
Erinyes, 100
"The Escaped Cock" (Lawrence), 35
Esslin, Martin, *185*, 213, 214, *216*, *217*
Estragon, 177
Eteocles, 21

Ethan Frome (Wharton), 144-148, *182*
Ethics (Spinoza), 143, *182*
Eurydice, 3, 21, 22, *30*
Eurynome, 22
Eve, 22, 128
Eve (of *Der zerbrochene Krug*), 198, *216*
Every Man in His Humour (Jonson), 190
Everything That Rises Must Converge (O'Connor), *122*
"Everything that Rises Must Converge" (O'Connor), 96
Exodus (1:5, 29:22, 29, 24:6-8), 11, 64
"The Experiment" (Brecht), 5
Ezekial (9:4), 92
Ezekial (the prophet), 67

*The Faerie Quee*ne (Spenser), 184
Failing, Mrs. Emily, 142
Fairchild, Sgt., 204-205
Falk, Signi, *60*
Falstaff, 189, 191
"The Farewell" (Böll), 210
A Farewell to Arms (Hemingway), 155, 159, 206
Father (of *The Empire Builders*), 214-215
Fathers, Sam, 166
"Fathers and Sons" (Hemingway), *120*
Faulkner, William, 3, 77, 82-83, 84, *121*, 163-166, *184*
Faust, 57
Faust, 198
Faustus, 129
Fedder, Norman J., *61*
Ferdiad, 13
Ferdinand, 190
Fever, Jesus, 89
Fever, Zoo, 89

Fezziwig, Mr. and Mrs., 135
Fidèle, 134
Fiedler, Leslie, *61*, 98
Finch (of *Home of the Brave*), 172-173
Finley, Heavenly, 174, 176
Finley, Tom, 174, 176
Finn mac Cool, 22, *30*, 196
Firkins, Oscar, *181*
Fischer, Doc, 72-76
Fisher, Pop, 99, 101, 115, *122*
Fisher King, 8, 65-66, 68-69, 72, 99-101, 109, 118, *119*, *120*, 130, *183*, *185*, 187-188, 196
Fitts, Dudley, *118*
Fitzgerald, F. Scott, 49, 68, *119*
Fitzgerald, Robert, *118*, *122*
The Fixer (Malamud), 44, *62*, 113, 115-116, *123*
Fleece, 132
Fliss, Avis, 116
Flite, Miss, 191
For Whom the Bell Tolls (Hemingway), *120*
Ford, Ford Madox, 148-151, 154-155, *182*
Forster, E. M., 141-142, 144, *182*
Forster, E. S., *28*, *29*
Fortinbras, 190
Foster, Richard, *181*
Frances Clyne, 69
Francis, St., 49-50
Frazer, Sir James George, 5, 12, 13, 16-20, 27, 29, 58, *61*, *62*, 64, 66, 175, *179*, *184*
Freud, Sigmund, 22
Friedemann, Johannes, 206
The Frogs (Aristophanes), 26
From Ritual to Romance (Weston), *29*, 66
Frome, Ethan, 145-148, 163
Frye, Northrop, 5, *9*, *123*, 128, 162, *179*, 192
Fuggerio (of "Mario and the Magician"), 207-208

Fulgentius, 12, 15
Furbank, P. N., 203

Gahmuret, *119*
Galatians (5:1), 93
Galileo, 129
Gary, Mr. (of *Plumes*), 155
Gassner, John, *216*
Gatsby, Jay, 68
"Der Gefesselte" (Aichinger), 212
Gene (of *A Separate Peace*), 161
Genesis, 10-11, 22, 24, 158, *182*
Georgette (of *The Sun Also Rises*), 69
Gerbert, *118*
Der gerettete Alkibiades (Kaiser), 200
Gersbach, Valentine, 111-113, 117
Gertrud (Hesse), 208
Das Gesamtwerk (Borchert), *217*
Gibson, William M., *181*
Gide, André, *119*
Gilley, Gerald, 45, 48, 116
Gilley, Pauline, 45-48, 116
Gimpty (of *Dead End*), 172
"Girl in Glass" (Williams), *121*
Gitche Manito, 13
The Glass Menagerie (Williams), 86-87, *121*
Go Down, Moses (Faulkner), *184*
Goat Song (Werfel), 199
God, 126, 135, 139, 140, 142, 148, 152, 158
"God Rest You Merry, Gentlemen" (Hemingway), 72, 73-75, *119*
Godot, M., 178
Goethe, Johann Wolfgang von, 107, 198
Gold, Herbert, *62*
The Golden Ass (Apuleius), 34, 60
The Golden Bough (Frazer), 27, 29, *62*, 66, *179*

Goldsmith, Oliver, 191
Golfing, Francis, *179*
"Good Country People" (O'Connor), 95
A Good Man Is Hard to Find (O'Connor), 95
Gorton, Bill, 156
Grail King, 101, *122*
La Grande et la petite Manoeuvre (Adamov), 213
Grand Inquisitor (of *The Brothers Karamazov*), 171
Grandma (of *The American Dream*), 102-103
Graves, Richard, *217*
Graves, Robert, 5, 18, 21, *29, 30, 31, 60, 61, 120, 179, 184,* 196
Gray, Louis, *27, 30*
Gray, Thomas R., *122*
The Great Gatsby (Fitzgerald), 68, *119,* 150
The Greek Myths (Graves), 20, *29, 30, 31, 61, 62, 120, 179,* 196
Grimm, Percy, 84
Guinea (Black Guinea), 134
Gutmann, James, *182*
Gwynedd, 13

Hackett, Tod, 85-86
Hale, Ned, 147
Halleck, Ben, 136-137, 141, 163, *181, 182*
Hamlet (Shakespeare), 126, *184*
The Hamlet (Faulkner), 164, *184*
Hamm (of *Endgame*), 177, *185*
Hanne (of *Dr. Faustus*), 208
Happy Days (Samuel Beckett), 177
Hark (of *The 13 Clocks*), 109
Harpocrates, 189
Harrison, Jane, 23, *30, 31, 61*
Harry (of "The Snows of Kilimanjaro"), 76-77, 176

Hassan, Ihab, *62*
Hatfield, Henry, *216*
Hatto, A. T., *119*
Hawkes, John, *122*
Heber, Reginald, Bishop of Calcutta, 140
Helen (Spartan moon-goddess), 54
Hemingway, Ernest, 4, 57, 68-72, 75-77, 84, *119, 120,* 155, 157, 158-159, 162, 188, 189, 206, 213
Henderson, Eugene, 57-59, 109, 192
Henderson the Rain King (Bellow), 57, 59, *61*
Hendrick, George, *60*
I Henry VI (Shakespeare), *185*
Henry, Lt. Frederick, 159-160, 206
Hephaestus, *3, 6, 24-26, 31, 123, 125,* 170, *179,* 195
Hera, 24, *31*
Heracles, 21, 127, *179-180, 208*
Hermes (Mercury), 26
The Hero (Lord Raglan), 18
The Hero with a Thousand Faces (Campbell), 18
Herodotus, *29*
Herzog (Bellow), 109-113, *123*
Herzog, June, 111-113
Herzog, Madeleine, 111-113
Herzog, Moses, 109-113
Hesiod, 6, 14, 24-25, *31*
Hesse, Herman, 208
Hetmann, Karl, 199
Hiawatha (Longfellow), 13
Hicks, Granville, *62*
Hidalla, oder Karl Hetmann der Zwergriese (Wedekind), 199
Hindemith, Paul, 205
Hinkemann (Toller), 201, *216*
Hinkemann, Eugene, 201-202
Hinkemann, Margaret, 202

Hobbie, Monroe, 91
Hobbs, Roy, 98-101, *122*
Hocart, A. M., *28*
Hoffman, Frederick J., 70, 76, *120,* 182
Hofmeister, Der (Brecht), 205
Hofmeister, Der (Lenz), 197, 205
Hohoff, Curt, *193*
Holmes, Urban T., Jr., *183*
Holy Grail, 65, 98, *185*
Home of the Brave (Laurents), 172, *184,* 214
Homer, 6, 11, 15, 21, 25
Hopewell, Joy (Hulga), 95-96
Horace ("God Rest You Merry, Gentlemen"), 72-74
Horus, 37, 189
Howard, Sidney, 171
Howells, William Dean, 136, *181-182*
Hoyt, Charles Alvah, *61*
Hu, 18
Hubbard, Bartley, 136
Hubbard, Marcia, 136-137
Huxley, Aldous, 77, 79-82, 84, 117, *120, 121*
Hyman, Stanley Edgar, 2, 5, 6, 9, *122*

Idabel (Thompkins), 89
Idmon, 22
Iliad (Homer), 10, 11, 21, 24, *31*
Ill, Anton, 212, *217*
"In Another Country" (Hemingway), 158
"in Just—" (cummings), 33
In Our Time (Hemingway), *120,* 158
Independent People (Laxness) 205
"Indian Camp" (Hemingway), 70-72, *120*
Invisible Man (Ellison), 101-102, *122*

Iolcus, 26
Isaac (Biblical), 184
Isaiah, 12, 94
Ishtar, 20
Isis, 20, *30*, 37, 55
Isolt, 25, 196
Israel, 24, *62*, 114, 126, 160
Istram, Tor, *28*

Jacob (Biblical), 7, 10, 14, 24, 26, *60*, 114, 126, 160, *184*, 195
Jacob (Grandfather in *Awake and Sing*), 172
Jackson, W. T. H., *119*
Jacobi, Yolande, *9*
James, Henry, 144, 148
Jason, 26
Jim (Conrad's Lord Jim), 57
Job, 11, 93, 128
Jocasta, *33*
Joe (of *They Knew What They Wanted*), 172
Johnson, Edgar, *122*, *181*
Johnson, Rufus, 97-98
Jones, Gwynn and Thomas, 27
Jones, Henry Stuart, *31*
Jonson, Ben, 189-190
Joseph of Arimethea, *119*
Joseph d' Arimathie (de Boron), *119*
St. Joseph, 209
Joshua, *62*
Julian, 96
Jung, C. G., 5, 6, *9*, 13-14, 23, 27, *30*, *31-32*, 33, *62*, *182-183*

Kafka, Franz, 200, 202
Kaiser, Georg, 199-200
Kalevala, 12, 27
Kapp, Yvonne, *9*
Kazan, Elia, 61
Kenner, Hugh, *178*, *185*
Kerkyon, 20
Khan, Zaman, 195

Keith, Marquis von, 199
The King Must Die (Renault), 20
Kingsley, Sidney, *172*
Kipling, Rudyard, 136, 137-140, *182*
Der Kleine Herr Friedemann (Mann), 206, *216*
Kleist, Heinrich von, 197-198
Klinschor, 107, *123*, 196
Knowles, John, 160-161
Koby (Dürrenmatt), 217
Kogin, 115
Kogin, Trofim, 115
Princess Kosmonopolis, 175-176
Krapp (of *Krapp's Last Tape*), 177
Krook (of *Bleak House*), 191
Herr Kuhn (Hesse), 208

Labove, 164
Lady Chatterley's Lover, 77-79, *120*, 188, 192, 206
Lafcadio, *119*
"The Lame Shall Enter First" (O'Connor), 96-98
Last Post (of Ford Madox Ford's *Parade's End*), 148, 151-154, *182*
Lattimore, Richard trans. *Hesiod*, *31*
Laüffer, 197, 205
Laurents, Arthur, 172, *184*
Lawrence, D. H., 7-8, 35-38, 39, 41, 47, 55, 59, *60-61*, 77-79, 80, 82, 84, *120*, 133, *180*, 206
Lawrence, Frieda, 80
Laxness, Halldór, 205
le Sage, Alain René, 196
Lear, 190
Lebedev, Nicolai, 116
Lebedev, Zinaida Nikolaevna (Zina), *62*, 116-117
Lemon, Iris, 48, 100-101, 116

Lenz, Jakob Michael Reinhold, *119*, 197, 205
The Lesson (Brecht), 205, *216*
Leverkühn, Adrian, 126, 208, *217*
Levin, Harry, 75, *120*
Levin, Seymour (Sy), 44-48, 116, 191, 203
Leviticus, 11
Liddell, Henry George, 31
Lie Down in Darkness (Styron), 83, 89-92, 117, *121*
Light in August (Faulkner), 83-84, *121*, 214
Lil (of *The Waste Land*), 67
The Little Crippled Devil (de Guevera), 196
Little Dorrit, 105, 107, *123*
Little Herr Friedemann (Mann), 206, *216*
little lame balloonman (Cummings), 33, *192*
Loeb, B. M., 21, *29*, 55, *62*
Loftis, Helen, 89-90, 92
Loftis, Maudie, 89-92, 117
Loftis, Milton, 89-92
Loftis, Peyton, 89-92
Logi, *123*
"Lohengrin 'o Death" (Böll), 210
The Long March (Styron), 166-171, *184*, 188
Longfellow, Henry Wadsworth, 13
The Longest Journey, 141-143, *182*
Loomis, Roger Sherman, *119*, *122*
Lowe-Porter (trans.), *123*, *216*, *217*
Lucius (of *The Golden Ass*), 34
St. Luke, 74

The Mabinogion, 27, *119*
Macauley, Robie, 148, *182*

Macbeth, 130, 190
Macculloch, John A., 27, *30*
MacMann (of *Malone Dies*), 177
MacPhail, 91
Mahood (of *The Unnameable*), 177
Malamud, Bernard, 8, 44-56, 59, 61-62, 95, 98-100, 109, 113-115, *122*, *123*, 188
Malcolm (of *Macbeth*), 190
Sir Maldemer, 99
Malin, Irving, 121
Malone, 177, 178
Malone Dies (Beckett), 177, *185*
Malory, Thomas, 66, *118*
Malraux, André, *120*, 206
A Man Could Stand Up (of Ford Madox Ford's *Parade's End*), 148, 152
Man Equals Man (see Mann ist Mann)
Mannheim, Ralph, 9
The Man Outside (Borchert), *217*
Man Who Died, 35-37, 43, 55, 60, 191
The Man Who Died (Lawrence), 35-38, 59, 60, 77
"The Man Who Would Be King" (Kipling), 136, 137-140
Manessier, 118
Mann, Thomas, *123*, 125, 179, 206-208, *216*, *217*
Mann ist Mann (Brecht), 204, *216*
Mannix, Captain Al, 167-171
Mario (of "Mario and the Magician"), 208
"Mario and the Magician" (Mann), 207-208, *217*
Der Marquis von Kieth (Wederkind), 199
Marlowe, Christopher, 129, 196
Mary (The Virgin), 209
Mary (of *Invisible Man*), 102

The Masks of God (Campbell),
   62
Math son of Mathonwy, 13, 196
"Maud" (Tennyson), 89
Maugham, W. Somerset, 143,
   182
McEachern (of *Light in August*),
   83
McCaslin, Ike, 166, *184*
McKenzie, Robert, 31
McNamara, Eugene, 168, 171,
   184
Mellors, 79
Melville, Herman, 1, 129-135,
   180, 199
Men Without Women (Heming-
   way), 158
Mendel, Vera (trans.), *216*
Menelaus, 54
Meng Tsao-Yu, 195
Mephisto, 199
Merlin, 118
"The Metamorphosis" (Kafka),
   200
Metamorphosis (Ovid), 27
le militant (of *La Grande et la
   petite Manoeuvre*), 213-214
Miller, Harry, 91
Miller, J. Hillis, 105, *122*
Milton, 174, *185*
Minogue, Ward, 48-50
Minos, *179*
Count Mippipopolous, 69, 156
Miss Lonelyhearts (West), 84-85
Miss Lonelyhearts, 85
Moby Dick, 129, 131, *180*
Moby-Dick (Melville), 129-132,
   134, *180*
A Modern Instance (Howells),
   136-138, *181-182*
Molloy, 177, 178
Molloy (Beckett), 177
Mommy (*The American Dream*),
   102-103
Montaigne, 15, *28*

Moor, Karl, 19
Moore, Harry T., *60, 61*
Mopsus, 21
Moran (of *Molloy*), 177, 178
Moses, 64
Motes, Hazel, 95
Mummah, 58
Munitus, 21
Murder in the Cathedral (Eliot),
   64-65, *118*
Murray, Gilbert, 26, *31*
Murray, Henry A., *193*
Mussolini, 207, 208
Mustard, Helen M., *118*
le mutile (of *La Grande et la
   petite Manoeuvre*), 213-214
"My Expensive Leg" (Böll), 210
Mylonas, George E., *32*

Nagg (Endgame), 178
Nana, 19
The Natural (Malamud), 44, 48,
   61, 98-101, 116, *122*
Neleus, 21
Nell (of *Endgame*), 178
Nellhaus, Gerhard (trans.), 205,
   216
Nelson, Benjamin, *60*
A New Life (Malamud), 44-47,
   61, 98, 116, 203
Nibelungenglied, 195
Nietzsche, Friedrich, 127, *179*
Nile, 13
No More Parades (Ford Madox
   Ford), 148
Noah, 54, 160
Numbers, 11
Nymph Eliza, 190

O'Connor, Flannery, 95-98, *122*
O'Connor, Jim, 86-88
Odets, Clifford, 172
Odin, 125, 140
Odysseus, 17, 23, 24, 26, 57
Odyssey, 10, 11, 15

Oedipus, 3, 25, *33*, 64, 65, 106, 126, 127, 195
The Oedipus Cycle (Sophocles), *118*
Of Human Bondage (Maugham), 143-144, *182*
Oisin, 13, 27, 196
Old Ben, 165-166
The Old Curiosity Shop (Dickens), 107, *123*
The Old Man and the Sea (Hemingway), 189
O'Meaghan, Mary, 42-44, 191
"On the Bridge" (Böll), 210-211
One Arm (Tennessee Williams), *185*
Onians, Richard Broxton, 14, 22, 27, 28-29, *30*
Ophion, 22
Orpheus, 15, *30*
Orpheus Descending (Williams), 39
Osiris, 7, 17, 18, 20, 22, 29, *30*, 37, 56, 106
Othello, 190
Othello, 191
Outside the Door (Borchert), 209
Other Voices, Other Rooms (Capote), 88-89
Ovid, 27

Paine, Thomas, 172
Pan, 44, 141
Parade's End (Ford Madox Ford), 148-154, *182*
Paris, 3, 16, 21, *179*, 190
Paris, Memo, *61*, 100-101, 116
Parzival, Parsifal, 98-99, 101, *122*, *185*
Parzival (Wolfram von Eschenbach), 99, 107, *118*, *119*, 196
Pascal, Blaise, 38, *60*

Passage, Charles E., *118*
Passover, *32*, 51, 62
St. Paul, 45-47
Pausanias, 29
Princess Pazmezoglus, Ariadne del Lago, 175
Peele, George, 190
Peg-leg, 134
Pelias, 21, 26
Pellehan, *119*
Pellinor, *119*
Pensées (Pascal), 38, *60*
Dr. Pep, 55-56, 59, 191
the *Pequod*, 130, 132
Percivale, Sir, 66, *119*
Percy, Sir, 99
Peredur, *119*
Peredur, *118*
Perken, *120*, 206
Perlesvaus, *118*
Perseus, 26
Perth, 132
Pesach (*see* Passover),
Philoctetes, 21, 23-24, 127-129, 166, *179*
Philoctetes (Sophocles), 21, 127
Philomela, 67
Phineas (of *A Separate Peace*), 161
Phlebas the Phoenician, 67
Pholus, 16, 21, *30*, *179*
Pierce, Zenobia (Zeena), 146-147
Pintias the Robber (Pontius Pilate), *60*
Pip, 131
Pitkin, Lemuel, 85
Plato, 28
Pliny, 11, 12, 14, 15, 27, *30*
Plume, Richard, 6, 154-155, 166, 190
Plumes (Stallings), 6, 154-155
Plutarch, 29, *30*
Podarces, *184*
Poeas, 21, *179*

Point Counter Point (Huxley), 77, 79-82, 117, *121*, 192
Pollitt, Brick, 39-42, 118, 191
Pollitt, Gooper, 40, 41
Pollitt, Mae, 40, 41
Pollitt, Maggie, 40-42, 118
Pollux, 21
Pasicles the Philosopher, 15
Polybus, 15
Polyneices, 21
Popeye (of *Sanctuary*), 164
Popkin, Henry, 174, *184*
Porter, David, *217*
Pound, Ezra, 148
Priam, 165, *184*
Procrustes, 4
Proetus, 21
Prometheus, 14, *123*, 129, 132
Pronko, Leonard, *185*
Prospero, 190
Ptolemy Hephaestionos, *30*
Pueblo Indians, 14

Quarles, Elinor, 79-81
Quarles, Philip, 79-82, 166
Quarles, Rachel, 81
Queste del Saint Graal, *118*
Quilp, 107
Quinn, Edward, *216*
Quirt (Sergeant), 6

Ra, 18
Raglan, Lord, 5, 18
Rampion, Mark, 80-82, *120*
Randolph (Cousin Randolph Skully), 89
Die Raüber (Schiller), 197
Rayber, George F. and Bishop, 97
Rektor Kleist (Kaiser), 200
Remus, 21
Renault, Marie, 20
"Revelation" (O'Connor), 96
Richard III, 63, 107, 189, 196

Richard the Third (Shakespeare), 63
Richman, Sidney, 48, 55, *61*, *62*, 122
Rigaud (*The Old Curiosity Shop*), 107-108
Rist, Jean, 214
Robinson, Edward Arlington, 199
Romero, Pedro, 69, 156, 157-158
Romulus, 21
Rosenfeld, Paul, 106
Rosenzweig Adam, 38-39, 158, 189, 191
Ross, W. D., *28*
The Royal Way (Malraux), *120*, 206
Ruprecht, 198, 216

Samsa, Gregor, 200-201
Sanctuary (Faulkner), 164
Sandbach, the Honorable Paul, 150-151
Sansom, Amy Skully, 89
Sansom, Edward, 88-89
Sansom, Joel Knox Harrison, 89
Santiago (of *The Old Man and the Sea*), 189
Princess Saralinda, 108-109
Satan, 75, 97, 107, *123*, 166, 168, 169, 171, *217*
Savill, Mervyn, *217*
Schill (*The Visit*), *217*
Schiller, Friedrich Von, 197
Schleppfuss (Mann), 208, *217*
Schmitz, Ettore (*see* Svevo, Italo)
Schmürz (Boris Vian), 215
Schorer, Mark, 79, *120*
Scott, Robert, *31*
Scrooge, 135, *180-181*
A Separate Peace (Knowles), 160-161

"A Sermon by Doctor Pep" (Bellow), 55-56, *62*
Servius, 21, *30*
Set, 18, 22, *30*, 34
Seward, Barbara, 33, *60*
Shakespeare, 34, 53, 63, 107, 174, *185*, 190
Shandy Tristram and Uncle Toby, 191
Shelley, Percy Bysshe, 175
Sheppard ("The Lame Shall Enter First"), 97-98
Sheppard, Norton, 97
The Sherwood Anderson Reader, 106
The Shoe-maker's Holiday (Thomas Dekker), 190
The Short Novels (D. H. Lawrence), *60*
The Short Stories of Ernest Hemingway, 120, 183
Shulman, Robert, 61, *122*
Sibyl (*The Waste Land*), 67
Silver, Mattie, 146-147
Sir Percyvelle of Galles, 118
The Skin of Our Teeth (Wilder), 160
Skipper (*Cat on a Hot Tin Roof*), 40
Smallweed, Grandfather, 105
Snopes, Ab, 3, 163-164, 166
Snopes, Flem, 163-165
"The Snows of Kilimanjaro" (Hemingway), 76-77, *120*
Socrates, 7, 200
"Socrates Wounded" (Brecht), 7, 200
Soergel, Albert, 193
Solotaroff, Theodore, 62
Sola (*Independent People*), 205
Some Do Not . . . (Ford Madox Ford), 148-151, *182*
Sone de Nansai, 118
Sophocles, 21, 34, *118*, *179*

"Sorrow Acre" (Dinesen), 161
Sosostris, Mme., 67
The Sound and the Fury (Faulkner), 82-83, *121*, 165, *184*, 192, 206
Spandrell, Maurice, 80
Spender, Stephen, *217*
Spenser, Edmund, 174, *185*
Sphinx, 127
Spinoza, Benedict de, 143, *182*
Stallings, Laurence, 6, 154-155, 190
Starbuck, 129, 131
Stein, Roger B., 88, *121*
Sterne, Laurence, 191
Stevens, Gavin, 164
Stirling A. H., *182*
Stories of Three Decades (Mann), 216
Stover, Clark Harris, 28
Stranitzky, 211
Stranitzky und der Nationalheld, 211
Streetcar Named Desire (Williams), 39
Studies in Classic American Literature (Lawrence), 133, *180*
Styron, William, 89-95, *121*, *122*, 166-171, *184*
The Sun Also Rises (Hemingway), 67-70, *119*, 155-158, 159, 192
Sun-go, 58
Sutpen, Thomas, 163, 179
Svevo, Italo, 202, *216*
Sweet Bird of Youth (Williams), 39, *61*, 174-176, *184*

Talos, 16, 21, *179*
Tamburlaine, 129, 196
Tammuz (Thammuz), 17, 19-20, 22, *29*, 189
Tanselle, G. Thomas, *120*
Tantamount, Charles, 80

Tantamount, Lord Edward, 80
Tantamount, Lucy, 80
Tarwater, Marion Francis, 97
Templeton, Colonel "Rocky," 167-171
Tennyson, Alfred Lord, 89, *118*, 199
Thackeray, William M., 137
Theseus, 26
The 13 Clocks (Thurber), 108-109, *123*
They Knew What They Wanted (Sidney Howard), 171
Thiddriksaga, 196
Thompson, D'Arcy Wentworth, *28*
Thompson, Stith, 122
"Three Dark Kings" (Borchert), 209
Three Plays (Wilder), *183*
Thurber, James, 108-109, *123*
Thyestes, 21
Tietjens, Christopher, 148-154
Tietjens, Mark, 149-154
Tietjens, Sylvia, 149-154
Timur-the-lame, 196
Tiny Tim (Cratchit), 135
Tischler, Nancy, *60*
Toby (*Der Besuch*), 217
Toller, Ernst, 201-202, *216*
Tommo, 132-133
Tony (of *They Knew What They Wanted*), 171
Tous contre Tous (Adamov), 214
The Town (Faulkner), 164, *184*
The Train Was on Time (Böll), 209-210, *217*
transatlantic review, *120*, 155
Trilling, Lionel, 140, *181*, *182*
Tristan, 25, *119*, 196
Tristan (Gottfried von Strassburg), *119*
Tristram Shandy (Sterne), 191

Trotter, W. F., *60*
Turner, Nat, 92-95, *121-122*
Turpin, Claude, 96
Mrs. Turpin (Ruby), 96
The Tutor (see Der Hofmeister)
Tynan, Kenneth, 176
Typee (Melville), 132-133
Typhon (Set), *30*
The Unnameable (Beckett), 177
The Unvanquished (Faulkner), 163

Updike, John, 55, *179*
Uranos (Uranus), 6, 18, 22, 25, *120*

Valency, Maurice, 217
Vanity Fair (Thackeray), 137
Varner, Eula, 164
Varnum, Ruth, 147
Vian, Boris, 214-215, *217*
Venus, 164
The Victim (Bellow), 109
The Violent Bear It Away (O'Connor), 97
Virgil, 21, *30*
The Visit (Valency), 217
The Visit of the Old Lady (Dürrenmatt), 211-212
Voltaire, 85
von Strassburg, Gottfried, *119*
Vulcan (see also Hephaestus), 96, 126, 140, 164

Wadman, Widow, 191
Wagner, Richard, *118*, 199
Waiting for Godot (Beckett), 177
Wanderer, Kommst du nach Spa . . . (Böll), 210
Wanderer, If You Come to the Spa (Böll), 217
Wariri (tribe), 57-58
Wannop, Valentine, 151-154

Warren, Robert Penn, 38, 59, 158, 160, 189
Wasserman, Earl R., *192*
The Waste Land (Eliot), 66-68, 80, 117, *119*, 192
Watling, E. F., *179*
Watts, Harold H., *121*
Wauchier, *118*
"A Way You'll Never Be" (Hemingway), 159
Wayne, Chance, 174-176
Wedekind, Frank, 199
Wee Willie Winkle and Other Stories (Kipling), *182*
Weisinger, Herbert, *28*
Werfel, Franz, 199
Werner, Alice, 27
West, Nathanael, 84-86
Weston, Jessie, *29*, 64, 66, *118*, *119*, 174, 175
Weyland, 25, 126, 140, 195
Wharton, Edith, 144-146, 182
What Price Glory? (Stallings and Anderson), 6, 154
White, W. H., *182*
The White Goddess (Graves), 27, *29*, *31*, *61*, *62*, *183*
Whiteside, Alexandra, 175
Wieger, L., 27
Wilcox, Doctor, 72-76
Wilder, Thornton, 158, 160, 162, *183*
Wilderness (Robert Penn Warren), 38, 160, 189

Williams, Tennessee, 3, 8, 39-42, *60-61*, 86-88, *121*, 173-176, *184-185*, 188
Wilson, Edmund, 66-67, *119*, 127, *179*
Wingfield, Amanda, 86
Wingfield, Laura, 86-88, 118, *121*, 166
Wingfield, Tom, 86-87, *121*
Winner Take Nothing (Hemingway), 159
Winnie (of *Happy Days*), 177
Winter's Tales (Dinesen), *183*
Wise Blood (O'Connor), 95
Wolfram von Eschenbach, 65, *118*
Wonham, Stephen, 141-143

Xavier, Val, 39

Yahweh, 22
Young, Philip, 157, 159-160, *183*

Zachanassian, Claire, 211-212, 217
Zeitlin, Jacob, *28*
Zeno, 202-204
Der zerbrochene Krug (Kleist), 197-198
Zeus, 12, 14, 24, 25, 26, 31
Zipes, Jack D., *216*
Zorn of Zorna, 109
Der Zug war pünktlich (Böll), 209-210